PSALMS

PSALMS

EVERYDAY BIBLE COMMENTARY

Robert L. Alden

MOODY PUBLISHERS

CHICAGO

We hope you enjoy this book from Moody Publishers. Our goal is to provide high-quality, thought-provoking books and products that connect truth to your real needs and challenges. For more information on other books and products written and produced from a biblical perspective, go to www.moodypublishers.com or write to:

Moody Publishers
820 N. LaSalle Boulevard
Chicago, IL 60610

1 3 5 7 9 10 8 6 4 2

CONTENTS

PUBLISHER'S NOTE

For over sixty years, the Everyday Bible Commentary series (formerly titled Everyman's Bible commentary series) has served millions of readers, helping them to grow in their understanding of both God and His Word. These commentaries—written by a wide variety of evangelical scholars who are experts in their respective fields—provide biblical interpretation that is both accessible and rich, impacting the daily lives of Christians from diverse cultural and theological backgrounds.

So why rerelease the Everyday Bible Commentary series given its immense success? These commentaries have served readers tremendously well in generations past, and we want to ensure that they serve many more for generations to come. While these commentaries are not new, they remain relevant as the content in each volume provides timeless scriptural exposition. And perhaps today more than ever, Christians need reliable biblical instruction that has stood the test of time. With so many voices vying for our attention and allegiance, Christians need to understand the voice of the One calling out to us in Scripture so we may faithfully live for Him and His glory. And it is to this end that these commentaries were written: that believers may encounter God through His Word and embody it in their everyday lives.

INTRODUCTION

No other Bible book has as many authors as the Psalms. And no Bible book except Genesis covers such a long period of time.

At least one psalm (90) was penned by Moses, who lived in the second millennium before Christ. Other psalms (e.g., 137) were written at least as late as the end of the Babylonian exile, some 500 years before Christ.

David is the best known and most prolific of the psalmists. If the expression "a psalm of David" in the title means that he is the author, then he is one of the most prolific of all Bible writers. That expression, however, may merely indicate that the psalm was about David or was written for him by a court poet.

Being poetry, the psalms utilize a literary form common to all Semitic poetry, called parallelism. Any psalm, and almost any verse in the Psalms, illustrates it. The writer says the same things in different words. Two such adjoining synonymous lines or stiches within a verse are a couplet.

Sometimes, however, adjoining lines are antithetical, saying contrasting things, such as in Psalm 1:6. Still other poetical devices occur and receive mention in the body of this volume.

Many commentators on the Psalms spend considerable energy trying to determine the life situation out of which the poems arose. Articles upon articles have been written to classify and categorize the Psalms into various groups. Naturally, there is much disagreement. Only a minimum of that is done here. By and large, the Psalms are without known context. Only occasionally are specific individuals, places, and events mentioned. Perhaps this lack of specificity contributes to the Psalms' popularity.

To many people the book of Psalms is simply a source of devotional material. Some people seem concerned only about the Messianic references in the Psalms. But an understanding and appreciation of the Psalter is incomplete until each Psalm is studied individually.

This first volume on the Psalms is intended to aid in the understanding of the hymnbook of ancient Israel. A commentary does not replace the Bible. It is not a paraphrase. It merely *comments* on the Scripture. An open Bible should be kept handy while reading this book.

This study seeks a balance between the obvious and the hidden, between the technical and the simple, between the historical situation and the contemporary application, between that which is old and well-known and that which is novel and perhaps provocative or even controversial.

Most of the translations are by the author, although in some instances, for the sake of accuracy or familiarity, the King James Version is used.

It is not in the New Testament that the greatest devotional literature is found but in the Old, in the book of Psalms. Because the psalmists often speak in generalities, the Psalms can be variously interpreted and widely applied. Here, more than any place in the Bible, the heartthrob of the saint is heard. Here are the most exalted expressions of God's greatness; here are the bitterest groans of the sinful and the afflicted. Here is something for everyone in every mood.

The prayer of the author is that the same Holy Spirit who moved holy men of old to pen the words of the Bible, and who has superintended its transmission over the intervening millennia, might illumine the Psalms through this commentary. Since He is also the Spirit of truth, may He also guard from misunderstanding and guide and confirm in all truth.

PSALMS 1–50: SONGS OF DEVOTION

....

PSALM 1

It is appropriate that an introduction such as Psalm 1 should begin this collection of songs and poems. Two ways of life are presented immediately. First there is the way of the righteous, the blessed, the lawkeeper, the avoider of sins. On the other hand, there is the wicked, the chaff-like man, who deserves no reward with the blessed. After all is said and done, are there not but two ways of life? We either fear and love God or we do not. The latter is one of the simplest definitions of sin.

The psalm is interesting in its structure as well as universal in its application. It has the typical parallelism of phrasing found throughout the poetical books of the Old Testament. The first verse is an example of this. Three things the blessed man does not do: he does not walk in the counsel of the ungodly; he does not stand in the way of sinners; he does not sit in the seat of the scornful.

More interesting, however, is the chiastic structure of the poem. *Chiastic* means that the first and last themes or ideas reflect each other and the middle ideas reflect each other—A B B A. In verses 1–2, there is the blessed man deciding for righteousness and against wickedness. At the end of the poem, in verses 5–6, the blessed Lord "decides" for the righteous man and against the wicked. In the middle of the psalm two pictures are drawn by the literary artist. Verse 3 is a picture of the righteous man as a green, fruitful tree in a fertile place. Verse 4 is a picture of a wicked man who is like useless chaff, fit only to be blown away by the wind.

Looking at the psalm in more detail, one sees what the blessed and wicked ways are. The man who does not follow bad advice, stand with sinners, or spend all his time criticizing is blessed. The verbs in verse 1 present a progression: walking, standing, sitting. But the three kinds of bad people are not progressively worse. Scorners are not worse than sinners.

What does walking in the counsel of the ungodly mean? It means simply following the advice of people who do not consider God. They do not mean to be anti-godly or atheistic, but they do not fear and love God. Hence when they give advice, God's claims and commands are of little moment. This verse is especially good for young people who are facing the major decisions of life: What and where shall I study? Whom shall I marry? What shall be my career? Shall I serve God?

Taking the advice of the ungodly leads to standing where sinners stand. We might put it in these terms: Ungodly advice leads to taking a sinner's stand on spiritual and moral issues.

The last term, *scorn,* is not too common in modern English but finds its meaning in our word *mockery.* People in the "scorner's seat" criticize many things but, in particular, God's people, God's Book, and God's way. They often mock God's Son and even the Father Himself.

But the Bible does not describe good merely in negative terms, and there follows here a description of what the blessed man is like. He thinks about God and His law, the Bible. This does not mean that he is a professional Bible scholar but, rather, that throughout the day and the waking hours of the night every happening of life prompts a reflection on something in the Bible.

Verses 3–4 present two pictures: verse 3 of the blessed man and verse 4 of the ungodly man. The former is like a green and productive tree because it is planted by a river (cf. Jer. 17:8). The ungodly is pictured as chaff, the refuse of the wheat-threshing operation. Bible students may be permitted to see some limited types here. The water is a source of life as Christ is our life. The unwithering leaf is the unblemished and untarnished testimony of the obedient Christian. The fruit (cf. Gal. 5:22f.) in season is the regular and abundant service which we ought to render to our Lord. In the second picture, the useless, inedible chaff is fit only for destruction. This corresponds to the eternal destiny of the wicked, who are utterly lost.

The *therefore* of verse 5 introduces the conclusion. Because the wicked are like chaff, they shall not stand at the judgment—they shall not be in the congregation of the righteous. When God executes His justice they shall not be able to withstand it. In verse 1, the blessed man chose not to stand or sit with sinners; now God justly forbids the sinner to stand or sit with His chosen. He knows and loves the righteous way of the righteous man, but the ungodly way of the ungodly man leads to peril and punishment.

PSALM 2

The second psalm is well-known for at least two reasons. It is the first Messianic psalm (verse 2 has in it the word *anointed,* which is *Messiah* in Hebrew and *Christ* in Greek). When Paul preached to the Jews of Antioch in Pisida, he cited the seventh verse (Acts 13:33). This is the only numbered reference to any Old

Testament passage in the New Testament. Hebrews 1:5 and 5:5 contain the same quotation. Revelation 19 has several allusions to phrases in this psalm. Psalm 2:2 may be the background of Revelation 19:19 and Psalm 2:9–10 of Revelation 19:15.

Psalm 2 has far-reaching implications and dramatic scenes. It is also interesting in its structure. The twelve verses may easily be divided into four stanzas of three verses each. In the first three verses the vicious but vain actions of the enemies of God are presented in the form of a rhetorical question. In verses 4–6 attention is focused on the almighty Sovereign of heaven and earth and His fearful reaction to hostile plots. Verses 7–9 are largely a quotation within a quotation. The Son relates His Father's instructions to Him. Finally, the last three verses are exhortations to the rulers to be obeisant and obedient to the Son. Thus we have:

The actions of earthly rulers (vv. 1–3)
The actions of God the Father (vv. 4–6)
The commands to the Son (vv. 7–9)
The commands to earthly rulers (vv. 10–12)

Note the parallelism, A A B B, and the chiasmus, A B B A. (See commentary on Psalm 1 for an explanation of these terms.)

The opening verses, which describe the actions of ungodly men, do so both in general and specific terms and with progressively more detail. The psalmist indicts the nations and the people in the first verse and the leaders of the people in the second verse. Their deeds are described in the first verse as generally mad and futile, but are narrowed down in the second verse to a specific plot to overthrow God and His Christ. The third verse gives the details of this evil plot. The same Hebrew word lies behind the "meditate" of Psalm 1:2 as the word "rage" in Psalm 2:1. Whereas the godly man uses his mental energies delighting in God's Word, the ungodly leaders use theirs to plot against God's rule.

This description of the unfortunate and uninformed state of the unregenerate mind is not unique to 1000 BC when David lived. The same thought patterns prevail more or less openly today. The world is at enmity with God, and rulers and ruled alike seek to escape the demands of God on their lives. They seek to outwit the Creator and to undo the mission of His dear Son.

The picture of God in the fourth verse is an unusual one. He laughs and derides. The laugh seems to be the kind of chuckle a champion gives when his opponent's defeat is imminent. The derision is probably mixed with the wrath and displeasure described in the following verse. He laughs at the futility of human actions, but He is angry at the whole idea of man trying to overthrow God. Rather than surrender His dignity, He commissions His king to execute wrath.

Because of the sixth verse, many liberal commentators see David and David only in this psalm. They call it a royal psalm and say it was probably composed for the enthronement of the monarch. The kingship of Israel was a divinely appointed office. The king was "set" or installed because of God's choice and was there to rule on God's behalf.

Such a limited application, however, is incompatible with the remainder of the psalm. Unless the accomplishments and promises of the Son are great exaggerations, they cannot apply to David, but only to David's greater Son, the Lord Jesus Christ. For this reason, and because the inspired authors of the New Testament so understood it, this psalm speaks of the commission and mission of Jesus the Messiah.

It helps to understand the third section of the psalm by supplying quotation marks in verses 7–9. The whole section is spoken by the Son, but He quotes His Father beginning with the words, "Thou art my Son." There is some question as to whether verse 7 should read "the decree of the LORD" or "the decree: the LORD said."

The words of the decree itself are all-important. God says to the Messiah, "Thou art my Son; this day have I begotten thee." Besides being an argument for at least two persons of the Trinity being mentioned in the Old Testament, it is also a statement of the relationship between these two persons. Paul used this verse in Acts 13:33 to support the resurrection of Christ. The Father offers the Son, for the asking, the world for an inheritance. The rebellious nations of verse 1 become the property of the Son. This truth is missionary as well as Messianic. Any passage which speaks of the ends of the earth in the plans of God is missionary. Here, however, more of the negative, judicial aspect of the Son's task is in view. Since the nations are rebels, He will smash them as one would smash a clay pot with an iron rod. The only way to avoid this wrathful punishment is to obey the commands of the last quarter of the psalm.

Verses 10–12 contain five commands to leaders of the nations: be wise, be instructed, serve the Lord, rejoice, and kiss the Son. A colloquial translation might render the first two: "Wise up; get smart." With such enlightened attitudes and divinely illumined spirits they then could serve, rejoice, and kiss the Son.

Perhaps the typical Protestant church needs verse 11b underscored: "Rejoice with trembling." We sometimes forget that it is possible to put these two things side by side. Often when we rejoice we lose our sense of dignity, and when we fear God we forget to enjoy our positions of sonship.

The translators of the Revised Standard Version presumed additional letters in the Hebrew text in order to produce their translation at this point: "Kiss his feet." The presence of the Aramaic word for son (*bar* rather than the Hebrew *ben*) perplexed them, but in recent years discoveries have shown that Aramaic is an older language than was thought. It is older than the writing of this psalm, and therefore it is not impossible that such a loan word could appear at this point, as the ancient inspired author sought for variety and color. Hence the older original reading, "Kiss the Son," is preferred. It means to do obeisance to Him. This is not the romantic kiss but the kiss on the feet, the hand, or the shoulder. His worshipers should reverence Him as vassals honored an ancient earthly sovereign. The word *little* may be a limitation of time or of quantity; that is, God's wrath may "soon" be kindled (NASB), or it may be kindled "but a little" (KJV). There are good reasons for either translation. The major concern ought to be that God be neither a little displeased with us nor soon be angered by us.

The last phrase describes the believer's place of blessedness. One arrives there by putting his trust in God. And so Psalm 2 ends with a promise, using the same line of thought with which Psalm 1 begins: "Blessed are all they that put their trust in him."

PSALM 3

The third psalm is the first one with a title. Mystery surrounds the origin of psalm titles. In most instances the title pertains to the contents of the psalm. Psalm 51 is a good example. The contents of Psalm 3 could describe any of several tight circumstances which David experienced.

The word rendered "psalm" in this title appears fifty-seven times in other titles. In most of these instances the Hebrew word describing the kind of a psalm is merely transliterated: *Shiggaion* (Ps. 7), *Michtam* (Ps. 16), and *Maschil* (Ps. 78). There is no reason not to believe that Psalm 3 describes David's sentiments toward his son Absalom (2 Sam. 15–18), as the inscription indicates.

Selah first occurs in this psalm, where it is found three times. Although many suggestions have been made as to the meaning of this little word, it remains quite uncertain. It is probably a musical notation having something to do with the tempo, volume, or accompaniment of the song, or with the participation or posture of the singer. All attempts to translate it have been unfortunate and ill-advised. For the sake of symmetry one would expect a *selah* after verse 6, but there is none.

Psalm 3 falls into the category of "trouble and trust" psalms, and is one of the shorter ones. David begins by crying out to God about his troubles, which come primarily in the form of enemies (vv. 1–2). Then follows a personal testimony of God's past favors and grace. Finally, as if to say, "Do it again, Lord," the psalmist prays for salvation for himself and blessing on his people.

The emphasis in the complaint section is on the great number of enemies (cf. 2 Sam. 17:1). Three times the Hebrew root for *many* occurs (translated "increased" in verse 1). Not only are these multitudes the enemies of David, but they are enemies of his God as well. Their accusation betrays this as they falsely charge, "There is no help for him in God." The word for *help* is the same word as *salvation* elsewhere (v. 8). Certainly these enemies had in mind temporal, physical salvation, although David might have meant his spiritual salvation as well. A similar range of meaning inheres in the word translated *soul*. Sometimes it means simply "breath." At other times the life principle is meant.

The testimony section begins, in general terms, in verse 3. God, says David, is my shield (cf. Gen. 15:1), my glory, and the lifter up of my head. The verb *lift* may echo an earlier use of the term in verse 1. Although his enemies rose up, God raised him yet higher. Verses 4–5 mention particular features of his deliverance. In the past he cried and God heard. In the past he slept soundly and God preserved him. Hence, with this new challenge, he testifies that he will not be afraid of myriads of hostile people all around him.

Some early Church Fathers saw the death and resurrection of Christ in verse 5, but most commentators see in these words simply a morning prayer.

The third section (vv. 7–8) contains a prayer for deliverance, but also includes statements of God's past accomplishments. Two verbs form the basis of the prayer: *arise* and *save*. Then, as if to remind God of His ability, the psalmist states how God had smashed the jaws and broken the teeth of former enemies. He thus likens his adversaries to disarmed animals, their weapons of destruction (jaws and teeth) now destroyed.

The last verse is somewhat like a benediction, but it is also a prayer. Salvation is God's. And since it is, the blessing is the people's. There is no salvation apart from God and He ever wants to give His people His blessing.

PSALM 4

Two additional technical terms are found in the title of Psalm 4. The *choirmaster* or *chief musician* occurs first and then the name of a musical instrument or a melody, *Neginoth,* follows. This, too, is a psalm by or about David, as the last two words of the title indicate.

It is difficult to know whom the author is addressing except in those verses where he clearly is petitioning God. Specifically, who are the "sons of men" in verse 2? Usually this term simply means "men" in the frailty of their human limitations (cf. Ps. 8:4, Gen. 6:2), including their propensity to sin. Were these merely the enemies of David, or did the inspired penman have all men in mind? Apparently the psalm is addressed to all men, for, apart from taking the advice of verses 3 and 4, all men love vanity and seek lies (which is the meaning of the word *leasing*, v. 2, in the KJV).

The psalm begins and ends with addresses to God. In the middle section (vv. 2–6) are admonitions to men.

The first verse is something of an introduction. There are three imperative verbs in this one verse: *answer* (rendered "hear" in the KJV), *have mercy*, and *hear*. In a manner typical of many prayers in the Bible, David reminds God of past deliverances. Things were tight for God's servant, but the Lord had released him and loosed the tension.

The first words directed to David's human audience are words of rebuke and reprimand. The three phrases are clipped and abrupt. To make the meaning understandable to the non-Semitic mind, translators must add phrases such as those indicated by italics in the King James Version. The "sons of men" turn the psalmist's glory into shame, they love vanity, they seek lies. Perhaps that first sin is their mocking or insulting David's God and making light of his devotion. (For a discussion of *selah*, see commentary on Psalm 3.)

In the rough chiastic arrangement of this psalm, verse 6 corresponds to verse 2. Again, David complains of those who ask ridiculing questions about his faith. Many of them wonder if there is any good any more. Assuming that their words continue through the end of the verse, they also ask whether God would lift up His countenance on them.

The central portion, verses 3–5, contains words of instruction. Count the commands: know, stand in awe, sin not, commune, be still, sacrifice, and trust. In verse 3 David wishes that we might know that God sovereignly sets apart the godly for Himself. It is interesting that coupled with that truth is the one regarding our ability to call on Him. So on the one hand God calls, or sets apart, the godly and on the other hand He hears those who call on Him. In the one instance God initiates the action, and in the other man does. The next four imperatives have to do with personal, private devotion. The first Hebrew word of verse 4 is rare and its translation here is uncertain. The Septuagint has "be angry." This is apparently the basis of Paul's use of the verse in Ephesians 4:26.

Perhaps if *selah* seems appropriate anywhere it is here, in view of the words "be still" which precede.

Verse 5 speaks of public worship: offer sacrifices. Then 5b has the final and yet most basic instruction: trust in the LORD (cf. Ps. 37:5 and Prov. 3:5–6). Sacrifices without trust are of no use. Works without faith are dead.

Having experienced God's salvation and continuing mercy and care, David concludes the psalm with two verses of praise. In terms understandable to farmers, he says that he is happier than at harvest. In contrast to this overt jubilation is his quiet confidence that lets him sleep soundly while God watches over his safety. *Peace* is a word loaded with meaning. One English word cannot do justice to *shalom.* Included in it are the ideas of economic and physical satisfaction, of health, and of peace with God and men. All this was possible in David's day and is also possible in ours because the Lord makes us dwell in safety.

PSALM 5

Like Psalm 3, Psalm 5 also may be a prayer or song for morning devotions, as verse 3 suggests. Like the other psalms in the beginning section of this book, it is a mixture of praise and prayer to God combined with complaints about enemies and about wicked men in general.

The title is similar to that of Psalm 4. Both have to do with the chief musician. But instead of being played on some stringed instrument (*Neginoth*) this poem is for the *Nehiloth,* which may mean "flutes."

The psalm has no easily discernible outline. Verses 1–3 and 8 are petitions. Four through six speak of God and His hatred of sin. Verse 7 contrasts the righteous behavior of the psalmist with the description of evildoers in the preceding verses and in verses 9 and 10. Verses 11 and 12 are a kind of benediction, which both admonishes and intercedes for the believer and praises God.

Three parallel but unbalanced lines, plus one odd line, make up the first two verses. *Give ear, consider,* and *hear* are the primary verbs. *My words, my meditation,* and *my cry* are the objects. O LORD, *my King,* and *my God* are the three vocatives. The words "consider my meditation" (or literally "groaning") in verse 1 are richer if understood as prayer that God will interpret those unintelligible noises that come from deep thought. The psalmist prays that God will understand (Rom. 8:26f.).

Verse 3 indicates that the psalm may have been composed for morning worship (cf. Ps. 3:5). If not, it may simply show that the psalmist considered prayer important enough to put early in his daily schedule.

Unlike the preceding psalms, where some verses are directed to the readers, this psalm in its entirety is addressed to God. The psalmist's complaints are not to men but to God. He urges not men but God. He communes not with men but with God. Even the criticism of the wicked is put in the form of praise: "The foolish shall not stand in thy sight; thou hatest all workers of iniquity" (v. 5).

In verse 6a is the only instance, in this psalm, of the psalmist's speaking of God in the third person. There he mentions what God Himself already knows. It is another instance of the one praying reminding God of His faithfulness. Later, in verse 10, he demands that God, who abhors unrighteousness, cast out the transgressors.

David asserts his own good intentions in verse 7. This is in contrast to the debauchery and deceit of the wicked described in the two preceding verses (5–6). In both Hebrew and English, verse 7 is a *chiasmus,* although translators have somewhat revised the structure. Literally it would read:

But I,

in the multitude of thy mercies, I will come to thy house
I will worship at thy holy temple in thy fear.

Following this interjection of praise, David prays specifically for direction (v. 8). After that, he again launches into a diatribe against the wicked. Apparently David had been the object of much verbal abuse. Verse 9 contains his counter invective. Paul used elements of this verse in Romans 3:13 where he, too, describes the wickedness of men.

Then in verse 10, with strong passion, David as much as commands God to destroy his enemies, to let them fall, and to cast them out. Then from a different viewpoint, he focuses on the righteous and prays that they might have cause to rejoice, to shout, and to be joyful (v. 11).

Verse 12 concludes the psalm on a note of assurance, with complete faith that the Judge of all the earth will do right (cf. Gen. 18:25). From past experience, and simply because he believes in the God to whom he prays, the psalmist boldly says, "With favour wilt thou compass [the righteous] as with a shield" (cf. Ps. 3:3 KJV).

PSALM 6

In the title of Psalm 6 is another uncertain musical term. *Sheminith* is related to the word for *eight* and so may refer to the eight strings of a musical instrument, or to an eightnoted melody to which the psalm was sung. Perhaps it is an ancient reference to the octave.

Psalm 6 is a kind of personal lament. The classification "trouble and trust" aptly describes this psalm, as well as many others. Toward the end, however, there is a note of hope.

The psalmist begins with a recitation of his troubles. That prompts prayer for deliverance, which culminates in an affirmation of faith and confidence of victory. The more we focus on God and His greatness the more insignificant our troubles become. Many believers let their problems block their view of God. Psalms such as this should remind us that He is the God of the impossible and He summons us to cast our burdens on Him and to spread our concerns before Him.

The source of trouble in this psalm seems to be both from within and without. The first three verses sound like a confession of sin, while mention of adversaries appears in verse 7 and following. We are always our own worst enemy. Even Paul often did that which he did not want to do (Rom. 7:15). We certainly need God's help to overcome the old nature. It may be that the psalmist is equating his enemies' onslaughts with God's punishment of his sins. This raises the larger question as to whether God immediately punishes the believer for his sins. The believer must discern between punishment for wrongdoing through the chastening hand of a loving heavenly Father and the malicious attacks of Satan, the accuser of the brethren. This was Job's dilemma.

The actual content of the psalm raises some interesting questions. From the first three verses, one might wonder to what extent grief affects physical well-being. In verse 2 the psalmist is withered and troubled in his "bones." The word "vexed," or "troubled," appears again in verse 3 and describes his soul. "Soul" recurs in verse 4 as the focus of God's deliverance. *Bones* frequently indicates one's inmost being.

Verse 5 raises the question of the psalmist's view of the afterlife. The Hebrew word *Sheol* here is parallel to "death." Often it is rendered "grave" and occasionally "hell." The psalmist is not denying consciousness after death. Rather he is saying that those who praise and thank God are the living. He is not addressing himself to the question of a conscious afterlife; rather, he is pleading with God for length of this life.

Perhaps the *withering* (KJV, weak) of verse 2 is to be understood with the profuse and bitter weeping of verses 6 and 7. So much water has flowed from the eyes of the grieved that he is literally drying up. As an adjective, this form of the word occurs only once in the Bible.

The turning point of this psalm is in the middle of verse 8, the first half of which is an imperative. The second half is declarative. It is almost as if a certain assurance of answered prayer suddenly flooded the psalmist. Why should he groan and complain any longer? The Lord has heard the sound of his weeping; He has heard his supplication; He will receive his prayer. These statements are the essence of the "trust" mentioned in this psalm. How the Lord, who has heard, will act is recited in the last verse. His enemies shall be shamed and troubled. The very words in verse 3a which describe his soul's condition now describe his foes in verse 10a. Now they shall be "greatly troubled."

In the course of this psalm the writer moves closer to God and thus relatively further from his enemies. God and the psalmist's adversaries are rather fixed entities in this drama. It is the psalmist whose position changes. When he is far from God, he is in jeopardy. But as he moves toward God, his enemy is disadvantaged, and the psalmist has his twofold problem solved. His fellowship with God is restored—the problem of the opening verses—and his vulnerability to his enemies is lessened. This pattern is the same for the Christian in his relationship to his Lord and to the enemies of the cross.

PSALM 7

Psalm 7 is called a *Shiggaion* of David. That technical Hebrew term occurs only twice in the Bible. Habakkuk 3:1 has the plural form, a verb meaning "to wander," which has the same root but does not explain anything about this psalm. It is best to offer no guesses.

Cush the Benjamite is not mentioned elsewhere in the Bible. He was probably a henchman of King Saul. This psalm probably comes out of the experiences narrated in 1 Samuel, when Saul relentlessly sought to destroy David.

Psalm 7 fits into the same category as the preceding one. It is, however, longer and more complicated. The mention of enemies appears again and again (vv. 1, 5, 6). Likewise, affirmations of trust in God occur throughout the psalm (vv. 1, 8, 9, 10, 11).

Verse 1 opens with a declaration of belief and trust. The Lord was David's God and in Him he took refuge. Then follows an imperative verb, a prayer, "Save me." Saul had shown himself ruthless before, and David feared he would be so again. He compared the king with a lion. From a poetic standpoint, notice *deliver* at the end of the first and second verses. In modern, non-poetic language we might say, "Save me while you can." These two verses are the essence of the psalm. The rest is elaboration on the two themes presented here: "The Lord is my God" and "Save me from my enemies."

Verses 3–5 are something of a self-imprecation. The writer calls curses on himself if he is not a man of integrity. The word *if*, which occurs three times, invites examination from God. The implication—rather, the assertion is that he has no evil; he has not done wrong. Having vindicated and exonerated himself and concluded with a *selah*, he continues to pray. Verses 6–9 are filled with appeals that God should act on his behalf: *arise, lift up, awake, judge*, and so forth. Even as the psalmist pleads his own righteousness in the verses above, so here he founds his case on God's justice. Note the number of occurrences in verse 8–11 of such terms as *judgment, judge, righteousness, integrity,* and *upright*.

The subjects of the verbs in verse 12 appear ambiguous, but most agree on an indefinite subject for the first verb. God is the subject of the ensuing verbs. The import is that, if the wicked man will not repent, God will whet His sword and punish him. But in verse 14 the wicked man is again the subject. Words usually used to describe childbearing appear here to describe the production of evil. Everything goes wrong for the wicked. He falls into the pit he dug to trap others, and all his evil plans backfire.

As if David saw victory already accomplished, he closes the psalm on a note of thanksgiving and praise. Once more he mentions the justice of God—the basis on which the evil are punished and the righteous are acquitted, justified, and avenged.

PSALM 8

Psalm 8 is one of the better-known psalms. The almost identical opening and closing verses often have been put to music. The fourth verse is well-known because the author of Hebrews quotes it and applies it to Jesus Christ.

The meaning of the word *Gittith* in the title of the psalm is unknown. Neither context nor related words reveals what it means. Psalms 81 and 84 use the word and they are works of jubilant praise. The two most common suggestions are that it is a tune or a musical instrument.

The psalm falls easily into the following chiastic outline:

> A   God's excellent name (v. 1)
>   B   God's rule (vv. 2–3)
>   C   Man's meanness (v. 4)
>   C´   Man's greatness (v. 5)
>   B´   Man's rule (vv. 6–8)
> A´   God's excellent name (v. 9)

The first half of the first verse is identical to the entire last verse and so these two elements are coupled in the outline. The two longer sections marked "B" describe God's rule and man's rule, respectively. The two middle verses (4, 5) are direct contrasts. First there is man's low view of himself as compared to God and then God's view of man.

The first verse is more extensive than the last. It states that God's name is excellent and worthy to be adored over all the earth, but it also states that His glory is set in the heavens. The latter part of verse 1 may belong with the next section of the outline.

From the suckling baby described in verse 2 on up to the highest heavens, God is Lord of all. Verse 2 is often recalled when a child says something very profound. Sometimes in their naivete children pronounce great truths which adults know but forget. One fall evening the neighbor children were playing beside our house. As it grew dark one of them said they should go home, but another responded: "Why should we be afraid of the dark? God's here." This is the meaning of Psalm 8:2. The expression *babes and sucklings* may indicate children old enough to talk. Hebrew mothers often nursed their babies for four or five years.

The purpose of using such feeble instruments to announce God's glory is to offend the adversary. How many unbelievers have been rebuked by the innocently offered remark of a child schooled in the basics of God-fearing living! When the children sang "Hosanna" on Palm Sunday, Jesus reminded the people of this verse (Matt. 21:16).

From the earthbound sphere of children, verse 3 lifts our attention to the heavens. They are the work of God's fingers. He has ordained the various heavenly bodies. The word "when" connects this verse very closely with the next.

Having focused the reader's attention on the heavens, the psalmist then wonders what dealings God would ever have with man. Why should a mortal be thought of or visited by Deity? The fifth verse answers that question immediately. It is because man is really just a little lower than God. The Hebrew word usually means "God," sometimes it means "gods," and, in a few instances, "angels." The point is that man is not just a little higher than the animals but a little lower than heaven.

Hebrews 2:6–8 quotes this passage and applies it to Christ. That New Testament passage shows that Christ is superior to angels. But because it seems to say much the opposite (the Greek word in Hebrews is "angels" and not "God"), some take the word "little" to refer to time. According to that interpretation, He was for a little while lower than the angels. This is supported by the commentary that follows in Hebrews 2:9. Psalm 8 doubtlessly is speaking of all men in general, but the writer of Hebrews, by divine inspiration, refers specifically and specially to Jesus Christ, the Son of Man and the Son of God.

Man, and particularly Jesus Christ, is crowned with glory and honor. His is a glory far grander than ours; nevertheless, the psalm can refer to both. God made everything in the world, and man is to rule it. Verse 6 says this in general terms and verses 7–8 in specific terms. Remember the chiastic arrangement of this psalm and note the references to the heavens in verses 3 and 8. God made the heavens; man is in control over the birds of the heavens.

The benediction which opened the psalm is repeated in the last verse. This time it has more meaning. God is worthy of more praise because of His love and concern for His creatures, including man. We are exalted to be His vicegerent. We, of all His creatures, are able to offer intelligent and voluntary praise. The Lord is our Lord. How excellent is His name in all the earth!

PSALM 9

Praise is the theme of Psalm 9, though the psalmist several times mentions his enemies and their certain destruction along with all the wicked. In the thirteenth and in the last two verses are brief petitions to God. But the main focus is on God Himself and His greatness.

Two technical terms appear in this psalm. First, the title indicates that it is *on* or *set to Muth-labben*. As with the other uncertain words in the titles, it is best to consider this one to signify either a tune or an instrument. There are many suggestions in ancient versions and modern commentaries which translate the words and make a connection between the contents of the psalm and some event in David's life. These suggestions are not very convincing, especially those which rely on altering the Hebrew spelling. The psalm itself speaks in general terms making it difficult to link it with a specific historical happening.

The second technical term is at the end of verse 16 where *Hig-*

gaion appears with *selah*. As with *selah* (see commentary on Psalm 3), we were uncertain about *Higgaion*. It seems to belong to the same root as the word usually translated as "meditate." Verse 16b however, does not mark a division in the psalm, and the terms may be musical notations with relatively nothing to do with the meaning of the poem.

Another peculiarity of Psalm 9 is that it is an alphabetic acrostic when joined with Psalm 10. Apart from some minor irregularities, every second verse begins with a consecutive letter of the Hebrew alphabet.

Four *I will*'s mark the first two verses. Actually, there are five things the psalmist determines to do: give thanks, show forth, be glad, exult, and sing praise. God and His work, of course, are the objects of all these verbs.

Verses 3–6 constitute the second section. Although the ancient worshiper continues to strike a note of praise, it is praise for the destruction of the enemy. This theme appears again in verses 15–17. At first, the "enemy" is the personal enemy of the psalmist. Later the terminology becomes more general. In verse 4, the jubilation over destroyed foes is interrupted, and David exults in his own vindication and justification.

Something should be said about the word *nations* (often "heathen" in KJV). It occurs in verses 5, 15, 19 and in many places in other psalms. The Hebrew word is *goiim* and is known by anyone having close Jewish acquaintances. The oldest meaning is "*nation*" in the sense of an ethnic group. Any political overtone is definitely secondary. Later the term came to mean all peoples other than Israelites, as today it means non-Jews. *Gentile* is a perfectly accurate translation but is often misunderstood. *Heathen* suggests someone from a primitive part of the world. *Nations* is the best meaning as long as it is not understood politically. Hebrew writers used *kingdom, house,* or the name of the political entity itself when they had governments in mind. *Goiim* is not so used, as the verses before us illustrate. The nations are here paralleled to the wicked, i.e., to wicked people.

The *name* at the end of verse 5 and the *remembrance* or *memorial* at the end of verse 6 point to another peculiarity of Semitic thought. A man's name is the man. His remembrance is his eternal life. That his name be blotted out and the remembrance of his acts perish is tantamount to being punished forever.

The psalmist changes focus in verse 7. The next three verses are not so much human expressions of praise as theological explanations of God and His justice. They are praise, nevertheless. The first declares God's eternality. Then follow three statements about His justice. The beneficiaries of His righteous judgment come into view in verses 8 and 9. The oppressed will find their advocate and defender in the Judge of all the earth. He will do right (Gen. 18:25). Verse 9, incidentally, is a fine example of progressive parallelism. ABC BDE is the pattern. The words *high tower* (or *refuge,* KJV) connect the two stichs.

The tower of a Palestinian town was the citadel, the innermost military stronghold. While the poor and oppressed were ordinarily forbidden its protection, they can find deliverance in the Lord.

Verses 10, 11, and 12 are the center of the psalm. These three verses capsulize the entire hymn. Included are a statement of faith, a declaration of God's attributes—His justice, in particular—and an injunction to praise.

Verse 13 is a prayer. It comes right after the statement that God remembers the poor or afflicted. David identifies himself with the afflicted and so justifies his petition. Then follows his promise to praise God faithfully.

The next section contains verses 15–18 and corresponds to

verses 3–6. Reports and predictions about the fate of the wicked, who bring trouble onto themselves, fill this part of the psalm. In verse 17, *nations* should be understood simply as "unbelievers."

The psalm concludes with five petitions to God. First is the positive appeal for God to arise. Then there is the negative, "Let not man prevail." Verse 19b puts the two together. Verse 20 continues the parallel with 19b. Both *nations* (or *heathen*) and *man* occur twice in these two verses. The point of the prayer is that God will fulfill His responsibility as Judge and that men should fulfill their responsibility in submissive trusting.

PSALM 10

Psalm 10 is the second half of the alphabetic acrostic that begins in Psalm 9. The natural division of this psalm falls after verse 11. Up to that point the psalmist describes the wicked. Beyond that point is the prayer to overthrow the wicked and to exonerate the righteous.

The opening verse is a complaint: "Why do You stand at a distance, Lord?" People do not want to get involved as witnesses to accidents. They walk on the other side of the road, as the priest and the Levite of the good Samaritan parable (Luke 10:30f.), when they see trouble. God, the psalmist charges, is only a fair-weather friend to the righteous. "Why do You hide Yourself in times of trouble?"

Verses 2–11 describe in detail the devious paths of the wicked man, but only in verse 2b is there an imprecation against him. Evil men are proud, boastful, and covetous. The word translated "blesseth" (v. 3) in the King James Version is interesting. The American Standard Version renders that Hebrew word with its polar or opposite meaning, "renounce." Several Hebrew words and several English words have such opposite meanings. "Stone" and "destone" are the same in Hebrew. "Go" and "come" may translate the same Hebrew word. Our English "let" can have opposite meanings.

Notice the arrogance of the wicked man's statements and thoughts in verses 4, 5, and 11. Not only does he say that God will not require anything of him, but he even thinks there is no God. He is more than a practical atheist—one who acts as if there is no God; he actually says there is none (v. 4b ASV). Yet that same wicked man declares that the God who does not exist has forgotten and hidden His holy face from those wicked deeds.

The metaphor of verses 9–10 illustrates the general statements of verse 8. The wicked man says and does what is false and wrong. His victims are the poor and the weak. As a lion preys on weak, slow, or ignorant animals, so the wicked takes every unfair advantage to gain mastery over other men.

The prayer of verse 12 through the end of the psalm is a welcome relief from the grim picture in the first half. The psalmist says in so many words, "Are You going to stand for this, Lord? Do something! Have You forgotten the poor and the weak? Will You tolerate this blasphemy?"

Verse 14 provides another instance of the psalmist exerting pressure on God with the lever of historical precedent. The helpless formerly committed their cause into God's hand and He delivered them. Will the Father of mercies now be untrue to Himself?

The strongest verse in the entire psalm is 15. Forgetting all courtesy and tolerance, the psalmist urges God to break the wicked man's arm—and so to divest him of his power. He strongly appeals to the Lord to uncover every wicked facet of this iniquitous operation. God should leave no stone unturned in order to root out evil and to right wrong.

Verses 16 to the end of the psalm are the benediction. They are written as if the prayer were already answered. The nations, unbelieving outsiders, are punished, while the meek are helped. The orphan and the oppressed will be vindicated and protected. The ravisher of the poor man's meager means will be a terror no more.

PSALM 11

Psalm 11 is another psalm of David for the chief musician. The theme is that God is a refuge from wicked men, a defense against their evil deeds. A lesson as simple as this is easily forgotten. Even Christians often fight fire with fire and sword with sword. In some very critical battles they forget that God has promised to be their refuge and defense. He delights to shield them and is honored by their requests for Him to do so.

Psalm 11 has several cryptic phrases which cannot be translated with certainty. The first is in the opening verse. Whom does the psalmist quote? Or who says the words, "Flee, bird, to your mountain"? How far should that quotation be carried? None of these questions has a certain answer, but it seems best to understand that the psalmist is referring to an evil taunt. "Bird," then, was a derogatory term as it is today when used to describe a person. The New English Bible seems right in carrying the quote through verse 2. The wicked is warning the believer, whom he calls a bird, to get out of the way because he has readied his bow to shoot down the prey.

The first two verses, taken as a whole, are a profession of faith in the face of threat. The God-fearing writer as much as says that he is not going to be intimidated by the challenges and warnings of the wicked, since he has put his faith in God.

Verse 3 is another difficult verse. The basic meaning of all the Hebrew words is clear, but not the syntax—how they are put together. The tenses are uncertain. The nature of the subjunctive is unsure. Should it be rendered *if, when, for,* or *since*? The word *can* is only in the text by implication. And there yet remains the question, "Foundations" of what? Society? True religion? Some literal building?

Some versions, such as the Revised Standard Version, understand this as part of the wicked man's taunt and close the quotation marks at the end of verse 3. Otherwise it sounds like a confession of despair. The good man apparently admits he can do nothing in light of the bad man's destruction of that which is vital and basic. If this latter is the better interpretation, then it forms an appropriate conclusion to the first part, the negative part of the psalm.

Immediately follows the only suitable answer. Remember that God is still on the throne. Though the walls seem to crumble around us, He is still there, watching, remembering, storing up judgment. Verse 4 begins the description of God, the object of the psalmist's trust. The God of all right will always do right. There are no English synonyms for "eye," so after the word is used once, the parallel Hebrew word is translated with the strange-sounding agent of God's justice, His "eyelids"! Some modern versions paraphrase to avoid this difficulty.

God tries or examines all men and all their deeds, good and bad. Especially will He put the wicked—those who love violence—on trial. God hates violence.

The picture in verse 6 is vivid and reminds us of the judgment on Sodom and Gomorrah, as well as of the fire and brimstone of Revelation 14:10, 19:20, 20:10, and 21:8.

The other side of the coin of God's perfect justice is His reward to the upright (v. 7). Since God is right and loves right deeds, He also loves righteous people. The greatest prize the poet can think of is to see God face to face.

Several gospel songs echo this hope. Carrie E. Breck (1855–1934) wrote one entitled "Face to Face." Another by Charles H. Gabriel (1856–1932) includes the lines:

When by His grace I shall look on His face,
That will be glory, be glory for me.
("Oh, That Will Be Glory")

PSALM 12

Psalm 12 is a chiasmus. The first and last verses contain the phrases "sons of men" and "children of men" (cf. ASV) and the basic contents of these two verses are parallel. The second verse describes the words of wicked men while the sixth and seventh verses describe the pure words of the Lord. The middle verses (3, 4, 5) portray the punishment God will pour out on the wicked and the deliverance He will give to the oppressed.

Psalm 12 is in the "trouble and trust" category. Because of the chiastic structure it is "trouble–trust–trouble."

Apart from the arrangement of the themes within the psalm there are vivid word pictures drawn by the ancient artist. In fact, the cutting off of lips and the severing of tongues may have been a method of torture common to those times. The figure of the mouth is not abandoned until the end of verse 5. Whereas the wicked talks himself into trouble with God, the oppressed pant after His righteousness.

In the psalms it is common to personify a virtue, a vice, or a condition. Righteousness is the righteous man; wickedness is the wicked man; poverty is the poor man; and so on. The faithful man stands for faith. Neighbor stands for society. This psalm is a mixture of such concepts and pictures. Verse 1 does not make it clear whether godliness or the godly man has ceased, or if righteous deeds or righteous men fail. Of course it is not crucial to the understanding of the psalm, but it is fascinating to see how concepts are actualized, and vice versa.

The psalmist's complaint is that bad men are everywhere and

good men cannot be found. He has an attitude similar to Elijah's. Elijah thought he was the only believer left when, in fact, God still had 7,000 others (1 Kings 19:14, 18).

For three verses the focus is on what the wicked say. Often our enemies hurt us more by what they say than by inflicting physical harm. James warned Christians that they are not exempt from committing sins of the tongue (3:5–10). Verse 2 contains an interesting Hebraism. Where we read with a "double heart" the original has "with heart and heart." That means that first he speaks from one set of principles and then from another.

Through the blasphemous din God still hears the groaning and gasping of the needy and oppressed. And the God of justice promises safety to these downtrodden objects of His love.

Verse 7 presents a textual problem. The verse might more accurately read:

> Thou wilt keep them [i.e., his words or the oppressed people],
> O LORD.
> Thou wilt preserve us from this generation forever.

All the standard translations make both objects either "them" or "us." We must try to determine what God inspired the psalmist to say and then accurately render it. Three interpretations are possible: God will preserve the oppressed; God will preserve those who believe in Him; God will keep His word. Which one does the psalmist mean in this passage? All are true.

PSALM 13

The question, "How long?" is typical of laments. Compare Psalms 6:3; 89:46; 90:13; and 94:3, 4. Psalm 13 has this question four times in the first two verses.

In characteristic "trouble and trust" fashion, this psalm begins with grievous lament and ends with genuine trust. These six short verses move from despair to rejoicing, from agony to ecstasy, from sorrow to song. Neither extreme is insincere. Both are marked by integrity.

The psalmist is like most other believers; he often cannot understand the ways of God. On the one hand, he knows that God never forgets, but on the other hand, God apparently has forgotten him. God is supposed to be everywhere, but at this critical intersection His location cannot be found. God should be the psalmist's counsel and comfort yet he has to find them in himself rather than in God. God is the Lord of hosts and yet the present enemy is winning the victory.

All Scripture is profitable for something, according to 2 Timothy 3:16. The profit of these individual laments must be in showing the modern saint that ancient saints had the same problems and questions. We are neither the first nor the last to wonder about God's sovereignty. David did it long ago.

In verses 3 and 4, the prayer changes from complaint to petition. See and do, Lord. Watch and act, my God. Consider and answer.

Verse 4 is the lever, noticed in other psalms, used to pry God into action with the threat that otherwise the adversary will be happy.

In the last two verses appears the declaration of trust. In spite of all he said before, the ancient writer asserts that he has trusted and that he will rejoice and sing. The bountiful dealings of God in the past outweigh any temporary discomfort. "Count your many blessings" is an appropriate commentary. Job lived out the details which this psalm only outlines in general terms. His testimony was, "Though he slay me, yet will I trust in him" (Job 13:15 KJV).

PSALM 14

Psalms 14 and 53 are nearly identical. The first three verses, which Paul echoes in Romans 3:10–12, have a familiar ring.

This is a wisdom psalm. The psalmist does not speak specifically of himself or of his people, except in the last verse. Personal pronouns are rarely found. The enemy, the fool, and the godly are mentioned in general terms.

Only a fool professes atheism (cf. Ps. 10:4). The foolish atheist is also a wicked man. He is totally depraved in the theological sense. He can do nothing to please God. That which man might call righteousness is still sin in God's eyes. A sinner can do nothing but sin. God cannot find a single individual who seeks Him. No man comes to Christ except the Father draw him (John 6:44). This truth drives us harder to our knees. By His sovereign choice, we are in Christ and by that same sovereignty He must lead any others who come. There is none who seeks God, not even one.

In a certain sense the unregenerate man can know nothing rightly. Workers of iniquity have no knowledge, especially the saving knowledge of God. All ultimate truth evades them as long as God's Spirit is not in their hearts.

The victims of the godless man's violence are the people of God. Though the godless man does not call on God, he survives at the expense of God's people.

Verse 5 presents some questions. Who is in great fear? And where is *there*? The first answer might be that the people of God are in great fear, for they are the most immediate antecedents. But in the light of verse 6, it might rather be the evil men. They are afraid because they see that they cannot act with impunity against the righteous, for God is with them. Those wicked ones are addressed in verse 6. If the verb is taken as inceptive, as the

Revised Standard Version does ("You would confound the plans of the poor"), the wicked are again seen as thwarted in their plan because God is the poor man's refuge.

The psalm ends with an invocation for God's salvation or deliverance. This anticipates the Messiah who would bring salvation to the elect of Israel when He comes to Zion. The name *Jesus* is from the Hebrew word for salvation, *yeshuah*. It is not necessary to understand this as an exilic psalm, for even in David's day, the captivity or bondage of sin prevailed. In a yet incompletely formed spiritual kingdom, the people were kept from rejoicing by the presence of so much wickedness. There are still people who deny God's existence and resist His Anointed, but someday the wicked will greatly tremble, while spiritual Israel will be glad.

PSALM 15

Psalm 15 was probably used in the tabernacle liturgy. The first verse asks two questions: the remaining four verses answer them. It is one of the more practical psalms with down-to-earth applications.

Verse 1 is a lovely example of Hebrew parallelism. After the initial vocative, "LORD," each element has its companion in the second half. *Sojourn* and *dwell* are synonyms; *tabernacle* and *holy hill* are virtual synonyms.

This is a psalm of David, and the reference to the tabernacle may further indicate the period when the psalm was written. It may, however, merely indicate God's earthly dwelling place—His tent. "Who can be Your guest?" is a homey paraphrase.

The hill of God's holiness, to render the Hebrew more literally, is, of course, the central sanctuary of Israel at Jerusalem. The question is: What are the requirements for citizenship in Zion?

There are eleven parts to the answer and a summary line at the end. Each verse has three stichs or lines.

The first three statements have to do with integrity in general. The man who would enter God's house must be truthful. He must walk, work, and speak in truth and righteousness.

The next three (v. 3) deal with friends and neighbors. In particular, they have to do with evil talk. Gossip was a social ill then as it is now. For the most part, gossip concerns friends and neighbors, not foreign enemies. The candidate for worship must not have a vicious tongue that shames and berates his neighbor in front of others. It would prove interesting if we made these same simple requirements necessary for participation in our church worship!

Verse 4 details matters of religious attitude. The worshiper must hate what and whom God hates. Sin must not be tolerated (cf. Deut. 7:5; 13:1–18; and Rev. 2:20). Some say that the phrase "them that fear the LORD" is a technical designation for uncircumcised Gentiles who nevertheless were adherents to the God and religion of Israel. If that is so, the question is raised of tolerating Christians who are not completely orthodox. What should our attitude be toward those who differ? How widely can they differ? What is essential to cooperation? Are all who differ from us, even in the slightest, reprobate? Or are there some God-fearers outside our own ecclesiastical orbit?

The last stich of verse 4 points up in a most practical way how a man of integrity acts. Even if it costs him money, he keeps all his promises. He does not try to escape commitments. How many missionaries have suffered untold grief because people and churches who promised support defaulted? Such a weasel should not presume to be a welcome guest on God's holy hill.

Money is the subject of verse 5. Israelites were not to lend to their poor countrymen at interest (Ex. 22:25). This is not, however, a prohibition of savings accounts or the stock market. Jesus

Himself commended wise investors (Matt. 25:14–27). Verse 5 condemns gross financial abuse of the poor. Bribing, the second matter, is also forbidden (cf. Ex. 23:8).

The psalm could be summarized: If you do all the moral and spiritual positives, and avoid all the negatives, you will never be moved from fellowship with God.

PSALM 16

Michtam is in the title of six psalms: 16 and 56–60. No one knows for certain what it means, and in most versions it is simply transliterated.

Basically, this is a personal testimony to the blessedness in the Lord which the psalmist enjoys. At the outset there is a petition, and in the course of the poem there is an overtone of a polemic against other gods. There is some difficulty in the Hebrew which has given rise to the variety of renderings in verses 1–4.

The psalm does not fall easily into an outline; rather, the author moves from theme to theme, sometimes with obvious logical connection and sometimes without.

A prayer for perseverance opens the work followed immediately by the reason. The psalmist says, in effect, that God owes him deliverance because of his trust.

The subject changes in the difficult third verse. If the traditional rendering is accurate, the psalmist declares his delight in God's people as well as in God. Incidentally, the Hebrew words for the last phrase are *kal-hephsi-bam* ("in whom is all my delight"), essentially the same as *Hephzibah,* the new name God will give to His people, according to Isaiah 62:4.

The faithful worshiper of Yahweh (or Jehovah) makes his anti-polytheistic punch felt in verse 4. He testifies that he has no part in giving gifts or drink offerings to anyone but the true God.

In fact, he does not even use the names of other gods.

In contrast to the divided allegiances of other people, the psalmist's sole hope for inheritance is in the Lord. This idea of inheritance ties verse 6 to the preceding verses. The boundary lines for his property have fallen in such a way that all the land is fertile, watered, and productive. He has inherited no rocky mountainside, no barren desert, no sterile wasteland. He is examining his spiritual heritage in picture form. He is a blessed man.

Unlike many of us, this singer recognizes how prosperous and happy he is. Sole credit goes to God for His sage advice and welcome nocturnal promptings to praise. Do we use the opportunities afforded by sleepless nights to sing His praise?

All the sermons in the New Testament are replete with quotations from the Old. Peter's were no exception. In Acts 2:25–28 he quoted Psalm 16:8–11 and later in verse 31 identified verse 10 as Messianic. Paul, too, cited the tenth verse as he preached the resurrection of Christ to the people of Antioch of Pisidia (Acts 13:35).

These citations confirm for us the Messianic interpretation of this psalm. Not only can these statements describe David, but they describe Christ our Lord as well.

The testimony in verse 8b echoes the same word that is sounded at the close of Psalm 15. With our eyes on God and our hand in His, there is no greater safety. Because of all these blessings, David rejoices. *Glory* here means "soul" or "spirit." Verse 10 parallels *my soul* with *your faithful* or *holy one.*

Sheol is the Hebrew word for the place of the dead. It does not necessarily connote punishment as the English word *hell* does. To that place God would not and did not abandon His Messiah. The word parallel to *sheol* is perhaps best translated "corruption" (v. 10b). Christ did experience the pit, i.e., the grave, but not the attendant dissolution of His body (cf. Acts 2:31).

The psalm ends with a three-part verse affirming in positive terms that which verse 10 said in negative terms. God leads His chosen ones to the path of life-everlasting life. This narrow road, in turn, leads to all sorts of delights, which are occasioned exclusively by the presence of God Himself. Compare the remarks on Psalm 11:7. The greatest prize of all is to see Christ and be like Him.

PSALM 17

The number of italicized words in the King James Version gives some indication of the difficulty in interpreting this psalm. All translators must make a number of guesses in order to provide a sensible English version.

Psalm 17 is a prayer. From beginning to end we witness the most agonized struggle of a man with his God. He needs protection. He needs assurance that he is in the right. He wants to see his enemies punished.

No neat outline fits this psalm. Several themes occur more than once, just as when we pray over a distressing problem and return again and again to it. Here is the psalmist's demand to be heard. It occurs in verse 1 and again in verses 2 and 6. "I am right" is another theme. It is in verses 1, 3, 4, and 5 (NASB). Specific prayer for protection appears in verses 7, 8, 9, 13, and 14. Verses 1b, 4b, 9, 10, 11, and 12 characterize the wicked. Verse 15 is a kind of testimony of hope.

Certain words and their synonyms occur again and again pointing to the unity of the work. *Cry, prayer, lips, mouth,* and *speech* belong in one group. *Ways, steps, paths,* and *feet* are roughly parallel. God is characterized by several anthropomorphisms. He has ears, a face, eyes, wings, hands, a sword, and a general bodily form, according to the last word of the poem.

Only five psalms are titled as prayers: 17, 86, 90, 102, and

142. Many more, however, are prayers. The word *prayer* actually occurs thirty-two times in the whole collection. No reason militates against the Davidic authorship of this psalm. A cursory reflection on the number of enemies he had gives ample substance to a prayer of this sort. Some enemies were foreign nations (e.g., the Philistines). Some were within Israel (e.g., Saul). Some were in his own family (e.g., Absalom). But his faithful ally was the God of Abraham, Isaac, and Jacob. The true disciple must expect enemies, perhaps even within his own household (Matt. 10:36). But we, too, have that Friend who sticks closer than a brother (Prov. 18:24).

The opening two verses introduce the prayer. Five pleading verbs are contained in this initial overture: *hear, attend, give ear, let,* and *look*. The word *right* or *righteous* stands without connection in the Hebrew of verse 1. Therefore it could be read: "Hear, O righteous Lord," or "Hear a righteous man," or "Hear what is right." In other words, the adjective could describe the Lord, the psalmist, or the prayer itself. The last is best because of the parallel "my cry."

His protestation of righteousness already appears in the first verse. Unlike his lying foes, his lips are free from deceit. In verses 3–5, that protestation of righteousness is elaborated on.

A legal tone permeates these opening verses, as revealed in such words as *right, sentence, equity, prove,* and *try*. The psalmist demands a hearing with the Judge of all men. He wants it because he knows he is right and the enemy is wrong. If God would only see that, then He would pay David damages and punish the enemies.

In verses 3 and following David reminds God that he has been proven and tried and found blameless. Even in the secret of night he asserts that God's all-knowing eyes have found in him nothing amiss. Neither his words nor his deeds condemn him. On the other hand, the ways, work, and words of wicked men are violent.

Verse 6 concludes the first section, sounding again the notes of verse 1.

The psalm continues with a positive petition that God would demonstrate His *ḥeseḏ*. This rich Hebrew word involves mercy, faithfulness to fulfill promises, and irrevocable covenant love. It is marvelous. The remainder of verse 7 is an elaborate description of God. The Hebrew is difficult and several translations are possible. The New English Bible has this fresh rendering:

> Show me how marvelous thy love can be,
>   who with thy hand does save
>   all who seek sanctuary from their enemies.

Because of the position of the words *your right hand* in Hebrew, it might better be understood that the enemies are "those who rebel against Your right hand." The preposition can be either *by* or *against*.

In verses 9–12 the enemies from whom David pleads protection are described. They are wicked. They oppress him. They are deadly. They surround him. They are fat, i.e., greedy, and full of pride. They are boastful of their vicious accomplishments. They encircle the saint. They have their eyes set on his destruction. They are like ravenous lions lurking in secret, waiting to jump their innocent victim.

David implores God to arise and free him from all these terrors (v. 13). "Confront him to his face, cast him down but deliver me . . ." A series of *froms* marks this section: "from the wicked that oppress" (v. 9), "from the wicked" (v. 13), "from men" (v. 14), and "from men of the world" (v. 14).

The latter part of verse 14 is probably the most difficult part of the psalm to understand. Most interpreters take it as a description of the wicked and of his rewards, which are only temporal. Maybe

David has his tongue in his cheek. The enemy, the man whose god is his belly, can only hope for transitory fortune, but God has "treasured up" for him only punishment.

In striking contrast is the hope of the believer. He, either figuratively in this present life or in reality in the next, will see God's face and behold His form. That is the only satisfaction he wants, for he knows that the righteous alone inherit that reward. Let the wicked have the cursed wealth of this condemned world. We shall see the King some day!

PSALM 18

What a beautiful way to begin a psalm! "I love you, LORD." And why not, since God was to David and did for him the dozens of things spelled out in the following fifty verses?

There is no reason to doubt the accuracy of the title to this, the fourth longest poem in the Psalter. Second Samuel 22:1–51 duplicates both the title and the psalm itself with minor variations. In that historical book is a kind of summary of David's life. Saul was now dead. Absalom was dead. The Philistines were subdued. David's kingdom was relatively secure.

A broad outline might be:

A praise introduction (vv. 1–3)
A picture of God the deliverer (vv. 4–19)
The basis of that deliverance (vv. 20–30)
Testimony of victory through God (vv. 31–45)
A praise benediction (vv. 46–50)

The opening three verses praise God in very general terms. He is the writer's strength, rock, fortress, deliverer, shield, horn of salvation, and high tower. All of these have to do with the military;

in fact, the whole psalm has a strong militaristic ring. Those over whom David triumphed were military foes.

Beginning with verse 4 and continuing through verse 6, David describes his deliverance, as it were, from death. *Saul* and *Sheol* have the same consonants in Hebrew; only the vowels are different. Because of this, some want to substitute *Sheol* for *Saul* in the title. *Sheol* is parallel with death here in verse 5.

Jonah knew this psalm and referred to verses 4–6 in his second chapter. The reference to "temple" in poetry does not prove that the poem is post-Davidic. This word is used in connection with the boyhood of Samuel many years before Psalm 18 was written (1 Sam. 1:9; 3:3).

Verses 7–15 contain an extended theophany. The earth and the foundations of the mountains shook, trembled, and quaked because God was angry. There is no record of an earthquake accompanying any of David's deliverances. All this may be a highly figurative description of the thundering army of the Lord of hosts.

The descriptions in verse 8 sound like a volcanic eruption but perhaps are only a thunder and lightning storm, as verses 13–14 indicate. Whatever its exact meteorological nature, this violent storm is evidence of God's vindicating, punishing power. The resultant flood from excess rain and melted hail washes bare the bedrock of the land (v. 15). The blast of the breath of God's nostrils is, of course, the wind.

The personal pronoun *me* appears again in verse 17. By all these natural and supernatural means God saves His saint from the hateful enemy. Even though they choose to attack David when he is down, thus multiplying his calamity, God chooses to bring him to safety. The *wide place* is in contrast to the narrow escape, the tight situation, the squeeze the enemy put on him.

It is an easy transition to the next point in the outline. The basis of God's deliverance is already indicated in verses 18–19, and 20–30 only elaborate on it. Simply put, the reason God saved David is that "He delighted in him." That answer sounds too simple to many unbelievers. Rather than believe Christ and win eternal life, they espouse a more difficult religion of works which brings no salvation at all.

Some might accuse David of arrogance and proud self-righteousness. But remember that ultimate righteousness comes from trusting God. This one "good deed" of belief in God's saving provision and forgiving power is counted by God to outweigh all sin.

Ten times over David tells why God dealt so generously with him. All of this is based on the one little statement in verse 19: "Because He delighted in me." If God chooses to be for us, none can stand against us (Rom. 8:31). We are His by sovereign election and He cannot forsake us. David was not saved by works—only by *the* work of faith (cf. John 6:29).

Verses 25–26 contain an interesting little series. God is what we are to Him. The good think He is good. The bad think He is bad. If we confess Christ before men, He will confess us before the Father. If we deny Him before men, He will deny us before the Father (Matt. 10:32–33).

In David's day, as well as in Peter's and in ours, God exalts the humble but humiliates the proud (1 Peter 5:5). With the figures of a lamp and a shield, the psalmist concludes this section. Verse 29b is one of this writer's favorite testimony verses. It comes to mind whenever a human impossibility is faced. "By my God I can leap over a wall!" Joshua and the people of Israel did it literally at Jericho. David and his army did it at Jerusalem. Why can't we?

The next large section (vv. 31–45) relates in glowing terms just how Yahweh, the only true God, gave David victory over his numerous antagonists. In figurative terms, God clothed him with strength and made his way perfect; that is, He completely prepared David. God made his feet like deer's feet, his bow like brass, and gave him the shield of salvation. (Compare verses 32, 34–35, 39 with Eph. 6:13–17.) Having so armed His king, God held his right hand and let him take giant strides, while not letting his foot slip. Thus he chased the enemy, stabbed them, and had them fall at his feet. Notice the typical Semitic repetition in verses 37–42. How many times and in how many ways does he repeat the fact of their annihilation?

From what seem to be local triumphs, the psalmist turns, in verse 43, to boast of the international fame that God granted him. Perhaps the first stich of verse 43 indicates that internal factions had ceased. He had consolidated all areas of Israel. In the balance of the verse the annexation of nations is the subject. For all this, the only credit he takes is that he trusted God. God gave the deliverances and deserves all the praise.

The last five verses of the poem are a benediction and summarize briefly all that was said above. The ideas of rock and salvation (v. 46) echo verse 2 in the laudatory introduction. The victories recited in verses 47 and 48 reflect the bulk of the central part of the work. The last two verses conclude both the benediction and the psalm.

Notice the evangelistic emphasis of this ancient, godly king. He declares that he will give thanks "among the nations"; that is, he will tell these recently conquered peoples of the greatness of his God. Why should such a man of faith not be concerned that his subjects, as well, know the true God?

Verse 50 has the word *messiah* in it (*anointed* in KJV).

The phrases "to his king," "to his anointed," "to David," and "to his seed" are parallel. That seed, we learn elsewhere, is none other than Christ our Lord.

To a certain extent we can share in the exultation of this psalm. Not only might we slightly resemble David in our faith, but because we are in Christ we share in His conquests as He builds and blesses His kingdom.

PSALM 19

Psalm 19 is a favorite psalm of many people. It is very clear in its arrangement and simple in its message. The author speaks of God's revelation in nature and in the Bible. Here is a three-point outline:

The World of God (vv. 1–6)
The Word of God (vv. 7–10)
The Way of God (vv. 11–14)

Men learn of God from the realm of nature, but more specifically from His written revelation. With the coming of Christ in the fullness of time the world received God's living Word (John 1:1).

The device of parallelism is apparent throughout this psalm. The first verse is a clear example of it. *Heaven* and the *firmament* (expanse or vault) are the two subjects, *declare* and *show* are the verbs, and *the glory of God* and *His handiwork* are the objects. A Bible student could profitably examine this entire psalm in the light of parallelism.

That God is evident in nature is believed by all except the most hardened of those who resist Him. Numerous and eloquent are the poems of men to this effect. Sunsets, seashores, starry nights, trees, flowers, waterfalls—all are the subjects men write about.

Poems are made by fools like me,
But only God can make a tree.

These famous words of Joyce Kilmer do just what the opening part of this psalm does: present the Creator through nature.

Verse 2 declares that night and day alike provide evidence of God's existence. The word rendered *uttereth* (KJV) has the sense of "gush" or "surge" behind it in the original language. Having spoken of a universal speech, the psalmist continues by saying that it is never heard. The word *where* does not appear in Hebrew, so what we have are three negative statements. "There is no speech." "There is no language." "Their voice is not heard." The first two-thirds of verse 4 complete this thought. The unheard speech, the words or message, is everywhere—to the ends of the earth. *Line,* which might be slang in our language, is not such in Hebrew. (Paul quotes the Greek translation of the Old Testament in Romans 10:18, which reads, "their voice" in the NASB.) The hymn "The Spacious Firmament" by Joseph Addison is a beautiful commentary on these verses. Here is just one of the stanzas:

What though, in solemn silence, all
    Move round this dark terrestrial ball?
What though no real voice nor sound
    Amid the radiant orbs be found?
In reason's ear they all rejoice,
    And utter forth a glorious voice,
Forever singing as they shine,
    "The hand that made us is divine."

To depict the worldwide communication of God's existence and glory, the psalmist chooses the sun's daily coverage of the earth. This picture continues through verse 6. But verse 5 is an illustration of an illustration. Evidence for God is like the sun. The sun, in turn, is like a bridegroom or a ready runner. These were the most glorious specimens the writer could use to characterize the beauty and strength of the sun. In its orbit it begins at one horizon, makes what appears from our perspective to be a high half circle, and goes to the other horizon. Everything derives warmth from it; all energy comes from it—a scientific truth recognized only in modern times.

Verses 7–10 speak of the Bible. Here are six synonyms for the Word: *law, testimony, precepts, commandments, fear,* and *ordinances.* Then there are the descriptive adjectives: *perfect, sure, right, pure, clean,* and the additional ones in verse 9, *true* and *righteous altogether.* Following each of the first five adjectives is a statement of what the Word of God does. It restores or converts the soul. It makes the simple wise. It rejoices the heart. It enlightens the eyes. It endures forever. An interesting study would be to rearrange the three elements of each of these strophes. There are more than fifteen possible combinations.

Notice in verse 7a that the first thing which the Word of God does is to restore the soul. This word can also be translated *converting* (KJV). The priority given to this word is intentional. Before we can be wise, before the heart really rejoices, before our eyes can be clearly enlightened, and before we find the Bible more precious than gold and sweeter than honey, we must be saved. Conversion is the first step.

The gold and the honey of verse 10 easily prompt many analogies. Like gold, the Bible is priceless. The Bible is the most valuable of all books. The Bible is enduring. The Bible serves as a standard. Like honey the Bible is sweet. The Bible is nourishing. The Bible has healing qualities. The Bible admits of no impurities.

The last four verses of the psalm tell us what the Bible does— what the way of God is. The writer, who calls himself a servant, testifies that there are to be found in the Bible both warning and reward—a hell to shun and a heaven to win.

Study of the Bible moves us to a consciousness of sin and to a sensitivity for holiness. Such is the gist of the prayer which continues to the end of the psalm. David knows that pride (presumption) can be the most deceiving of all sin, so he prays for cleansing from it. The sister of pride is hypocrisy; hence the petition in the last verse of the psalm that his thoughts might correspond to his words. When Christ rules our minds, and our words speak His mind, we will not have to worry. Paul urges us in 2 Corinthians 10:5b to bring into captivity every thought to the obedience of Christ.

PSALM 20

All the verbs of the first half of Psalm 20 can be rendered two ways. For example, the first line can read, "The LORD hear you" or "The LORD will hear you." In grammatical terms the first form is a jussive and the second a simple future. In Hebrew they often cannot be distinguished. The difference in the total interpretation of the psalm is that it is either a prayer or a prediction. Most standard translations opt for the former.

Essentially, this is a prayer *for* David. The problems then arise: Did David write it or did someone write it about him? The word translated *of* could as well mean *for* or *concerning*.

Assuming that the prayer is for King David, the psalm is a beautiful expression by a devoted subject. With slight modification, parts of this prayer could be adapted for our own political leaders.

The first three verses are an uninterrupted series of petitions. Notice the interesting parallel in verse 1 of "The LORD" with "the name of the God of Jacob." His name is Himself. Even in the New Testament, the idea persists that the person is the name. So we are urged to call on the name of the Lord, believe in the name of Christ (John 1:12), and pray in Jesus' name (John 14:13). *Name* occurs again in verses 5 and 7.

A *selah* appears at the end of verse 3 but the reason is unknown. It concludes two verses which speak of liturgy, but it is not a major break in the prayer.

The fourth verse continues in the form of a prayer wish. The desire of the heart of the godly man should correspond to the desire of the heart of God (Ps. 37:4). When we delight in the Lord, He will delight in us and give us what we want. When we are near God, we want what He wants. Jesus said essentially the same thing in the Sermon on the Mount: "Seek ye first the kingdom of God, and his righteousness; and all these things shall be added unto you" (Matt. 6:33 KJV).

Verse 5 is a transition. Here first person pronouns appear and continue to the end of the psalm. The Revised Standard Version continues the form of the verbs as in the previous verses, understanding them as cohortatives: "May we shout for joy," "May the LORD fulfil."

Verse 5 is also the last verse of the prayer. Verses 6–8 are a testimony. Anticipating a response the psalmist with conviction affirms his knowledge of God's salvation. The "anointed" (Heb. *messiah*) is David in this context, but a Messianic allusion cannot be ruled out.

The word *trust,* or *boast* (v. 7), does not appear in the Hebrew, but is clearly implied by the parallel line. Zechariah 4:6 echoes the sentiment of this verse: "Not by might, nor by power, but by my spirit, saith the LORD of hosts" (KJV).

In America it is very easy to trust something or someone other than the Lord. Our economic bliss gives us a false feeling of security and independence. Often, it is only in times of crisis that we are cornered into trusting God. Perhaps we should pray for more "heat and pressure" on our faith in order to produce more holiness and piety. Then we will witness the unbelievers' bowing, not to us as their conquerors but to Christ, their newly claimed King. This is the reason we stand upright (v. 8).

The concluding verse is another prayer. The plea, "save," is "Hosanna" used on Palm Sunday.

But who is the king (v. 9)? Though some modern translations take David to be the king, the Hebrew has it parallel with the Lord. That means that ultimately the prayer is not that King David, but the King of kings Himself, should save us.

PSALM 21

Psalm 21 falls easily into two main parts. The division is between verses 7 and 8. The first half expresses the king's gratitude for blessings. The second half describes God's overthrow of the enemy. The first and last verses are complementary. The phrase "in your strength" appears in both. In the first verse the king rejoices in God. In the last verse we, the worshipers, sing and praise His power. The psalm was probably used in the divine services in Jerusalem.

After the introductory verse stating that the king does rejoice, the ensuing six verses tell why. God gave him his heart's desire. (Compare the commentary on Psalm 20:4.) God answered his prayer. He crowned the king with a golden crown and let him have a long life.

But the thing in which the king gloried most was God's salvation (v. 5). The writer may have had a military victory in mind, or the higher, ultimate purpose of God's deliverance, that is, eternal life. We ought to enjoy temporal blessings but also to remember that the source of greatest joy should come from our hope of everlasting life.

As in verses 6–7 of Psalm 20, verse 7 of this psalm points up the king's trust in God's never-failing, covenant love. Only as he trusts will he not be moved, regardless of the foes who stand against him.

A contrast begins with verse 8. Whereas in the first half positive words abound—blessings, goodness, life, glory, salvation, honor, majesty, trust, and loving-kindness—now negative words are abundant. In verses 8–12, these terms color the picture: *enemies, hate, anger, wrath, destroy,* and *evil.*

This second half of Psalm 21 describes God's dealing with the enemy. In verse 8 He finds out who they are. The punishment begins in verse 9. *Anger* and *wrath* poetically relate the first two stichs of verse 9 to each other; *swallow* and *devour* relate the second and third stichs; while *fire* occurs in the first and third.

Verses 10–11 show God frustrating the selfish human hopes and dastardly designs of the enemy. The heirs who would enjoy their fathers' ill-gotten wealth are destroyed. They are caught in their own traps. Their bows literally backfire; they shoot themselves. That is the lot of the godless. All this gave the ancient Israelites great comfort and a basis for praise. They blessed God who had destroyed their enemies.

The last verse wraps up these sentiments. *We,* the worshipers of the true God, who make the Lord our strength, will sing of and praise God's power.

PSALM 22

The word *Messiah* (Christ) does not occur in Psalm 22, yet no other psalm speaks so specifically of our Lord Jesus Christ and His passion. The opening phrase was the cry of the Savior while He hung on the cross. The vile taunt of verse 8 was on the lips of the thoughtless crowd around Calvary. Three gospel writers cited verse 18 when the soldiers gambled for His robe. And the author of Hebrews (2:12) quotes verse 22 and applies it to Christ.

In the title, *Aijeleth ha-shahar* (Heb.; cf. NASB) may be translated as "deer of the morning," probably the name of the tune to which this psalm was sung.

Verses 1–21 constitute a prayer of the righteous sufferer; 22–25 are praise; 26–31 are a prediction.

Within the first twenty-one verses, the sufferer goes from complaint to trust and back again several times. Verses 1–2, 6–8, and 12–18 are complaints. Verses 3–5, 9–11, and 19–21 are prayers of trust.

The *Eli, Eli, lama sabachthani* of Matthew 27:46 is the Aramaic of Psalm 22:1. This expression is the traditional fourth word from the cross. When the Son of God uttered these words, the greatest transaction of all time occurred. The Righteous died for the guilty. The guiltless One bore the sin of many. The "many" need only believe and live. We live because He died.

The opening words could apply to David only in a hyperbolic way. That which could apply to him only by way of comparison applies to Christ quite specifically. Yet even the *bulls* of verse 12 must be understood figuratively. Neither David nor Christ was literally surrounded by angry bulls.

The complaint continues in verse 2. Night and day witness the sufferer's plea for a hearing.

Beginning with verse 3, the psalmist turns to an argument from history. He reminds God of His past faithfulness and former deliverances and attempts to force Him to act. Sometimes such a tack is for the benefit of the one praying. We sometimes forget that God is altogether good, that He cannot deny Himself, and that He does nothing except for our welfare. A brief reflection on our spiritual pilgrimage can be most helpful and therapeutic.

Verse 6 again takes up the complaint. The agonizing saint says he is the lowest of all animals. He is far below human status. He is a worm and, as such, is despised by all. Shooting out the lip is like sticking out the tongue or razzing. Both Matthew (27:39) and Mark (15:29) report on the wagging heads of the bewildered onlookers. But the more vile of Christ's enemies gave vent with the seething taunt: "Let God save him." These words faintly echo those of Satan during the temptation in the wilderness (Matt. 4:6). In verse 9 the pendulum swings back the other way again.

Once more the psalmist reflects on God's former mercies. From birth until now he has seen only love and concern. Now that trouble besets him he prays that God will be near to help (v. 11). The author is not a foxhole convert; he is not a crisis Christian. He is a well-established believer with experience in prayer and faith. He has seen God work in the past.

The long, descriptive complaint of verses 12–18 contains many direct and indirect allusions to the events of Passion Week. The Bashan bulls represent the established religion of Judaism and the powerful Roman government. For years they had surrounded Christ waiting for the opportunity to "gore" Him. As a hungry, salivating lion they lurked in secret to take Him. And now they have Him on a cross—dehydrated and hungry, seemingly helpless and hopeless. But note that it is God, not the enemy, who has brought the sufferer to death. Still He acknowledges God's sovereignty. Still He sees Himself as part of the divine plan of the ages. Though dogs and evildoers nail His hands and feet, though soldiers crucify Him at the command of the government and the urging of the maddened throng incited to hate by the Jewish leaders, yet it is God His Father who brings Him to the dust of death (v. 15b). That is the key verse in this psalm; it is one of the essential doctrines of the Christian faith. God *willed* that Christ should die.

Some Bible students see many more details in these verses. For instance, the reference to water might be connected with the piercing of the Savior's side. Blood and water poured out of that laceration (John 19:34). The bones being out of joint may refer to the fact that Christ's bones were not broken (John 19:33), only out of joint because of the hanging. Verses 19–21 are the last in the prayer cycle. Some of the animals named above reappear in this prayer. The word *darling* (KJV) of verse 20 is interesting. It is built on the word *one* or *together* and probably has reference to the composite person—body and soul.

The psalmist asserts that he will praise God (v. 22). Then he adjures his audience to praise Him (v. 23). Apparently the prayers of the first half of the psalm were answered, at least the eye of faith saw the answers, for the content of the praise is in verse 24. God did not ignore the afflicted. He did not hide His face but listened and answered.

With the praise went vows (v. 25). The inspired author probably vowed to tell others faithfully of his deliverance. He promised to testify of God's keeping power.

The concluding six verses are primarily in the future tense and sound like predictions. Since God has heard, the meek shall eat and be satisfied. Then all the remote parts of the world will learn and turn to the Lord. The kingdoms of this world will become the kingdom of our Lord and of His Christ (cf. v. 28; Rev. 11:15). The rich and the poor, the living and the dead will all eventually bow. Generation after generation will recite the deeds of the Lord. People not then yet born would learn what Christ would do and has done.

PSALM 23

The twenty-third psalm is the favorite of millions. No other psalm comes close to its popularity. There are dozens of translations, paraphrases, and hymn arrangements.

The psalm is basically a testimony of great faith. The first four verses use pictures from the pastoral life that David led before he was engaged by Saul for palace service. The fifth and sixth verses have multiple metaphors.

With brief strokes the picture takes shape. First there is a shepherd, who is the Lord. Then there is a satisfied sheep, the psalmist. The pasture is green and the stream trickles through it. It is a beautiful picture of the believer and his Lord. Jesus used the illustration of sheep and shepherds many times (e.g., Matt. 7:15; 18:12f.; 25:32f.; John 10:2f.).

Sheep are among the most helpless and stupid of animals. They desperately need guidance and assistance. Probably for this reason God's people are likened to them.

Verse 3 gives an interpretation of verse 2. As sheep's appetites are satisfied with ample grass and abundant water, so God restores the soul of the spiritually fatigued. The verb *restores* might be translated "converts," which would load the psalm with additional theological meaning. The *leading* by still waters of verse 2 is paralleled by the leading in righteousness of verse 3. For His own sake He leads us to do right. If we sin we offend Him and tarnish His reputation. So, for the sake of His own name, as well as for our good, He points us in the right direction.

Verse 4 again takes up the figure of shepherding. The famous opening phrase can be translated either "shadow of death" or "deep darkness." The latter should not detract, however, from the use of the psalm in connection with death. The sheep should never fear, whether it be light or dark, whether it lives or dies. Two trusty implements are in the shepherd's hand. One is a club for beating off the enemies of the sheep, the other is a stick for nudging the sheep along. God both defends and directs the believer. He protects him and points out the way. The mere knowledge that the shepherd has these two instruments comforts the flock.

The metaphor of verse 5 is that of a banqueting victor. It may have been the practices in ancient times for the winner to feast in front of the starving prisoners of war (cf. Judg. 1:7). Anointing or perfuming of the banquet guests was a gracious gesture by the host. When the guests were prepared to dine, their cup was filled to overflowing. These three pictures—the table, the oil, and the cup—all typify God's provision for His people. The table may be the Lord's Supper; the oil, the filling of the Holy Spirit; and the cup, the daily benefits with which God loads His people.

The last verse is more than a picture. In truth, God has a "house" in which believers will live eternally. Otherwise Jesus would not have told us so (John 14:2). God's goodness and covenant faithfulness will accompany us not only in this life but in the life to come.

It may have been David's hope to live, while on earth, at the temple which he wished to build, but his eternal hope was to be where God would be, in heaven. Three possibilities exist for translating verse 6b. The well-known "I shall dwell" is one. "I shall rest" is a second. "I shall return to" is a third. All of these suggestions are grammatically, exegetically, and theologically possible. It is clear that David anticipated being forever where God is.

PSALM 24

Psalm 24 was doubtlessly a liturgical hymn. The question-answer motif in verses 3–5, 8, and 10 indicates that the psalm was probably sung antiphonally. One choir or soloist asked the questions and another responded.

The psalm is in three parts. Verses 1–2 express in grand and cosmic terms the extent of God's domain. Verses 3–6 are an examination for participation in the worship at Jerusalem. This section is reminiscent of Psalm 15. The third section is verses 7–10, and sounds like a triumphal march. Verse 1 declares that

God owns everything. Verse 2 states that He made everything. In more modern language, "The earth is the Lord's and everything that fills it." The parallel to *earth* is *world* and to *fullness* is *they that inhabit it.* In other words, everything and everybody belongs to God.

With verse 3 begins the liturgical examination. Who may go and stand in the sanctuary? Four stipulations are found in verse 4. First, the would-be worshiper must have clean hands—a symbol of a clean and faultless life. Second, he must have a pure heart—a symbol of a right attitude. Third, he must not have lifted his soul to vanity, meaning that he does not have an appetite for foolishness. Fourth, he must not swear deceitfully; that is, he must be a man who keeps his word and pays his bills. In general, terms these two positive and two negative requirements cover most of life.

The man who passes these tests is the man whom the Lord will bless and admit into His presence. He is a member of the generation which seeks God. *Generation* (v. 6) here means family, species, or kind. *O Jacob* is elliptical for *O God of Jacob.*

Verses 7–10 may have been sung when the ark was brought to Jerusalem (cf. 2 Sam. 6:12ff.). This anthem may also foreshadow both the Messiah's coming to Jerusalem on Palm Sunday and His victorious reentry into the Father's presence at the ascension. Verses 7 and 9 are identical; verses 8 and 10 are almost identical. The two *selahs* in this psalm are appropriately placed at the ends of major divisions, but no indication of their meaning is apparent.

PSALM 25

The author of Psalm 25 employed two fascinating literary devices. The psalm is an alphabetic acrostic. It is also an elaborate chiasmus.

Every verse, with only minor exceptions, begins with each successive letter of the Hebrew alphabet. In the second verse only the second word begins with the second letter of the alphabet. Verse 5 must be divided in half and assigned two letters. Verse 18 should begin with a *qoph* instead of a *resh,* as does verse 19. Verse 22 is beyond the end of the alphabet. Here is the chiastic outline:

1	A	"I lift up my soul unto them"	
2	B	"Let not shame"	
3	C	Treacherous shamed	
4–5a	D	Three petitions for guidance	
5b	E	Psalmist's salvation	
5c	F	"I wait"	
6	G.1	God's mercy	
7	G.2	God's goodness implored	
8–9	H	God's instruction of the meek	
10a	I	God's faithfulness	
10b	I′	The faithful	
11	J	"Pardon me"	
12–13	H′	Instruction of God-fearers	
14–15	G.1′	God's friendship and covenant	
16a	G.2′	"Have mercy"	
16b	F′	"I am desolate"	
17a	E′	Psalmist's troubles	
17b–19a	D′	Three petitions for salvation	
19b	C′	Psalmist's enemies	
20	B′	"Let not shame"	
21	A′	"I wait for thee"	
22	J′	"Redeem Israel"	

Such an elaborate arrangement could not have been accidental. Perhaps this was an aid to memory just as the acrostic feature was. But imagine the ingenuity of the poet who put this together with these two features intermingled and still produced such a meaningful psalm!

A third, less rigid device also marks this work. Many of the verses are linked by key words. A verse may pick up a word from its preceding verse and be connected to the following with yet a different word. This is how it works: Verses 1–2 are connected by the first person singular testimonies, "I lift up" and "I have trusted." Verses 2–3 are connected by the idea of *shame*. *Teach me* occurs in both verses 4–5. *Remember* appears in 6–7. In verse 7 we read of God's goodness and in verse 8 that He is good. The word *way* links verses 8–9. The pattern continues, with irregularity, through this and many other psalms. This feature is part of the Semitic thought pattern. Even the apostle Paul often used it in his epistles (e.g., 2 Thess. 1:3–10).

There is a simpler outline to this prayer which is based on the use of pronouns and other features of the content. Verses 1–7 are petitions of the psalmist. Verses 8–10 are statements about God's character and deeds. Verse 11 is like a parenthesis, as seen in the chiastic outline. It also marks the halfway point. Verses 12–14 contain more statements about God's deeds. Verses 15–21 revert to the petition form. Verse 22 is a kind of summary, communal petition (as verse 11 was a personal petition) marking the end of the second half of the psalm.

The prayer is very personal, yet the subject matter is very general. Both the nature of the enemy's oppression and the character of the deliverance sought are universally applicable. For this reason some think this is a liturgical psalm fitted for any number of occasions.

The first verse is a statement of faith. But from verses 2–7 a series of imperative verbs forms the content of the prayer. The first four petitions, those in verses 2–3, are negative: "Let me not . . . Let not my enemies . . . Let none that wait. . . Let them be ashamed. . . ." Then follows a series of positive imperatives: "Show me. . . teach me. . . guide me. . . teach me. . . ."

Verses 6–7 are marked by *remember* and *don't remember*. On the one hand, the prayer is that God would remember His mercy and His commitment to love. *Ḥeseḏ* (see notes on Ps. 17:7) appears a second time in the middle of verse 7. On the other hand, the prayer is that God would forget the petitioner's sins and transgressions. Within verses 6–7 is a simple chiasmus.

> Remember your mercy. Remember not my sins.
> Remember me according to your mercy.

Verses 8–14 (with the exception of verse 11) provide additional bases for a man coming to God in prayer. God is good and upright. He does instruct, guide, and teach. Verses 8–9 have some of the same words used in the prayer of verses 4–5. Verse 10 teaches that all that God does for those who fear Him is based on His consistent, faithful love and truth. The estate of such a man blessed by God is portrayed in verses 12–14.

In verse 15 the first-person pronouns again appear and in verse 16 imperative verbs once more set the style. Because of the faith asseverated in verse 15, the psalmist is bold to pray as he does in the following verses. "Turn and have mercy." "Bring me out." "Consider my affliction." "Forgive my sins." "Consider my enemy." "Keep and deliver me." "Let me not be shamed." "Let integrity preserve me." Note the identical word *consider* (*look* in KJV, v. 18) which begins verses 18–19. He prays: "Consider me and consider my enemies."

The psalm concludes with a general prayer for Israel's redemption. If the psalm is a communal prayer, then this seems to be a fine summary and benediction. All the individual petitions can be wrapped up in the one word, *redeem*. And all the people and problems they need deliverance from can be wrapped up in the word *troubles*. The complement to this last verse is verse 11, where the psalmist uses the argument, "For thy name's sake." All deliverance, all redemption, and all salvation are for His glory and our good. By these mighty acts His name is honored.

PSALM 26

Psalm 26 is classed as an individual lament. In this psalm David demands of God a hearing so that he may be vindicated. The first two verses are his demand. The third through the eighth verses are his protestations of innocence and righteousness. Verses 9–12 contain a mixture of petition, promise, and testimony.

Four imperative verbs make up the appeal for justice in verses 1–2. In verse 1 the plaintiff is convinced of his integrity—a theme he expands in verses 3–8. He swears that he has walked in uprightness and has trusted. His is not a plea for forgiveness but a demand for divine exoneration. The older word *reins* (v. 2 KJV) in newer translations is *mind* or the like. The ancient seat of the emotions was thought to be in the lower torso.

The protestation of integrity in verses 3–8 contains testimony to the avoidance of sins of both omission and commission. The psalmist did walk in truth. How can a man expect to place a claim with God if he is not a man of truth? He did not sit with men of falsehood. How can God's people expect to entertain successfully both right and wrong? He loved God's house. Why should we go if we do not? He hated the assembly of evildoers. Who, today, are the companions of God's people Monday through Saturday?

Having disclaimed in verses 4–5 any evil associations, David relates his going undefiled to the sanctuary. Washed hands symbolize a sinless life. Then, in general terms, he promises to relate all God's wonderful works.

The third section of the psalm contains more petitions, but it also reflects the testimony and promise features of verses 3–8. The requests are *gather not* (v. 9) and *redeem me and be merciful*

(v. 11). Verse 10 is a relative clause describing wicked men among whom he does not want to be counted. They are men of blood, that is, murderers. They take bribes. But the psalmist walks in integrity. He stands on level ground (v. 12). That phrase may be understood several ways. He is a man "on the level," so to speak or he dares to approach the Lord on the same level or he is in a position where he cannot fall. The phrase may be in contrast to the last phrase in verse 1 which, in the King James Version, is rendered, "I shall not slide."

As with other psalms, David concludes this one as if God had already answered his requests. Because of those unrecorded answers he declares that he will bless the Lord in the congregation. Sometimes God's people are long on asking and short on thanking and blessing. Even if we do not receive an immediate answer, shouldn't we bless God nonetheless?

PSALM 27

This psalm of David focuses on that ancient king's fearless trust in God. He trusts his God for strength (vv. 1, 14), for safety (vv. 2, 3, 12, 13), for instruction (vv. 4, 11), for salvation (vv. 1, 9), and for answered prayer (vv. 7–10). Sometimes the psalm is outlined simply as David's testimony (vv. 1–6) and his prayer (vv. 7–14). But it is interesting that much testimony is also reflected in the prayer.

According to verse 1, the Lord is light, salvation and strength. Therefore the believer has no cause to fear. Perhaps these three things refer to the three elements of our person. He is light for our otherwise darkened minds. He is salvation for our otherwise lost souls. He is strength for our otherwise weak bodies (cf. Isa. 40:31).

David testifies, in verses 2–3, of deliverance from adversaries, and prays for a continuation of the same in verse 12. Other psalms record the inhospitality and outright hatred he had for his enemies. He resisted them because they were the enemies of Israel and of God.

The deepest desire of the king's heart is exposed in verse 4. He wants to be near God, where it is beautiful, where his inquiries can be answered, where it is safe. We may seek the Lord wherever He is found, and that is everywhere. We may call on Him when He is near, and that is all the time. Here David prays to be in God's house all his days, while in Psalm 23:6 he prays to be there for eternity.

Some question may arise regarding the reference to the temple, which was not built in David's lifetime. It seems that he was searching for a word to parallel "house" and "tabernacle," even though *the* temple had not yet been built. On the other hand, he may have had his eye on the heavenly temple, the life after death when such a privilege would be available to him.

The latter part of verse 5 contains a precious picture. The writer hopes for a tent (tabernacle) to shelter him. God is such. David hopes for a solid rock on which to stand. And God is such also.

Verse 6 summarizes the psalmist's testimony. It mentions deliverance from enemies. It mentions his joyous activity in the tabernacle. And it mentions the purpose for it all—to give glory to God.

The seventh verse begins the prayer proper. This section, too, has some fascinating interplays with words. Notice how each successive verse is connected to the preceding one by a catchword. The word "face" connects verses 8 and 9, and the word "forsake" connects verses 9 and 10. By saying his parents have forsaken him, he probably means that they have died.

The matter of enemies and adversaries occurs toward the end of the prayer even as it occurred near the beginning of the testimony. The *plain path* (KJV) of verse 11 might better be translated "straight" or "righteous." As Christians we must have impeccable lives before those who are enemies of the cross. To lead such sterling lives would be impossible if it were not for Him who lives in us and for the hope which lies before us. Unless we had believed to see the goodness of the Lord in the land of the living (v. 13), we would have no hope of eternal life or purpose for this one.

At the very conclusion of the psalm is a timely word for us. Incidentally it is in chiastic arrangement:

Wait on the LORD.
  Be strong.
  Let thy heart take courage.
Wait on the LORD.

PSALM 28

Typical of the personal laments is Psalm 28. It evidences a common outline:

Invocation (vv. 1–2)
Imprecation (vv. 3–5)
Intercession and praise (vv. 6–9)

God is addressed in verse 1 as "my rock." This appellative, rock, is found sprinkled throughout the Old Testament (Deut. 32:4, 15, 18, 30, 31; Ps. 18:2, 31; 19:14; et al.). Perhaps this is a subtle reference to Christ (cf. Matt. 16:18; 1 Cor. 10:4).

The *lest* (v. 1) is the "lever" David uses on God to move Him to act. He asks God if He is willing to let His servant go to the grave unrewarded and unvindicated. In verse 2 he begs that the sound of his supplications be heard as he raises his hands toward the holy of holies. The English word *oracle* correctly translates the Hebrew *debir.* That root means *to speak.* This word and the Holy of Holies are put together in 1 Kings 6:16, 19. No one but the high priest, and he but once a year, actually entered that sacred inner room, but both layman and priest prayed facing it. God dwelt in that holy place in a special way. Here David lifts his hands toward it in a gesture of unfeigned desperation.

The content of the supplication is in verses 3–5. Mostly it is a plea for the punishment of the wicked. Such curses are called "imprecations." Verse 3 details the nature of evil men. They are insincere, saying one thing but doing another. They greet a neighbor with *"shalom"* (peace), but plot his downfall in their minds. Verse 4 is the essence of the curse. Basically David prays, "Do to them what they have done to others." Their sinful ways are the result of ignoring God. This is the diagnosis of every sinner's problem—he does not know God. He has not heard or does not believe that God is, and that He is a just and holy God. In the end He will break down and not build up those who choose to be His enemies. These last two verbs in verse 5 make an interesting couplet.

In verse 6 the psalmist takes his eyes off the enemy and focuses on God. The familiar, "Blessed be the LORD," begins this praise section. Again, note that it is written from the perspective of a prayer already answered. Or it may be understood that he blessed God in the light of former prayers and in anticipation that this one, too, would shortly get a response.

Verse 7 is rich with praise and joy. In military terms the psalmist asserts: "The LORD is my strength and my shield." He testifies that he trusts with his heart, not just with his lips. But it is with his lips that he will sing his song of praise. The beneficiaries of God's blessing, as described in verse 8, may be plural or singular. The text can read either "The Lord is his strength" or "The Lord is their strength." Perhaps David refers to himself in verse 8b, for he, as a king of Israel, is one of God's anointed. His prayer definitely is not selfish as he concludes this psalm. God's people and His inheritance are one and the same thing.

At the very end of the psalm, David moves to a pastoral figure of speech as lovely as those in the twenty-third psalm. Among the tasks a shepherd has is to carry the lambs. We are God's lambs, and He will carry us forever.

PSALM 29

In this psalm God is exquisitely portrayed through the storm in verses 3–10. This hymn begins with two verses enjoining worshipers to ascribe glory to God. It ends with a benediction for God's people.

The opening lines illustrate a variety of staircase parallelisms (ABC, ABD, ABE). The first two important words (*give, Lord*) in each of the first three lines are the same. The third element changes. In the first line, the third element is *sons of the mighty.* Then it is *glory and strength.* In the third line it is *the glory of His name.*

For the difficult term in verse 1 (cf. Gen. 6:2), the King James Version has "O ye mighty" and the Revised Standard Version renders "O heavenly beings." Are these angels? Are they heathen deities? Are they extra strong, mighty men? Are they the spiritual sons of God, the true worshipers, the devout Yahwists? The last seems best. Furthermore, the parallel in the benediction (v. 11) is *His people.* The last part of the fourth stich (v. 2b) has given rise to at least three interpretations. When rendered *holy array* (ASV, RSV) it seems that the worshiper or, at least, the officiating priest must be dressed in a certain way. The translation *in the beauty of holiness* (KJV) suggests the splendor of a place of worship. A third interpretation places the focus on the beauty of the Lord Himself, "at the manifestation of His holiness" (author's trans.). He, the holy One, is arrayed. The middle section, the hymn itself, has many fascinating features. The name of the Lord appears in almost every stich—a total of eighteen times in the entire psalm. The expression "the voice of the LORD" occurs seven times. Another feature is the poetic balance within the entire section. *Waters* and *flood* appear in verses 3a and 10a, respectively. The *thunder* of 3b corresponds to the *lightning* of verse 7. The *power of His voice* in verse 4 corresponds to its shaking the desert in verse 8. The calf and the calving of verses 6 and 9a correspond.

Obviously the psalmist is illustrating the glory of God from natural phenomena. In this section there are no people—just God and nature. His power is most evident in the middle of a raging storm. It is impossible to explain all these figures from a scientific viewpoint. But witness the glory of God in the violence of nature as well as in the ancient poet's description. The worshiper hears God's whisper in the rain and His shout in the thunder. It is a powerful and majestic voice. Even the cedars of Lebanon, among the strongest trees in the world, break in the wind and are splintered by lightning bolts. The cedars of Lebanon prompt the psalmist to think of the mountains of Lebanon and of Sirion, as Mount Hermon was called (Deut. 3:9).

Verse 6 should be scanned so that one geographical reference occurs in each of the two stichs (cf. RSV, NEB, JB, etc.). So not only the trees on the mountains sway, but the mountains themselves appear to shudder at God's voice. Anyone who has ever been caught on a mountain during a storm can testify to the awesomeness of the experience.

Lightning is described in verse 7 as God showering sparks as He strikes flinty stone with a metal tool. The uninhabited areas near Kadesh (probably the Kadesh to the north of Palestine), likewise tremble (v. 8).

Some translators alter the Hebrew slightly to make the *deer* (*hinds,* KJV) into *oaks* in verse 9a (RSV, JB). Such a change fits the immediate parallel with 9b much better, but it destroys the parallel with the *calf* and *young wild ox* (v. 6). (The KJV's *unicorn,* a fabled creature, is not an accurate translation of the Hebrew.)

Verse 10 provides a transition to the benediction. *Flood,* the translation of a Hebrew word found only in Genesis 6–11 and here, may refer to God's agent of punishment during the time of Noah. In fact, the entire hymn may be a veiled allusion to His wrath on His enemies, who are depicted here as stately trees and lofty mountains. Most of the figures used in the poem are also found in Ugaritic poems sung to Baal.

The benediction (v. 11) can be translated as a simple future or a jussive: "The Lord will give . . ." or "May the Lord give. . . ." Whereas His people had ascribed strength to Him (v. 1), He now gives strength to them. He will bless His people with *shalom*—physical, emotional, mental, financial, spiritual, and social well-being. It means peace with God, peace with others, and peace with oneself.

PSALM 30

Psalm 30 is a song of thanksgiving for deliverance from death. Some of the verses suggest it was a narrow escape from enemies (e.g., v. 1b) while others point to some physical illness (e.g., v. 2). Most of the content focuses on the actual plight of the poet rather than on the delivering power of God. It is very personal and therefore very easily applicable.

The title to this psalm seems wholly inappropriate. Some have suggested that the psalm titles, or parts of them, belong at the end of the psalms and not at the beginning. That suggestion is welcome in this case, for at least the temple was mentioned in

Psalm 29 (v. 9). If the dedication of the house refers to the events of 1 Kings 8, where Solomon dedicated the temple he built, then there is a problem with the Davidic authorship of this psalm.

The psalm does not quickly betray its outline. Verse 1 is an introduction, while verses (11–12) are the conclusion. The body has several major themes: verses 2–3 constitute a testimony of salvation; verses 4–5 are instructions to others; verses 6–10 are a recitation of the actual lament uttered during the crisis.

David was disliked by many. From the time he killed Goliath until his own death, jealous men on all sides, and even within his own household, tried to kill him. Any one of those narrow escapes might be the basis for this song.

This poet, as all poets, must be granted some license to exaggerate. *Sheol* is the place of the dead. No mortal man returns from that place. It may seem that death is all around, but, in fact, the psalmist is kept alive, as the latter part of verse 3 indicates.

Verse 4 contains two noteworthy expressions. *Saints* is from the Hebrew word *ḥeseḏ*. It means faithful, covenant love. Usually God possesses *ḥeseḏ,* not men. Nevertheless, the Hebrew describes the beneficiaries of *ḥeseḏ* with the same word. The Hasidim, a very orthodox Jewish sect, derive their name from the same word. The other noteworthy expression is *memorial* or *remembrance*. A literal translation might be *the memory of His holiness.* It means: "We shall give thanks every time we remember how holy our God is." The pleasure of that memory is elaborated in verse 5.

Among the lovely twists and turns of this poet's pen are the heart-warming phrases of verse 5. There is no better way to say it than as he said it. Here is a literal translation:

> For a moment is His anger.
> For a lifetime is His favor.

For an evening weeping lasts,
But in the morning, singing.

If verse 6 sounds like boasting, it is only boasting in God. The psalm is written by a man who lived a God-centered life. When he was in danger, God delivered him; when he was ill, God healed him. Now, God has allowed him to fall into trouble, and the psalmist seeks His help. The opening of the lament evidences a belief that God will not let him fall. He is sure of his deliverance, but this is a discipline of faith and patience.

In verse 9 the sufferer uses an old tool to move God to respond. It is a variety of the "for-Your-name's-sake" argument. Like a bargainer, he makes God weigh the cost against the benefit, the price against the worth.

Apparently the device worked, for the psalmist testifies that God turned his mourning into dancing. He removed his funeral garb and dressed him with joy—both interesting metaphors. For this and other benefits he sings praise and gives thanks forever. The highly personal psalm ends, as it began, jubilantly.

PSALM 31

Psalm 31 is a blend of lament, prayer, testimony, and admonition, but none of these themes is dominant. Verses 1–18 are mostly prayer and lament. Verses 19–24 are mostly testimony and admonition. As with the preceding psalm, the troubles seem to be both illness and enemies. The figures used are vivid and colorful.

Despite confessions of trust sprinkled throughout the first part of the psalm, the content is basically a complaint. The opening line is a statement of faith, but then the psalmist launches into petition. The ancient saint feared the shame of defeat. Any kind of loss not only humiliated him but his family, his tribe, the cause he struggled for, and his God. The psalmists founded many of their arguments on the basis that God might be shamed. Spelled out more fully, the last stich of verse 1 argues: Lord, if You are righteous You will deliver me. If deliverance doesn't come, You will be accused of unrighteousness.

The same logic shows up again in verse 5. These words used both by Christ and by Stephen (Luke 23:46; Acts 7:59) could be connected with what follows by the word *since*. We should entertain no hesitancy in committing ourselves to God, who has committed Himself to redeem us.

Other verses containing testimony of faith are 6–8, 14–15. Other verses with petitions in them are 2, 3, and 15–17. Verse 3 in particular illustrates the way the psalmist "pressures" God. He reminds God that His reputation is at stake.

The enemy is amply described in the other parts of the first eighteen verses. In the prayers for deliverance from them and in the imprecations against them, we have a vivid picture. According to verse 4, they secretly spread a net for the righteous. According to verse 6, they are the guardians of vain lies.

Beginning with verse 9, either the enemy is the "sickness" or David describes the physical effects of being hated. Diagnosis of a disease he may have had is impossible from these sketchy poetic phrases. His eye *wasted*. His strength *failed*. His bones *wasted*. Because of the phrase tucked away in verse 10, "because of my iniquity," the great enemy may have been within—his own sinful proclivity. Perhaps this psalm should be read with Psalm 51, the one connected with the king's confession of sin with Bathsheba. Notice verses 11 and 12, especially, in light of this suggestion.

Another suggestion for the life situation of this psalm is David's feigned insanity recorded in 1 Samuel 21:13. Verse 12a may allude to that incident.

The end of verse 13 marks a minor turning point in the psalm. In verse 14 the frustration and pessimism immediately give way to exuberant, positive faith. The little words *but God* make all the difference in the world. Though the enemies surround, though mortal life is in the balance, though personal sins weigh heavily, though the dawn appears never to come, yet we trust. And we say with David, "Thou art my God. My times are in thy hands."

Verses 15–18 contain a series of imperatives calling for God's blessing on the suppliant and for His curses on the wicked.

Blessing begins in verse 19. That verse and the following are addressed to God. Verse 21 speaks of God in the third person. These triumphs are uttered from the perspective of answered prayer. The "trouble and trust" sequence is once more demonstrated. Whether these ancient writers had an about-face as they voiced their complaints to God, or whether they recorded their spiritual pilgrimages from the perspective time provided, is unknown. The important thing is that we bear in mind, even in times of deepest despair, that God is good.

The last two verses are injunctions to believers. The first command is to love God. Remember that these words were written by a man acquainted with the Ten Commandments. Seeing the first and greatest commandment in this context should be no surprise. The second and third admonitions are "be strong" and "take courage." These are similar to the orders given to Joshua (1:6–7, 9). If we hope in the Lord as we say we do, then we should be strong and courageous of heart. In the past, God has mercifully preserved the faithful. He has adequately and abundantly punished the proud.

PSALM 32

Several verses of Psalm 32 have a familiar ring to them. Some are quoted in the New Testament. Others simply have endeared themselves to God's people over the years.

In this psalm, David draws special attention to the blessedness of sins forgiven and of a wholesome trust in the never-failing God. He had experienced sin and he had experienced forgiveness and therefore was qualified to write this poem.

Verses 1–2 introduce the subjects of sin and forgiveness. The word *blessed* is the same as the one that begins the first psalm. It could be translated "happy." Verse 1 is a close parallelism while verse 2 is freer poetry.

When the apostle Paul discussed imputation of sin in Romans 4 he alluded to these two verses (Rom. 4:7–8). The doctrine of imputation is a great and precious one. Unfortunately, it is often misunderstood. Verse 2 does not say that certain men may sin and yet be innocent. It does not teach that some men have not sinned. Rather, the doctrine is that when God forgives sin it is reckoned to us no more. The New Testament elaborates on this by making clear that our sin is imputed to Christ and His righteousness is imputed to us (Rom. 4:24, 25; 5:19, etc.). Verse 2 cannot be understood apart from verse 1. If one should have a guile-free spirit it is because God has forgiven his transgressions and covered his sin. True bliss, genuine happiness, comes from the assurance that God has forgiven sin. However incomplete was David's understanding of God's plan of salvation through Christ, he knew this one basic truth—God must forgive his sin.

Verses 3–7 describe the spiritual pilgrimage from the agony of unconfessed sin to the joy of certain deliverances. First, the psalmist relates the physical torment he endured. The price of keeping silent was wasting bones, day-long groaning, and dehydration. David understood what modern psychology has only recently discovered—many ills are caused by unconfessed sin. Many diseases are purely psychosomatic. Spiritual maladjustment often provokes physical ailment.

The turning point and apex of the psalm are verse 5. The sinner acknowledged his sin. He stopped trying to hide his iniquity. He confessed his transgressions. Then he arrived at that blessed state which the opening verses described—the state of forgiven sin.

Verse 6 is a homily on the preceding experience. Any believer can be godly. Any believer can pray. Any kind of trouble can threaten him, but never should it harm him. God is the hiding place for the saint. He will preserve him and circle him with song.

Another *selah* closes this major section as others did the minor breaks at verses 4 and 5.

The subject of verse 8 is uncertain. This may be one of the "songs of deliverance" that God gives, or it may be the advice of the experienced psalmist to his fellowman. The former is the usual interpretation of this dearly-loved promise. The picture is one of a father or a teacher closely watching every move of the son or the student. Unbelievers are unhappy at the thought that God sees everything they do, but this same fact is a source of comfort and joy to the child of God.

A most homey and rural illustration follows in verse 9. Everyone knows how much discipline dumb animals need. The exhortation is not to be like them. The interpretation of the American Standard Version is preferable for the end of verse 9. As draft animals need trappings to bring them into line so, too, God's children need discipline to keep them in line.

Verse 10 begins the conclusion to the psalm. As the poem started in general terms, so in general terms it ends. The wicked will reap sorrow, but believers inherit God's never-failing, covenant love.

The congregation and the reader are encouraged to gladness and joy in the concluding verse. Three imperative verbs outline this exhortation: *be glad, rejoice,* and *shout for joy.* The basis for such jubilation should be our standing in Christ. We are the happy ones whose transgressions are forgiven and whose sins are covered.

PSALM 33

Psalm 33 is a hymn. It has no title indicating the author, the occasion, or the purpose. After three verses of introduction enjoining worshipers to praise God, comes the body of the psalm (vv. 4–19), describing God's character and achievements. The last three verses constitute the pledge, promise, and prayer of the worshipers.

Five imperatives are in the opening three verses. Verse 1b is not an imperative but a novel twist on words to urge people to praise. It is a lovely thing for the upright to praise the Lord.

Several themes appear in the body of the psalm. Verses 4–5 speak of the faithfulness of God. Verses 6–9 focus on the creation by divine fiat. Verses 10–12 concern God's role in international politics. Verses 13–15 have to do with God's omniscience. And verses 16–19 teach the futility of trusting in human means and methods and the surety of God's deliverance.

Christians constantly need to be reminded of God's sovereignty. As verse 4 teaches, all God's doings are right and faithful. God is not prompted by selfishness or greed. He sets the standard of righteousness. All truth, all right, all justice are measured against His norm. Entire studies could be made on each of the key words in verses 4 and 5: *right, faithfulness, righteousness, justice,* and *loving-kindness.*

Perhaps even better than Genesis 1, the section beginning with verse 6 and ending with verse 9 teaches that God created the world out of nothing simply by speaking. The term *Word* suggests the second person of the Trinity (John 1:1–3). The word *breath* in verse 6b might even allude to the third person of the Trinity since *breath, wind,* and *spirit* are the same word in Hebrew. The term occurs in Genesis 1:2.

Verse 7 is a simile. Following the Greek and Latin versions, some modern translations read *wineskin* instead of *heap.* Implicit in verses 6–9 is the command of verse 8.

From the subject of the world in general, the hymn moves to the nations and peoples who occupy them (vv. 10–12). Whereas human plots and programs are often vetoed by God, His counsels and thoughts endure forever. No one can frustrate divine plans. Notice the perfect parallels in verses 10–11 and how the words *counsel* and *thoughts* tie them together. Unlike other nations, whose schemes fail, the God-fearing nation will enjoy only success. With the Lord as their King, subjecting themselves to His gracious rule, they will be blessed indeed.

As noted above, verses 13–15 deal with God's all-seeing ability. Not only does He see every move men make and hear every word they say, but God also has made all men and can discern even their motives and attitudes.

The weak arm of the flesh and the strong arm of the Lord are the subjects of the following four verses. These verses also teach God's sovereignty. It is not the size of the army that wins the battle. It is God. It is not the strong man's strength that saves him. It is God. If God does not deign to deliver, then to rely on a horse is vain. Psalm 127:1 is a commentary on these thoughts:

Except the LORD build the house,
   they labor in vain that build it:
Except the LORD keep the city,
   the watchman wakes in vain.

Sure deliverance comes only to those who fear God and hope in His covenant faithfulness, which evidences itself in constant loving-kindness. God can also save their souls. Horses, strength, and armies cannot. When God's people face starvation, physical or spiritual, God will provide.

The concluding three verses express the self-dedication of the worshipers. They correspond to the hymns of commitment that close many modern church services. Each verse has two parts, an effect and a cause. The worshipers say, "Our soul has hoped in the Lord," the reason being that He is their help and shield. They promise that their hearts shall rejoice, the reason being that they have trusted in His holy name. They pray for God's loving-kindness on themselves, the reason being that they have hoped in Him.

PSALM 34

O magnify the LORD with me
and let us exalt his name together. (v. 3)
The angel of the LORD encamps round about them that fear
him, and delivers them. (v. 7)
O taste and see that the LORD is good. (v. 8a)

These and other verses in Psalm 34 have endeared themselves to God's people over the centuries. This psalm is a personal song of thanksgiving, on the one hand, and a wisdom psalm on the other. In it David recounts his deliverance and adjures others likewise to trust in God.

The title alludes either to 1 Samuel 21:10–15, where David feigned madness before King Achish of Gath, or to some unrecorded similar incident. Achish may also have been named Abimelech. There is nothing in the text of the psalm which helps to pinpoint the situation.

Psalm 34 is another acrostic. Although there are the expected twenty-two verses corresponding to the twenty-two letters of the Hebrew alphabet, the letter *vav* is missing and verse 22 is beyond the end of the alphabet. The psalmist apparently labored to fit his material to this scheme, for there is a certain lack of logic to the content. The subject matter and the addresses change several times in the course of the twenty-two verses.

Opening the psalm are two verses of personal praise. In rather general terms, David sets the tone of the hymn.

Verse 3 is the first verse of exhortation. These words, which frequently have been set to music, urge the listeners to join the psalmist in exalting God's name.

The personal testimony begins in verse 4 with the statement that God has answered and delivered. Except for verses 11 and 13, the balance of the testimony is in the third person. It is clear, however, that David includes himself among those who fear God (v. 7) and are righteous (v. 15). The *they* of verse 5 is without direct antecedent, but it must refer to the meek of verse 2 or the God-fearers of verse 7. Countenance reveals whether or not a life is lived by faith. Believers should be radiant. Confused looks and anxious faces belong to unbelievers. God's angel is our safety. From Hagar in Genesis 16:7 to the last book of the Old Testament, the angel of the Lord ministered to God's people.

Verses 8–9 continue the admonition to commitment. An invitation that is still valid is, "Taste and see that the Lord is good." A man cannot know blessedness until he takes refuge in God. A man cannot know freedom from want until he fears God. Verse 10 ends this brief section with a tidbit of wisdom akin to the Proverbs: Lions may get hungry but God's people will never lack.

Almost as if David were beginning a new psalm, verse 11 reinvites listeners to live God-fearing lives. This is followed by a series of proverb-like instructions. All men fit into the category of verse 12—all men want to be happy and live long. The how-to-do-it comes in verses 13 and 14. The timeless maxim of guarding the tongue appears here 1,000 years before Christ. What we say probably provokes more anguish than any single thing in our lives. The tongue is capable of the grossest iniquity. With it we can curse men or bless God.

The second set of instructions (v. 14) is general but universally applicable. "Seek good and not evil" was reiterated by the prophets (Isa. 1:16–17; Amos 5:14–15). "Seek peace" is echoed by the apostles (Rom. 14:19; Heb. 12:14). Elsewhere the manifold meaning of *shalom* (peace) is found (cf. Ps. 29:11). The command is to do all you can to have everything right within yourself and with you, your neighbor, and God.

Verses 15–16 go together. The eyes and ears of the Lord are ready to see, hear, and help the good. But His face—meaning His favor—is against the wicked. The lot of evildoers is to have their remembrance removed from the earth. Would that only good men were remembered and the wicked forgotten. The word *remembrance* also has the meaning of *posterity.*

The testimony of praise resumes in verse 17. David probably is making veiled references to himself in these verses. The truth remains, however, that God loves and saves the humble from all sorts of grievous troubles. In specific terms, God does not let even a bone be broken. Some read into this verse an allusion to the fact that Jesus died without any bones broken. Such an interpretation is forcing a Messianic reference into the text.

The psalm concludes with two verses that form a pair much as verses 15–16 do. First the psalmist predicts the fate of the wicked and then testifies to the deliverance of the servants of God. The verdict will be "innocent" for those whose refuge is in

God. Whereas the wicked condemn the righteous (v. 21), God vindicates them (v. 22).

PSALM 35

Psalm 35 is an imprecatory psalm. In it David calls down numerous curses on his enemies. Then he looks forward to rejoicing when God will punish them for all their wrong. The first complaint section runs from verse 1 to verse 8. Then follow two verses promising praise. Verses 11–17 are a mixture of accusation and self-justification. Verse 18 corresponds to verses 9–10 as a vow to give thanks. The imprecations continue in verses 19–26. The psalm concludes with yet more pleas for and pledges of praise.

In the light of the teaching of our Lord Jesus Christ, many find it hard to understand such cursing on the enemy as occurs in this and other psalms. How could God inspire a man to pen such venom? How can a psalm like this serve as a stimulus to piety? Should a Christian use such imprecations against others? Such questions are not easily answered.

Perhaps one explanation is found in the nature of the hatred mentioned here. It is a holy hatred. David viewed these enemies not so much as his own personal foes, but as adversaries of God and of God's nation, and of God's plan. The king so identified himself with the kingdom of God on earth that any opposition to it was opposition to God. The enemies were not under God's covenant. They were not believers. They were not concerned with the progress of Israel. Therefore, they must be cursed.

Secondly, a difference between the Old and New Testaments admittedly does exist: missionary obligations were nonexistent or unclearly understood by our Old Testament forebears. In their minds, God had only one chosen people and they were the citizens of Israel. Only with the coming of Christ did it become unquestionably obvious that God has chosen people from all nations, that His kingdom is not of this world, and that He loves all men.

A third answer is in the cold facts themselves. Men were trying to kill David. It is the normal reaction of regenerate and unregenerate men alike to resist death and to love life. These wicked men were liars, cheaters, defrauders, murderers, and false accusers. David could not have been expected to condone and bless their evil.

A fourth answer or application is to recognize that the enemies of the gospel are either willing agents or unconscious tools of the devil. These psalms can be used in our spiritual warfare described in Ephesians 6:11–18 to fight the wicked one who is the mastermind behind the human persecutors.

In the first eight verses are seven verbs in the imperative and seven in the jussive form ("let them . . ."). Most of them are curses on the enemy; a few are prayers for the protagonist himself.

The Jerusalem Bible has a very clipped but accurate rendering of the first verse. The translation is very close to the Hebrew.

Accuse my accusers, Yahweh,
    attack my attackers.

The terminology of the first four verses is military: "take hold of shield and buckler . . . draw out the spear." From these the poet turns to expressions which might be found in the everyday life of hunting and agriculture: "chaff . . . a dark and slippery way . . . their net," etc. Note the presence of the angel of the Lord in verses 5–6. In the former verse he drives them like chaff and in the latter he chases them down a muddy path at night. Verses 7–8 are linked in a manner typical of the psalms. Whereas the enemy hid a net and dug a pit to trap the righteous, the prayer is that God would use these same devices to trap the wicked.

The first promises to praise are in verses 9–10. As though he anticipated the answer to his prayers, David pledges his praise to God for his deliverance. The expression "all the bones" means simply "with the entire being" (cf. Ps. 34:20). The section from verses 1–17 is a mixture. Verses 11–12 are complaints against the activity of the ungodly. The scene is in a court of law and the complaint is against lying witnesses who bring trumped-up charges against the psalmist.

Verses 13–14 are David's self-justification. Perhaps Christians ought to focus on these verses rather than on the imprecations. Despite all the evident hatred David had for his enemies, there is no reason to doubt the boasts of verses 13f. He declares that he sympathized when they mourned and felt afflicted himself when they grieved. But most of all he withdrew his prayer against them, at least temporarily. When his enemies suffered, then he treated them as brothers.

Such a gracious spirit does not last long, for complaints about the enemies' antagonistic activities resume in verse 15. They mocked. They gnashed. They rejoiced at David's calamity. A plea for God to act closes this section. It is as if the cases have been laid before the judge and now the accused, speaking on his own behalf, begs for a favorable and just decision from the bench.

Again, in verse 18, he promises to thank and praise God when it is all over. This verse corresponds to 9f. and 28.

The imprecations of verses 19 and 25f. introduce and conclude, respectively, the complaints and pleas of verses 20–24. In particular, verses 20–21 describe the conspiracy the enemy concocted against the righteous. With winks and chuckles they enjoyed their crafty prosperity. So David pleads with God to wake up, take notice, and do something to vindicate him. Four curses in the jussive form constitute verses 25–26 and close the imprecatory parts of this psalm.

The same verb form continues in verse 27 as David prays that the righteous be given cause to rejoice. That cause is a verdict of innocence for the good and a sentence of guilty for the wicked.

The last promise to praise comes as a benediction and conclusion to the entire psalm. As a result of a favorable and just decision, the psalmist vows that his tongue shall talk of God's righteousness and praise all day long.

PSALM 36

Psalm 36 partakes of the characteristics of the imprecatory psalms but only in a minor way. A better balance prevails between complaints because of the wickedness of sinful men and praise for the loving-kindness of God.

The opening four verses describe the wicked. The closing two verses are prayer and prediction of deliverance. The middle section, verses 5–10 focuses on God's benign attributes.

Some key words expand this rudimentary, chiastic structure. The words "wicked" and "iniquity" appear in verses 1–4 and 11–12. "Loving-kindness" and "righteousness" link verses 5–6 to verse 10.

Modern comparative Semitic language study has discovered that the difficult *my heart* in verse 1 can be read "his heart." This does not alter the Hebrew text and at the same time provides an easier reading. The verb in verse 1 (*saith*) is the usual word for divine utterances and generally is found when the prophets introduce God's speeches. Here the point must be that wicked men listen to their hearts rather than to God. So they come up with the blasphemous attitude described in verse 1b and following (cf. Rom. 3:18).

Through verse 4 the servant of the Lord delineates the wicked man's thought pattern. He begins with a certain godlessness. Then pride pervades his thinking. Soon he is convinced that his sin will not be discovered or punished. He proceeds to voice his plots, which are neither wise nor good. Having worked out the iniquity while lying in bed, he then executes his wicked chicanery.

A major break in the subject matter comes with verse 5. Now the mercy, faithfulness, righteousness, and justice of God are in view. These attributes, limitless in their scope, sustain the universe. God preserves man and beast, but particularly man. He may enjoy the shade from His wings. He may feast on the abundance of His house. He may imbibe the water from the river of His pleasures.

God is the source of all life and light. A preferable translation makes verse 9b into a prayer: "In thy light let us see light." This simple half verse could be expanded in several directions. The first and most obvious interpretation is that we are blind apart from the divine illumination of the Holy Spirit. Or the phrase may be a prayer to see things from God's perspective in the light of eternity. A third line of interpretation is that the study of God's Word under godly instructors affords an appetite and an ability to understand even more truth. Such an interpretation is borne out by verse 10. David prays that God's loving-kindness and righteousness might endure and multiply.

The prayer portion of this psalm may begin in the middle of verse 9 or only at verse 10. Either way verses 10–11 form a couplet. Verse 10 is positive. Verse 11 is negative. In the former, David begs for continued mercy. In the latter he pleads deliverance from evil of two sorts. He needs to be saved from the sin of pride (cf. v. 12), and he needs to be rescued from the wicked hands of godless men.

The last verse elaborates on the fate of those iniquitous men. They are fallen, thrown down, and made unable to rise. Judgment always has two sides. The righteous are exonerated and delivered while the wicked are convicted and punished. Christians have been saved from hell and for heaven. Sinners forfeit heaven and inherit hell.

PSALM 37

The English reader does not appreciate the alphabetic outline of Psalm 37 but it is nevertheless there. The psalmist sought to begin every other verse with each successive letter of the alphabet. Verse 1 begins with the first letter of the Hebrew alphabet, verse 3 with the second, verse 5 with the third, and so forth.

Besides being alphabetic, the psalm is also an elaborate chiasmus. Here is that outline:

1–8	A	The righteous are exhorted to ignore the wicked and trust God.
9	B	Wait and inherit the land.
10–15	C	The righteous inherit but the Lord destroys the plotting wicked.
16	D	The poor are blessed though poor.
17	E	The Lord upholds the righteous.
18a	F	The Lord guides the righteous.
18b	G	The righteous inherit.
19	H	The righteous get.
20a	I	The wicked perish.
20b	J	The wicked are like a sacrifice.
20c	J′	The wicked are like a sacrifice.
21a	I′	The wicked give not.
21b	H′	The righteous give.
22	G′	The blessed inherit.
23	F′	The Lord guides the righteous.
24	E′	The Lord upholds.
25–26	D′	The blessed may be poor but not forsaken.
27–33	C′	The Lord loves the righteous who will live and inherit, but the plotting wicked will die.
34	B′	Wait and inherit the land.
35–40	A′	God destroys the wicked but saves the righteous.

Such devices have nothing to do with the meaning of the psalm, but to learn of such fascinating details can draw from us a greater interest in and appreciation for the literary excellence of God's holy Word.

A simpler outline based on broad themes might be this:

A. Counsel for the meek (vv. 1–11)
B. Warning for the wicked (vv. 12–20)
C. Reward for the righteous (vv. 21–31)
D. Contrasts of retributions (vv. 32–40)

The basic message of the psalm is the safety and blessing of those who trust in God and the insecurity of the ungodly. Many of the verses are proverb-like, and for this reason we might classify it as a wisdom psalm. Proverbs 24:19 is almost exactly like verse 1:

> Fret not yourself because of evildoers,
>   and be not envious of the wicked.

The sixteenth verse is like Proverbs 15:16 and 16:8:

> Better is a little with righteousness
>   than great revenues with injustice.

In addition, there are several well-known proverbs found only here. One of them is verse 21. It reads:

> The wicked borrows and pays not again,
>   but the righteous deals graciously and gives.

Verse 25 is used in the Jewish prayer after meals:

I have been young, and now am old;
　　Yet have I not seen the righteous forsaken
Nor his seed begging bread.

The imagery of verse 35 is also well known:

I have seen the wicked in great power,
　　And spreading himself like a green tree.

The first seven verses of the psalm are hortatory, and with these we will deal in some detail. A numbering of the imperatives reveals that there are four *do nots* and eight *dos*. Verses 1, 7, and 8 instruct us to "fret not." Basically the meaning of the word is "to anger yourself." A colloquial translation would be, "Don't fume" or "Don't get burned up." Although there may be a place for righteous indignation, Christians by and large ought to refrain from anger. "Fret not." In view of eternity, in view of the fact that we are called to please God and not men, in view of the uselessness of getting angry, in view of the coming judgment, and in view of our God who will adjudicate all injustices, we ought not to fret because of evildoers.

The second negative imperative is like the above: "Be not envious." Although jealousy can be commendable in cases such as that of Phinehas (Num. 25:11–13 NASB), generally it is not a wholesome characteristic. Rachel, Joseph's brothers, and Absalom are examples of the bad kind of jealousy or envy. For the reasons noted above, envy is warned against.

The other two warnings are in verse 8: "Cease from anger, and forsake wrath." These are obviously parallel to the above two warnings, except that the words are prohibitions in themselves and do not need the particle *not* to make them negative.

The eight *dos* are the heart of the psalm and are found in the most popular verses. Verses 3–5 enjoin us to trust the Lord. Coupled with our spiritual, or soul, reaction is the practical injunction, "do good." In terms of God's economy, good deeds done prior to faith are of no avail. On the other hand, "faith without works is dead" (James 2:20).

The latter half of verse 3 also has two imperatives, though they are not so rendered in the Authorized Version. Listen to the translation from the 1901 American Standard Version:

Trust in Jehovah and do good;
Dwell in the land, and feed on his faithfulness.

The last word might also be rendered *truth*. With the elimination of the added word *his* it would read: "Feed on truth."

Verse 4 has both a command and a blessed promise. The linking of these two is significant. When we delight in the Lord, we want what He wants. Then what we ask will be in His will. The desires of our heart will be the desires of His heart.

As noted above, verse 5 begins with the third letter of the Hebrew alphabet. The inspired author chose the word which has the basic meaning of "roll." Hence the imperative "commit" could be translated "roll." This idea is reflected in 1 Peter 5:7: "Casting all your care upon Him; for He cares for you." A popular chorus goes "Every burden of my heart rolled away." Proverbs 16:3 has the same verb and thought.

The last two commands of this section are in verse 7 and are parallel. "Rest in the Lord, and wait patiently for Him." *Wait patiently* really means "to writhe," or "to wrestle in conflict," hence to make fervent supplication to God. So here is a paradox: rest, but wrestle. Sometimes this is the hardest command of all to obey.

Yet this is just what some of God's people need most. This is advice for the sick, the fretful, the anxious, and the faithless.

The remainder of the psalm is to encourage the saints of God, to show them the end of the wicked and the blessed destiny of the righteous. That destiny is found, among other places, in the last verse:

> And the LORD shall help them, and deliver them:
> He shall deliver them from the wicked, and save them,
> Because they trust in him.

PSALM 38

Psalm 38 is an individual lament. A reading of the opening verses leaves the impression that David was physically sick. One might follow two lines of reasoning to explain this and similar psalms. First, he may be writing with the idea in mind that sickness is a punishment for sin. If he is not, at least his associates thought that. The other line of reasoning is that sin does have its psychosomatic effects. Ulcers, headaches, and hypertension are just three common maladies provoked by worry, jealousy, or guilt.

Some of the verses are very much like Job's complaints. The expression "arrows" of verse 2 is in Job 6:4. The reference to *bones* in verse 3 is similar to Job 33:19. The aloofness of friends was the lot of this psalmist and Job alike. Compare verse 11 with Job 19:13–19.

Psalm 38 is very human. The view of God is not too high. David seems to understand sickness as God's wrath (v. 13). Many of God's children have felt the same way. As the psalm develops, however, it becomes clear that God is only indirectly responsible, for sin has its own reward. To suffer for ignorance, foolishness, or disobedience does not require a special act of God's retributive justice. Many daily illustrations prove that if we do not "follow the directions" we suffer.

Verses 2–11 are written out of genuine agony. The sufferer creates a word picture with deftness and vividness. God's arrows stick into him. God's hand squashes him (v. 2). The ancient understanding of anatomy as simply flesh and bones appears in verse 3. Neither of these basic elements enjoy *shalom-health.* The pictures in verse 4 are of a man crushed by the weight of his sins. These figures are sustained in verses 6–7. Verse 5 describes open wounds while verse 7 may allude to some digestive disorder. Verses 8 and 10 show a man dizzy and bruised, with an overworked heart, tired muscles, and eyes without sparkle.

Only verse 9 is a breath of fresh air in this catalog of grief. David stops a moment to restate his confidence in God. On the other hand, he may be giving a gasp of despair. He says, in effect, God is my last and only hope. All the doctors, all the medicines, all the counsel, and all the advice have failed. As a last resort he hopes in God. How much like God's modern children! Instead of God being the first resort, He is often the last.

Sometimes the hardest pain to face is that of friendlessness. Verse 11 indicates that even his closest friends and relatives avoided him. Perhaps he had a contagious disease. Perhaps he was just a miserable person to be with and no one elected his company. Christians ought to examine their personalities, for often harbored in them are some horribly offensive spiritual diseases.

From bodily disorders, David turns in verse 12 to the troubles caused by his enemies. Even though he had alluded to his own sin (vv. 3–4) he still finds some comfort in cursing his enemies for his misfortunes. This may also be a spiritual illness on our part—blaming others for troubles that we bring on ourselves.

The psalmist asserts his innocence and nonretaliating spirit in verses 13–14, and gives the reason for such patience in verse 15. Verse 15 corresponds in its sentiment to verse 9. Verses 19–20 elaborate on the description of David's enemies.

If there is any development in the psalm, it begins in verses 16–17. There the psalmist sees the wisdom of affording the enemy no opportunity to rejoice over his plight. And again he sees the necessity to confess his sin and repent of his iniquity.

The psalm concludes with two verses of petition which answer to the opening plea of verse 1. "Forsake me not. . . . be not far from me . . . make haste to help me." These wrap up the anguish and agony of a despairing saint. In the end, there is no salvation from Satan, from physical pain, from guilt-ridden lives, or from the hateful adversary other than in God and His never failing mercy.

PSALM 39

Jeduthun, who appears in the titles of Psalms 39, 62, and 77, was a musician mentioned in 1 Chronicles 16:41 and 25:1. The old questions rise again. Did Jeduthun write this about David? Was Jeduthun the chief musician? Is David the author of the words and someone else the composer of the tune to which they were sung? To none of these inquiries is there any definite answer.

Psalm 39 is both a wisdom psalm and a lament. It contains the personal complaint of a suffering saint (cf. v. 10). But it also has pithy bits of wisdom such as verse 5. Verses 5–6 in particular sound like the book of Ecclesiastes.

If *selah* does indicate some sort of a break, then its two occurrences in this psalm are somewhat appropriate. Verse 6 introduces a section focusing on the vanity of mankind in general and prompts a reaction from the psalmist. Verse 12 begins the concluding prayer.

Up to the middle of verse 3, the psalmist reflects on how

quiet and patient he was about his troubles. Recognizing that the tongue produces innumerable problems, he decided at first against using it. But, as verse 3 indicates, all those pent-up feelings, all those harbored grudges, and all those unspoken emotions burned within him as he thought on them. The expression, "while I was musing, the fire burned," is often misunderstood. It is not a picture of a thinker in front of a fireplace but of a man with a fire on his insides. Jeremiah had a similar problem of God-sent heartburn (Jer. 20:9).

Finally the silence breaks in verse 4. The words are a prayer to understand the frailty and brevity of life. The confession of verse 5 is pessimistic and discouraging, but also true. God can live without us. But without God, our lives are pure vanity.

The transition to verse 6 is very smooth as the psalmist enlarges on the subject introduced in verse 4: "Let me know how frail I am." The opening line of verse 6 more accurately translates as "man walks in a shadow." It may mean that man never sees things in full light and as they really are. Or it may mean, as some versions have it, that man's life is as brief and unimportant as a shadow. The things men fight for are usually fleeting. What a man gathers is soon dissipated, or dispersed to those who neither understand nor appreciate it.

All this pessimism prompts the confession and prayer of verses 7–8. While other men are hopeless, the psalmist affirms his hope in God. To the believer, life has direction, purpose, and fulfillment. Verse 8 has the only specific reference to sin. In the event that his troubled spirit is a result of sin, the psalmist prays for deliverance.

That plea is partly prompted by a fear of embarrassment. But the end of the psalm does not lead to the belief that in this poem the author was truly penitent.

More of the feelings of the protagonist surface in verse 9.

Here he begins to blame God more directly for his troubles. The complaint against God grows more specific in verse 10 as he lays the heavy charge on God for the strokes and blows he has gotten. The complaint becomes even more bitter in verse 11, as he charges God with making men be consumed like moths as a price for their sin. A moth is a very short-lived insect, and man's life is very short and vain as well.

In spite of the overwhelming despair of the entire psalm, verses 12–13 emit a vapor of hope. It is not enough, however, to turn the tide of pessimism. Acknowledging that he is but a guest with God, he prays nevertheless for mercy during his brief stay. No glimmer of hope of an afterlife brightens the conclusion of this psalm. Rather, an embittered plea for respite from the avenging hand of God ends this bleak poem.

PSALM 40

Psalm 40 can be divided into two parts. Verses 1–10 constitute a hymn of praise while verses 11–17 are a prayer for deliverance. Psalm 70 is virtually identical to Psalm 40:13–17.

Personal praise marks the first two and a half verses. The description of the trouble David was in is very graphic. "He brought me up also out of a horrible pit, out of the miry clay." Jeremiah really had this happen to him (Jer. 38:6). David may be speaking in figurative terms just as we do when we sing the gospel song based on those words. Some Bible students make the entire psalm refer to Christ. On that basis, these opening lines cannot be the believer's testimony, for they are the Messiah's words. Such an approach is dangerous and open to abuse because it has no guidelines.

In the middle of verse 3, and continuing through verse 5, the worshiper speaks more often in corporate terms. "Many shall see . . . Blessed is the man (any man) . . . many are your thoughts to us." In other words, in the middle of his testimony he turns to preaching.

If this song immediately followed an illness such as those alluded to in the preceding psalms, then it provides an interesting illustration of the benefits of sickness. Sometimes God makes His children look up by putting them flat on their backs. When things go well, it is easy to forget God and our necessary dependence on Him. Only after God forced him to take the time, did David realize just how many are God's wonderful works and thoughts toward men. They are innumerable. The gospel song "Count Your Many Blessings" by Johnson Oatman Jr. teaches the same truth in the line, ". . . name them one by one, and it will surprise you what the Lord has done."

The author of the epistle to the Hebrews quotes most of verses 6–8 (Heb. 10:5–7) and applies the testimony to Christ. Verse 6 repeats the truth Samuel told Saul (1 Sam. 15:22). Isaiah echoed the same principle several hundred years later (Isa. 1:11). In the New Testament the doctrine is fully expounded. God does not want endless blood sacrifices. From the beginning, He has been interested in obedience. God knew that one day His Son would end all sacrifices in His own death.

The New Testament quotation of Hebrews 10:5–7 is from the Greek translation of the Old Testament. That translation paraphrased the Hebrew "Ears thou hast digged for me" into "A body thou hast prepared for me." No other suitable explanation exists other than that the Septuagint scholars thought a paraphrase rather than a strict translation would best communicate the truth. The truth is that God must prepare the servant to understand. The unregenerate man has no capacity either to believe or behave rightly. A supernatural act of "fashioning the body" is required.

Verse 7 can be interpreted in two ways. One is that the *volume of the book* predicts the delight the Messiah will have in doing God's will. The other interpretation is that the "volume of the book" contains instructions to the saint to make God's will his delight. The Hebrew can be read either, "written to me" or "written of me." It is a toss-up as to which the ancient poet meant, since both renderings are grammatically correct, exegetically possible, and orthodox. The message remains: Christ did God's will and Christians are to be Christlike.

The first half of the psalm concludes with the testimony of verses 9–10. A mixture of positive and negative declarations mark these two verses. The psalmist did *not* refrain his lips. He did *not* hide God's righteousness. He did *not* conceal God's loving-kindness and truth. Rather, he *did* proclaim the good news. He *did* declare God's faithfulness and salvation. We might take a lesson from the nature of these statements. Not praising God is a sin. Perhaps among the sins of omission, one of the most frequently "committed" is thanklessness, or ingratitude. Worship does not end at noon on Sunday. Appreciativeness should be a way of life for the Christian. Those for whom God has done so much should ever be ready with a psalm, a hymn, or a spiritual song.

Prayer, confession, and imprecation mark verses 11–17. Confession is limited to verse 12 and the first line of verse 17. Not only have troubles from without disturbed David's fellowship with God, but sin from within weighed heavy on his spirit.

The imprecations are found in verses 14–15. The two verses divide into three synonymous parts. Three compound curses open each of the three parts and three phrases describing the enemies' acts close each part.

Balancing these prayers *against* the foe is the prayer *for* the fellow believers in verse 16. The remaining verses of this section (vv. 11, 13, 17) are David's prayers for his own deliverance. First he asks for mercy, loving-kindness, and truth (v. 11). Then more specifically he asks for help and deliverance (vv. 13, 17). The psalm ends on a note of urgency: "Don't wait, O my God!"

PSALM 41

A simple chiastic outline fits Psalm 41.

Praise to God (vv. 1–3)
    Prayer for mercy (v. 4)
        Trouble from the enemy (vv. 5–9)
    Prayer for mercy (v. 10)
        Triumph over the enemy (vv. 11–12)
Praise to God (v. 13)

Obviously the larger blocks of verses deal with suffering from enemies. But the psalmist is also suffering from some illness or wound, if verse 3 is taken at all in its plain sense.

Inasmuch as verse 9b was quoted by Jesus in reference to Judas in John 13:18, this is also a Messianic psalm. Some not-so-conservative interpreters go a step further and make the entire psalm fit with the life of Christ. Such a course of interpretation requires that many of the details be ignored which more literally may have been applied to David.

Psalm 41 is the last psalm in the first book of the Psalter. (Other divisions begin after Psalms 72, 89, and 106.) It begins with the same word that began Psalm 1: *blessed* or *happy*. A different Hebrew word, however, lies behind the *blessed* of verse 13.

The opening three verses describe the man who considers the poor and weak. What God will do for such a man makes up the content of those verses. By this means the psalmist gradually comes around to the subject of his own suffering. He hints at trouble in verse 1b; the idea takes shape in verses 2–3; finally in verse 4 he makes his point, "Heal me." The preceding generalities suddenly give way to specifics. All the introductory verses speak in the third person of a suffering man. Now in verse 4 it is "I . . . O LORD."

As in other psalms, the connection between sin, sickness, and enemies is not clear. Perhaps the poet's line of reasoning went this way: sin removed God's blessing, which in turn resulted in a military defeat in which the hero was wounded. While recovering from those wounds he found time to think on God's faithfulness and justice, and on his own sin. Then he mixed his prayer for recovery and his confession with maledictions on the foe.

The central section, verses 5–9, contains some particularly caustic remarks. Verse 5 is especially cruel, for the enemy wished not only for the king's death but also for that of his entire family. *Name* can and should be understood to mean all the descendants who bear the progenitor's name.

Even the brief prayer for mercy in verse 10 has retaliation as its purpose. Notice the source of assurance in verse 11. David knows God is with him because God is against his enemy.

Verse 13 concludes both the forty-first psalm and the first book within the Psalter. It echoes both verse 1 of this psalm as well as parts of Psalm 1. The Hebrew word for *forever* occurs once in verse 12 and twice in verse 13. Not only does David trust that God will give him everlasting life but also that God will get everlasting praise.

A double *amen* concludes the verse, the psalm, and the book (cf. Ps. 72:19; 89:52; 106:48; 150:6). *Amen* is one of those few words that migrated intact from one language to another. Attempts to translate it—such as, "so be it," "it stands," or "I believe it"—lack the force of this one pure Hebrew word, *amen*.

PSALMS 42-43

Psalm 42 and 43 together constitute a single poem of three stanzas. A nearly identical chorus follows each stanza (42:5, 11; 43:5). That Psalm 43 has no title is additional reason for putting the two together.

The title of Psalm 42 indicates that the psalm (or psalms) is for the chief musician, as many of the preceding ones have been. It also claims to be a *maschil* (a kind of psalm) of the sons of Korab. (Compare the titles in Psalms 44–49.) The Korahites were one of the families appointed to the ministry of music by David (cf. 1 Chron. 6:31–37).

The first two stanzas, i.e., the whole of Psalm 42, are basically a personal lament. In the third stanza, Psalm 43, the psalmist turns to petitioning God. The psalms fit the "trouble and trust" category as well.

The opening verses are dear to many of God's children to this day. The picture is of a thirsty deer panting for a drink from a mountain brook. So the psalmist's soul, meaning the man himself, is anxious to meet God again. Until God satisfies his thirst, he must drink his own tears while plagued by adversaries who ask the taunting question, "Where is your God?"

The content of the recollections in verses 4–6 suggests an exilic background for this psalm. With fond memories and anguished yearning the psalmist brings to mind the delights of temple worship (v. 4), the thronging crowd of worshipers, the magnificent house of God, the enrapturing music, and the annual festivals.

We gain a different perspective on the church when its fellowship is denied us. That which can become so ordinary and even boring takes on different meaning when we are separated from it. After we had spent a week in an Islamic country on a Holy

Land trip, a cathedral was the first stop in the next country. One pastor remarked on how refreshing it was to be in a church of any kind after being exiled, so to speak, in a culture with almost no Christian influence.

The chorus which closes the first stanza (v. 5) is a one-man dialogue. The poet addresses a question to his own soul and then proceeds to answer himself. In his mind he vacillates between pessimism and optimism, between despair and trust, between walking by sight and walking by faith, between looking at himself and his circumstances and looking at God and His will and ability.

Though the fifth verse ends on a somewhat positive note, verse 6 resumes the discouraged tone which prevails through these two psalms. This time, rather than remembering the temple worship, the exiled Judean brings to mind what may have been his homeland, the hills large and small along the Jordan valley. Especially in the flatlands of Mesopotamia, where the psalmist may have been exiled—would the recollection of mountains be particularly nostalgic.

Verse 7 is difficult to interpret. It is unlikely that the psalmist is drowning, which is the surface meaning. The latter half of the verse was quoted by Jonah, who could apply it to himself quite literally (Jonah 2:3). Perhaps this is a highly figurative expression for being overwhelmed with trouble. We use the expressions "snowed under" or "buried." Some scholars say that this verse, and perhaps the preceding one, is written from the vantage point of *sheol,* the abode of the dead. Even that would be hyperbole.

In the wavering course between despair and confidence in these psalms, verse 8 is again on the positive side. Not only are these lovely poetic lines, but they bespeak a wholesome and refreshing heart attitude. Elihu told of God's giving "songs in the night" (Job 35:10).

A mood of despair takes over in verses 9–10, which in turn

introduce the chorus again. In verse 9 the psalmist, with conviction, blames God for absenting Himself in troublous times. Yet in other parts of the psalm the writer appears to be a man of little faith. He is unable to lift his eyes off the problem-plagued horizon and gain a clear perspective of God, whom he claims to trust.

The third stanza (Ps. 43) begins with a plea for justice and an appeal for deliverance from deceitful and unjust men. The *ungodly nation* in verse 1 may be the Babylonians, who captured the psalmist and his people. Verse 2 is similar to Psalm 42:9 in that the latter halves are identical.

The appeal of verse 3 is addressed to God. The verse has been misapplied and used as an injunction to Christian witness and missions. The psalmist is in the dark and surrounded by deceitful men. Against this background he prays for some word from God to give him direction. He wishes to go to Jerusalem, God's holy hill, and to God's dwelling place there. Then he wants to go to the altar and join the orchestra that praises God. On this happy note the refrain begins for the third and last time:

Why are you cast down, my soul?
   Why are you disquieted within me?
Hope in God;
   For I shall yet praise him who saves my face,
My God.

PSALM 44

Psalm 44 can easily be divided into three parts. Verses 1–8 recollect former deliverances and victories. Verses 9–16 lament present trouble and defeat. Verses 17–26 are a mixture of protestations of trust and innocence with pleas for help. Basically this psalm falls into the category of communal laments. It may have been written against the background of a specific military loss or in the light of the Babylonian exile itself. There is nothing else to indicate the occasion which prompted the poem.

The opening section (vv. 1–8) in and of itself is a fine hymn of praise. As with the entire work, a militaristic and mercantile vocabulary is present.

The psalmist recounts past deliverances which his forefathers benefited from and enjoyed. His purpose is to build up his historical argument. By this means psalmists and prophets, as well as modern believers, have hoped to move God to beneficent action. It is as if they were saying, "You did it before, Lord; do it again."

Notice the parallels in the first verse: "We heard . . . they told . . . In their days, the days of old." After this introduction, the psalmist begins to spell out the conquest of the land in simple, graphic, but general terms. Verse 2 is a fine illustration of antithetic parallelism. The first and the third lines tell what God did to the other nations, while the second and fourth lines tell what God did for His people. The first two lines of verse 3 are negative, while the latter two lines are positive. The first half tells how God's people did *not* fight and the second half tells how their God *did*.

Verse 4 is somewhat of a change of pace. It has the first occurrence of the word *my*. Only two other verses in the psalm are similarly personal, verses 6 and 15. Otherwise the work is strictly communal, that is, *we, us,* and *our* are the characteristic pronouns of the protagonist. Verse 4 is also a prayer which interrupts what is otherwise a praise section. Furthermore, there is a change of subject after verse 4.

In verse 5 the emphasis changes to trust. Inasmuch as the fathers were delivered from their enemies, so the psalmist hopes that his generation will enjoy similar victories. Verse 6 is like the first half of verse 3. Verse 7 probably recalls a more recent deliverance—one within living memory which prompts the statement of faith in verse 8. The expression, "all the day long" occurs again in different contexts in verses 15 and 22.

If there ever was an appropriate place for *selah,* it is here at the end of verse 8, where it marks the major turning point of the psalm.

All the happy and inspiring reminiscences and pledges of trust in verses 1–8 give way to bitter complaint in verses 9 and following. God is charged with casting off and dishonoring His people. According to the psalmist, he has not accompanied the army, which was another cause for their defeat. That defeat is elaborated on in verses 10–11. It is the latter part of verse 11, together with verse 14, that particularly points to an exilic origin for this psalm.

The motif changes in verse 12 to that of a bad bargain in the market. God is accused of selling His people and losing money in the deal. The anguish is made more bitter by the rejoicing of blasphemous enemies (vv. 13–16).

The third section starts at verse 17 and continues to the end. Verses 17–18 are protestations of innocence and fidelity. The singers of this lament assert four times that they have not wavered in their allegiance to the one true God. In this respect this psalm is like the book of Job. For no reason apparent to the psalmist, God has dealt harshly with His own people. From time to time Christians are thrust into similar circumstances. Only an understanding of the kinds of suffering, and an unfeigned faith in the God who does only what is right, help in such trying times. Here, in outline form, are the different kinds of suffering mentioned in the Bible.

1. The natural results of foolishness or stupidity, illustrated in the parables and the proverbs by the poor investors (Matt. 25:14–30; Prov. 20:4).

2. God-allowed but Satan-sent, persecution of believers, illustrated by the troubles that beset the apostles in the book of Acts.

3. God-sent punishment for disobedience, illustrated by Korah and his rebellious company (Num. 16) and by Ananias and Sapphira (Acts 5:1–11).

4. God-sent discipline to believers, illustrated by Moses not being allowed into the Promised Land. This kind, like the one above, has a didactic purpose.

5. God-ordered suffering sent to edify, but not caused by disobedience. It does not have correction as its aim but, rather, the glory of God and the building up of the saint. The man born blind (John 9:3), the parable of the vine (John 15:2), and Job illustrate this type.

The testimony of the sufferers in Psalm 44:17–19 then would classify this under the fifth type of suffering.

Verse 20 starts with *if* and is a kind of self-malediction. The believers invite God to search their hearts and check on secret sins (cf. Ps. 19:12–13). Verse 22 contains more embittered complaint. Paul chose to cite this verse in Romans 8:36, where he certainly was thinking of undeserved suffering, possibly through Satanic persecution. Strictly speaking, only verses 23 and 26 are prayers. "Awake and arise . . . rise and redeem." In between are two additional verses of complaint. Verse 24 charges God with unconcern and forgetfulness, while verse 25 describes the extreme humiliation the people of God were enduring.

The psalm ends on a slight upward swing. The mention of God's mercy, or loving-kindness (Hebrew *ḥeseḏ*), reflects at least the beginning of an understanding of undeserved suffering. Psalm 136 remains in the Psalter. Twenty-six times it repeats, "For his mercy endures forever." God will never break the covenant He made by oath to His people.

PSALM 45

Psalm 45 describes a royal wedding. It is also Messianic, for Hebrews 1:8–9 quotes verses 6–7. Among other things, the title indicates that this is a love song. *Shoshanim,* meaning "lilies," is perhaps the tune to which it was sung.

Older rabbinic commentators applied the psalm to the love of God for His "wife," the nation Israel. Christian commentators apply it to the love of Christ for His bride, the church. In this respect the psalm is very close to the Song of Solomon, which is similarly applied.

This psalm was probably composed for the wedding of a king, but several of the grandiose terms point beyond to the union of God and His people. Verse 6 is difficult in the former regard. By the same token, many of the expressions do not fit a Messianic interpretation, except by the most radical adjustment of the plain meaning. Verses 9 and 12, for example, are difficult to apply to the figures of Christ and the church. The interpretation is preferable which sees one major lesson or application. Just as this king was supernaturally endowed, so Christ is the ideal King, the very Son of God. And just as this bride abandoned her family to join her groom's, so believers are to forsake the carnal life when they are adopted into the family of God.

One additional consideration before studying the psalm verse-by-verse: Many Old Testament writers were doubtlessly not clear in their own minds about the first and second advents of Christ. They did not realize that God planned the interim of the church age, in which Christ's kingdom would be only spiritual. When He returns, that kingdom will then be political as well as spiritual. Many of the terms in Psalm 45 refer to the earthly, sociopolitical kingdom that Christ will one day set up. Mention of sword and scepter point to this millennial kingdom. Likewise the wedding is viewed in Christian theology as an eschatological event, not one which happened at the first advent.

The author of this psalm makes the first verse his introduction and the last verse his conclusion. Only those two verses contain references to this one whose "tongue is the pen of a ready writer." In a way, he is like the editor of the social page of a big city newspaper and the story of the year is this royal wedding. Hence his heart literally "bubbles up with the goodly matter." He has a story on the king!

Verses 2–9 describe the groom and verses 10–16 pertain to the bride. In ancient Semitic weddings the man was more important than the woman. He was dressed elaborately. All the guests waited to see his clothing and his attendants. The grand march played for his arrival, not the bride's—a reversal of our custom.

Accolades are exaggerated as the groom is made "king for a day." In reference to Christ, they are not exaggerated. Such praises as those in verse 2 cannot suitably fit any mere human being. Only the Son of God is fairer than the sons of men. The eternal blessing of God on the groom mentioned in verse 2 is parallel to the never ending throne of verse 6 and the everlasting thanksgiving of the people in verse 17. Verse 3 begins the description of the king's attire. The sword, though decorative in the wedding, is symbolic of his strength and his execution of justice. Verse 3 calls him the "Mighty One," a term similar to one of the epithets of the Messiah in Isaiah 9:6.

In verse 4 the king rides forth, probably on a donkey, since that animal, rather than the horse, was the customary royal mount (cf. Zech. 9:9). This is one of those passages, such as Psalm 2:7–9, where the inspired penman sees both the present ministry of Christ and His eschatological triumph in the same glance. Now

Christ works truth, meekness, and righteousness. Some future day His right hand will execute terrible things. Then the enemies of the gospel will feel His arrows in their hearts (v. 5).

Verses 6 and 7 are quoted in Hebrews 1:8–9 and are applied directly to Christ to assert His superiority over angels. This New Testament commentary also bolsters the total Messianic interpretation of this psalm and is a declaration of the deity of Christ. Verses 6b and 7a list additional virtues the king possesses.

The *ivory palaces* of verse 8 may allude to the ivory inland work of walls and furniture which archaeologists have discovered in the ruins of buildings in the Holy Land (cf. 1 Kings 22:39 and Amos 3:15). A gospel songwriter has used these words to describe heaven; which Christ left when He was incarnated at Bethlehem.

Verse 9 concludes the description of the groom's side of the wedding. The references are to international participants and guests. Solomon had such international relations, but perhaps this points as well to Christ's kingdom which will host citizens of every tribe and tongue.

The bride receives two basic instructions (vv. 10–11), which begin the section pertaining to her. She must leave her family (v. 10) and to her husband she must cleave (v. 11). These verses underscore the believer's duty to his Lord. We were born into the family of Satan. The house of that "father" we should forget. Christ is our new Lord and loves and desires us. We must reverence Him. Just as Paul taught that a woman should submit to her husband (Eph. 5:22–23), so these verses teach that a Christian should submit to the Lord Jesus Christ.

The king had female attendants (v. 9) and the bride, as well, had the daughter of Tyre in her retinue (v. 12). Although historically Solomon had good relations with the kingdom of Tyre (2

Chron. 2:3f.), this reference may point to the universal constituency of Christ's church.

Verses 13–14 specifically describe the bride. An ellipsis in verse 13 leaves the meaning of *within* open to guesses. Is she beautiful inside *the palace* where no one can yet see her? (cf. ASV italics). Is it that the girl is beautiful underneath all the heavy veils which customarily covered the bride? Or is she an uncomely girl who, nevertheless, has a certain inner beauty (cf. 1 Peter 3:4)?

The procession continues through verse 15 into the palace where the wedding will occur. Then verse 16 jumps ahead to speak of the offspring of this union. No longer will the bride boast in her parentage but, rather, in her children. For Christians, as ties are severed with the old life, pride is then in the groom as he begets additional "royalty" through us (cf. 1 Peter 2:9).

The poet concludes this brief but complete song with the hope that he will make it last to all generations. And as long as Psalm 45 is in our Bibles his hope is fulfilled. We who live centuries away from him still read, enjoy, and benefit from what he wrote. We are part of that people who give thanks to *the* King forever and ever.

PSALM 46

The three occurrences of *selah* divide the three stanzas of the familiar forty-sixth psalm. In fact, verses 7 and 11, which close the second and third stanzas, are identical.

Essentially all three stanzas say the same thing: Though the world is in turmoil, in our God there is quiet and safety. Martin Luther paraphrased the opening lines of this psalm in his German hymn which has come to us as "A Mighty Fortress Is Our God."

This communal psalm of confidence begins with a statement that God is both the defense and the offense of His people. He protects them as well as fights for them. That is the meaning of *refuge* and *strength*. (The *refuge* of verses 7 and 11 translate differ-ent Hebrew words.) Quite different is the confession of verse 1b from the complaint of Psalm 44:23–24.

The four stichs making up verses 2 and 3 describe violent natural catastrophes. The description sounds like a combination of earthquake, landslide, ocean storm, and flood. Without press-ing the meaning of the figures, the passage simply means that no storm of life can assail us and no disaster in nature can overwhelm us since we are safe in God. From the violence of verses 2 and 3 the psalmist turns in contrast to the tranquility of the streams that water the city of God. Isaiah reversed these figures when he warned King Ahaz that, when he turned from the waters of Shiloah that flow softly, he would experience the flood of Assyrian soldiers who would inundate the land (Isa. 8:6–8).

In actuality no river flows by Jerusalem. Its water comes only from two springs, Gihon and En-Rogel. In the idyllic language of hymnody such imprecision is not only permissible but desirable to bring across the lesson intended. Both Isaiah (33:21) and Ezekiel (47:1–12) refer to a future river near Jerusalem. Verse 5 completes the pacific scene begun in verse 4. God makes His home among the citizens of Zion who sing of their safety and bliss.

With verse 6a comes another scene of terror and confusion. But peace and victory come in the latter half as God merely speaks the word. By the word of His mouth He created the world and with the utterance of His voice He makes it dissolve.

The third stanza begins with an invitation to observe God's work in the world (v. 8). That is followed by a description of His work which consists of winning wars and guaranteeing peace. The bows, spears, and chariots are destroyed as He puts an end to war.

We can enjoy this hymn as poetry, but we can also anticipate the day when this will be literally true. Christ's kingdom will enjoy a rule of absolute peace.

Verse 10 is a favorite of many people. The Hebrew word for *be still* is the same as *cease* in Psalm 37:8. The command is to let go and let God do the work. The word *know* is another very broad term in the Old Testament. Here it means "to admit," "to realize," "to acknowledge," "to experience," "to enjoy," or "to appreciate." All of God's children need to be reminded regularly of how great He is. As we fail to look at God and His Word, or fail to speak to Him in prayer, He grows smaller and weaker in our view. On the other hand, the more we study about Him, the more often we invite Him to help us, the more He will help us and the more we will *know* that He is God.

Then not only will His reputation increase in our eyes, but the unconverted of the world will also be led to recognize and exalt Him. When God is given a chance to prove His love and might, we will be prompted and required to confess that the Lord of hosts is with us, the God of Jacob is our refuge.

PSALM 47

Psalm 47 is a short hymn which was probably sung at one of the annual festivals. A *selah* divides the work roughly in half, but the content is quite homogeneous throughout. The psalmist may have had the literary device of chiasmus in mind, for a number of repeated words suggest such an inverted parallelism. *Peoples* occurs in the first and last verses. Verses 2–4 and 7–8 are linked by the terms *king of all the earth and nations.* That leaves verses 5–6 as the middle of the psalm.

The opening verse hints at the exuberance with which God's ancient people praised Him. In view of the disdain many Christians have for hand clapping and other expressions of rhythm accompanying hymn singing, and in view of the total inappropriateness of applause for God in our worship patterns, this verse is an interesting commentary on the way God's chosen people worshiped Him in olden times. Perhaps the church is not excited enough about the things God does. Maybe our worship is too solemn. On the other hand, worship must ever seek that delicate balance which Psalm 2:11 spells out:

Serve the LORD with fear,
And rejoice with trembling.

The second verse of Psalm 47 immediately turns from the ebullition of the worshipers to the terror and greatness of the Worshiped. Never let it be forgotten that He about whom gospel ditties are sung is also the great and terrible King over all the earth.

In verses 3 and 4 ancient Israelites reflected on what God did for them. Primarily He chose the patriarchs from a sea of heathendom and then brought their descendants into the Promised Land.

With verse 5 the praise is in more general terms. The use of the words "go up" has led some commentators to see this as an enthronement psalm. Such songs were used by the nations neighboring Israel when the statue of their god was paraded through the city and deposited in his sanctuary. If such a background influenced this psalm, it certainly was written from a more enlightened theology. The God in this psalm is the God of all the earth who reigns over the nations and who owns the shields of the earth (vv. 8–9). He is not a local deity who is revered by only one city-state.

"Sing praises" occurs four times in verse 6 and once more in verse 7. It sounds like it may have been a chant that the laity on the sidelines sang as the priests and the Levites executed their functions in the temple precincts.

Verses 8–9 have an eschatological ring to them. References to nations, peoples, the whole earth, and God's universal rule usually point to the future era when men from many lands and languages will join the covenant people of God, and God's kingdom truly will be worldwide (cf. Zech. 14:9).

PSALM 48

As Psalm 47 praised the God of Zion, so Psalm 48 exalts the Zion of God. It may be the psalm was written to commemorate the salvation of the city from the planned attack of Sennacherib in 701 BC (cf. Isa. 36–37). Verses 4 and 5 in particular support such a guess. Other Bible students wonder if this psalm does not commemorate the rebuilding of Jerusalem by Nehemiah (Neh. 12:27). Verses 12–13 bolster that suggestion.

Since Jerusalem is the city God chose for His name to dwell in, it partakes of the praise that is given to God Himself. Just as the name, the remembrance, and the deeds of God get praise, so too His city is honored. Although some of the epithets are exaggerated, Zion, to use the poetic name, was a beautiful place.

The psalmist is careful not to let the city, apart from its God, become the focus of worship. Such a form of idolatry is always imminent when the place of worship is beautiful and tends to replace the person of worship. Some people choose a church on the primary basis of architecture. All bragging about the church building and its attendant facilities runs the risk of the sin of idolatry. Zion is only beautiful and glad because the temple is there and in that temple the God of heaven made His earthly sanctuary.

The opening verse focuses praise on God and then the subject turns to the city situated on God's holy mountain. It took a poet to pen the words of verse 2. Although Jerusalem is set on a hill it is only 2,500 feet above sea level. Located on the spine of the north-south ridge, it is also in the morning shadow of the Mount of Olives which rises 100 feet higher.

Beginning with verse 3 is an account of some deliverance which God wrought for the city. According to verse 3 He was known, i.e., appreciated or recognized as the real refuge for the people. So when hostile kings plotted an attack, they suddenly retreated. The psalmist does not tell what amazed and dismayed them, but for some reason they began to shake and writhe as a travailing woman. The figures of verse 7 even more graphically magnify their fear as the hostile kings are compared to wind-wrecked, oceangoing ships.

Selah concludes verse 8, which is a summary to the foregoing incident. That act of supernatural deliverance elicited a pledge of unwavering faith from the citizens of Jerusalem.

Particularly in the temple of Jerusalem did God reside. According to verse 9, every sight of it prompted thoughts of God's loving-kindness and mercy. Is that what we think of when we drive by our church? Or does the sight of the building remind us instead of problems, impossible people, and preachers? Would that every church house moved us to speak the words of verse 10:

According to Your name, O God,
So is Your praise to the ends of the earth.
Your right hand is full of righteousness.

In highly figurative terms the citizens of the city are urged to rejoice. Of course a mountain cannot be glad, and the command is not just to the women of one tribe.

Despite the detailed accounts of the temple and the many references to the city of Jerusalem, it still is difficult to reconstruct them as they stood in Old Testament times. But from verses 12 and 13 they must have been both beautiful and strong.

Some modern translations have altered the traditional last words of Psalm 48 from *unto death* to *forever.* This may be correct for several reasons. *Unto death* does not fit with the sense and makes a bad parallel line. The Greek translators of the Old Testament read it as meaning *eternity.* This is entirely possible with a text that has no vowels. The two Hebrew words can also make another word which is the *alamoth* in the title of Psalm 46 (cf. 1 Chron. 15:20). So the expression may belong with the title of Psalm 49 and not at the end of Psalm 48. Or it may be read as *forever.*

Whether the traditional text or the emended one is correct, the truth is not altered. God is our God and our guide, now, at death, beyond, and to eternity.

PSALM 49

Psalm 49 is a wisdom psalm. In it the wise are warned against trusting in wealth. It will perish as the rich man whose fate is no better than an animal's.

The first four verses are the introduction. After that, only in verses 5 and 15 does the psalmist speak of himself. The body of the work is in verses 6–14, while the five concluding verses are didactic and repetitive.

Verses 1–4 each contain pairs of very strict parallels. The summons to attention goes out to every one of every class of society. The sage announces his intention of speaking in a proverbial form, while accompanying himself on the harp. Verse 5 is an interlude and a transition. It sounds like the poet is eliminating himself from the upcoming indictment of the rich and foolish. The things that ordinarily shake up other people will not move him.

The actual message begins in verse 6. The subjects are sketchily described by the two synonymous phrases of verse 6, and the acts they cannot do are spelled out in verse 7. The psalmist is obviously saying that money cannot buy off God. The word "redeem" (v. 7) is not used in the economic sense but in the spiritual. This truth hardly needs repeating—the rich, either with money or good deeds, cannot produce enough to pay the cost of a soul. If it took the shed blood of Christ to satisfy the just demands of God, then surely material means are inadequate. Not only are they insufficient but they are not even comparable, since the spiritual dimension demands another medium of payment. Furthermore, there may be a link, as often there is elsewhere in the Old Testament, between evil (v. 5) and wealth (v. 6). Often the rich are so only because of exploitation, bribery, and crooked business practices. Certainly it is not always so, for elsewhere in Scripture certain rich men are described as commendable and godly (e.g., Abraham, Solomon, and the centurion of Matt. 8).

The sentence begun in verse 6 actually continues through verse 9 (it may even have started in verse 5). The additional message of verse 8 is that no amount of money will ever suffice for the price of a soul. And the additional message of verse 9 is that a rich man cannot preserve himself from death and corruption.

The book of Ecclesiastes, in a manner of speaking, is a commentary on verse 10. Rich or poor, wise or foolish, all men die, and that which they have must be left behind. How or by whom their inheritance will be used is something hard to control.

Some people build monuments to themselves—gravestones, churches, schools—and even name streets, cities, and countries after themselves. Such means do not preserve their souls (v. 11) regardless of how hard they work or how rich they become. Verse 12 repeats the inevitable truth—men die like beasts. This verse forms a conclusion to the first stanza and is repeated at the end of the psalm.

It is folly for a person to think he will not die. It is stupid to welcome the congratulations of men without reckoning with the judgment of God. The end is like that of a sheep in the slaughterhouse. Houses and wealth will be consumed in the fires of destruction.

In the middle of verse 14 are a glimmer of truth and a sparkle of hope for those who are trusting in something other than wealth: "The upright shall have dominion over them in the morning." This is one of the relatively few references to the afterlife in the Old Testament. *In the morning* can refer to nothing other than life after death. In that great day all injustices and all inequities will be rectified. At the great reckoning the upright will plead the death and life of the crucified Son of God as their redemption.

That ray of light in verse 14 undoubtedly prompted the personal testimony of verse 15. While the rich man could not redeem his own soul (vv. 7–8) the psalmist declares that God will redeem his (v. 15).

Because of this truth and in the light of eternity, we are enjoined not to be afraid of the rich man in the big house. Just a little reflection will remind us of the brevity and futility of life not lived by faith. The rich may have many friends and be happy while he lives (v. 18). But in a few brief years he will join his ancestors in the grave, where there is no light.

Verse 20, which is similar to verse 12, concludes the second stanza as well as the whole psalm on the dismal note which must be continually sounded in warning to unbelievers.

> Man that is in honor and understands not
>> Is like the beasts that perish.

PSALM 50

Asaph is connected with twelve psalms, 50 and 73–83. He is undoubtedly the singer mentioned in 1 Chronicles 15:19 and elsewhere. He served the tabernacle during the time of David. Most of the psalms bearing his name are longer praise psalms, but some include imprecations. Others, such as this one, are really sermons directed to God's people.

It is not hard to understand why Asaph, a professional singer, also should be a composer. But we cannot be sure of what the word *of* means in the expressions "a psalm *of* Asaph" or "*of* David."

Here is one outline for the psalm:

Introduction (vv. 1–6)
God's dissatisfaction with insincere sacrifice (vv. 7–21)
Warning and promise (vv. 22–23)

A *selah* concludes the introduction, which has two thrusts to it. First is the announcement of God's coming. Second is the summons to saints to stand trial. Although the opening couple of verses sound like a praise psalm, the fire and tempest of verse 3 suggest that God has unpleasant business in mind. In verse 4 that purpose is specifically stated: He is to judge His people.

In verse 5, the worshipers are summoned to give account of their integrity in the matter of sacrificing. They must have been unfaithful to the covenant they had made with God or such a charge would not be warranted. The use of the word *saints* may be a sarcastic, tongue-in-cheek insult. That Hebrew word, when not a participle, is usually rendered *loving-kindness, faithfulness,* or *mercy.* God, the Judge, is about to accuse His people of not possessing these qualities.

123

The body of the psalm has two parts. Verse 7 introduces the long quotation of God in verses 8–15. Verse 16 introduces God's words against the wicked (vv. 16b–23). The first part is an attack on insincere sacrifice. The second half is broader and is an attack on unethical practices among the people of God.

God makes it very clear that He neither needs nor really wants sacrifice. In this respect the psalm shares the insightful theology of Isaiah and Amos. God's first requirement is integrity. Sacrifices only show a worshiper's overt obedience. Even for Christians it is often easier to do the overt thing rather than have a heart right toward God. To some people, regular attendance at the church services is more important than the "weightier matters of the law." To others, giving to missions is far easier than being a missionary to unsaved relatives and neighbors. So for the ancient people of Israel, sacrifice replaced true service, and burnt offerings substituted for inward piety.

The point is obvious: God does not drink the blood nor eat the meat of sacrifices but He examines the motives of the believer. More important to Him is the sacrifice of thanksgiving and the paying of vows, i.e., the keeping of promises. 1 Samuel 15:22 and Psalm 51:16–17 also emphasize this basic truth.

God concludes the first half of the psalm with an invitation to call on Him in time of trouble (v. 15). "Let Me deliver you and you glorify Me," God says.

The second major section of the psalm (vv. 16–21) is much more caustic and accusing. Perhaps the two sections are tied together with this line of reasoning: there are certain sins for which there is no prescribed sacrifice. So the inadequacy of the old sacrificial system is especially shown by the nature of these offenses. Among them are hateful attitudes (v. 17), sharing with thieves and adulterers (v. 18), lying (v. 19), and slander (v. 20).

The twenty-first verse culminates the list by charging that the people hold to the misconception that God is like men who tolerate sin and accept bribes. His silence, however, does not indicate His forgiveness but only His patience. God is waiting until the cup of iniquity is full. Then He proceeds to warn before it is too late.

The conclusion (vv. 22–23) is twofold. Verse 22 is a warning to the wicked against coming judgment, and verse 23 is a promise to the righteous. It is the offering of true thanksgiving that glorifies God. And the one who watches his step and examines his way of life (*conversation,* KJV) sees the salvation of God.

PSALMS 51–100:
SONGS OF
DEDICATION

....

Within the group of Psalms 51–100 are some well-known ones. The very first, Psalm 51, is the classic Bible passage on repentance and rededication. Psalm 69 is a most insightful prayer by a suffering servant. The New Testament quotes several of its verses. The tender sentiments of Psalm 84 are especially beloved: "How lovely are thy dwelling places," and "A day in thy courts is better than a thousand." The prayer of Moses, Psalm 90, focuses on some of God's eternal attributes as no other portion of Scripture does. Psalm 91 is the source of the expression, "under the shadow of the Almighty." And Psalm 100 has been paraphrased into one of the most famous anthems in our hymn books.

All of these psalms were written by dedicated saints of old, motivated by the Holy Spirit. They display their love for God, their hatred of sin, their pain, and their joy. They have bared their souls to all who take time to read and study this very intimate part of God's Word.

The author's prayer is that his comments on these abiding

songs of dedication will move people to true piety, biblical obedience, and fruitful service.

PSALM 51

The well-known confession of David opens this second volume on the Psalms. Several phrases from Psalm 51 have etched their way into the thinking of haunted sinners who searched for words of regret and repentance. The tenth verse is perhaps the best known: "Create in me a clean heart, O God; and renew a right spirit within me."

The rather lengthy title to Psalm 51 provides a setting for the prayer. There is no reason to question the suitability of this confession for the situation. David's adulterous relationship with Bathsheba and his provision for Uriah's death are the blackest of scars on that godly king's character. In 2 Samuel 12 is recorded the encounter between Nathan, the reprimanding prophet of God, and the guilty king. This psalm, David's prayer to God for forgiveness, is in general enough terms so that all sinners, as well as sinning believers, may echo its sentiments.

The opening two verses contain four prayer verbs: "have mercy" and "blot out," "wash" and "cleanse." The first couplet (v. 1) is formed by the phrases "according to your loving-kindness" and "according to the multitude of your tender mercies." The second couplet (v. 2) has the parallel words "iniquity" and "sin." These are not two varieties of evil any more than God has two varieties of mercy. The concepts of God's grace and David's sin are intensified by the use of synonyms which help fill out the total picture. Verses 7 and 9 are similar to these opening two and will be considered in order.

Whereas verses 1–2 are essentially petition, verses 4–6 are basically confession. David acknowledges the several facets of the classic doctrine of sin, called hamartiology in theology texts. First he confesses in the most general terms that he has sinned. In the middle of verse 4 he defines sin. Sin is to do what is evil according to God. Apart from a standard of right, there can be no transgression of that standard (cf. Rom. 4:15). Laws make criminals possible. God's holy Law, which demands perfection, makes us all sinners. Verse 4 concludes with a note of praise for God's justice.

Verse 5 points to the doctrine of total depravity. It does not state that David was the product of an illegitimate union. Traditional Protestant theology recognizes that all men are born sinners and that they all sin volitionally, as well. Here David recognizes these two aspects of guilt.

Verse 6 is another interjection of praise, while verse 7 picks up the petition for forgiveness begun in verse 1. Forgiveness involves two parties, the offender and the offended, the forgiven and the forgiver. The forgiven is restored to a place of joy and health (v. 8). The forgiving party—in this case, God—must put away the accusations. So verse 9 points to His part in this transaction. However, it is not until verses 16–17 that the price of pardon is mentioned.

The concluding four petitions (vv. 11–12) are in pairs, two negative and two positive. David prays *not* to be cast away and *not* to have God's Holy Spirit removed. Notice that "spirit" occurs in verses 10, 11, and 12. The "restore" and "uphold" of verse 12 indicate this is a believer's prayer. The unregenerate has never had the joy of salvation.

David promises to give God service (vv. 13–14). The sincerity of his confession, like the sincerity of ours, will be demonstrated by obedient service. Forgiveness is, in a sense, removal of the evil, but there must follow the execution of the good. These promises predate the Great Commission by 1,000 years; yet they underscore the great twofold task of the church of Jesus Christ. We must bring sinners to the knowledge of God and we must praise God's righteousness. One can hardly be done without the other.

Furthermore, David recognizes that he needs divine enablement in this matter of witnessing. He prays what every hesitant Christian should pray: "Lord, open thou my lips."

The concluding verses (16–19) focus on the sacrificial system and its basic inadequacy. Like all perceptive Old Testament saints, David realized that God really did not want or need blood sacrifices as much as He demanded right attitudes which produced good deeds. The penitent must come not only with burnt offerings, but also with broken hearts. Repentance is more than doing penance. These well-known lines by Augustus M. Toplady express this truth:

> Nothing in my hand I bring,
> Simply to Thy cross I cling. ("Rock of Ages")

Good deeds must accompany good promises. The proof of David's sincerity would be his building the walls of Jerusalem. This divine-human intention he makes both a prayer to God and an instruction to himself and other confessors. Only as good behavior follows noble vows can any of the externals of the Old Testament religion be acceptable to God. Sacrifices of righteousness must bolster the offered bullocks. Otherwise the temple becomes merely a slaughterhouse and not the scene where men are reconciled to a holy and offended God.

PSALM 52

The record of Doeg the Edomite's coming to Saul and announcing that David was at Ahimelech's house is in 1 Samuel

22:9. It unfolds into a bloody massacre as Saul, jealous of David's growing popularity, has Doeg slay all the priests of Nob, including Ahimelech. Though no certainty should be attached to the titles of the psalms, this particular one is not at all unsuitable.

The "mighty man" of the opening verse is, then, King Saul. While he boasts in badness, God continues to deal with goodness. Apart from this initial reference to God's goodness (v. 1b), His loving-kindness does not appear until verse 8. The largest part of this complaint poem—first in a series that continues to Psalm 59—focuses on the wickedness and judgment of David's enemy.

The image of verse 2 likens the tongue to a razor: devising, deceiving, and cutting. The Revised Standard Version arranges the lines differently, effecting no basic change in meaning. The "all the day" of the newer scanning applies to the tongue's devising wickedness rather than to the loving-kindness of God.

A typical synonymous parallelism constitutes verse 3. Those who say *selah* means "think of that" have difficulty explaining why such an instruction should occur at the end of this verse. The Hebrew is better understood as some musical direction regarding volume, key change, posture, or antiphonal choirs.

Verses 2b–4 form a concise chiasmus. Note the deceitful tongue in the opening and closing lines, the word "love" in the intermediate parts, and the second half of verse 3 as the central stich.

The turning point comes with verse 5. Now the judgment of God and subsequent ridicule by the righteous are in view. This verse contains four varieties of punishment God will execute: He will destroy them; He will take them up; He will pluck them out; and He will root them from the land.

Verses 6–7 predict what the righteous will do when the wicked are judged. They shall learn the importance of reverencing God and His righteousness and rejoice that the wicked are punished.

Rejoicing at the downfall of the wicked without fearing their own would leave out an essential. The punishment of criminals should serve to instruct the rest of the people. The opposite is an unfortunate modern phenomenon in America. Since many criminals go unpunished, fear of the law is lost. As a result, crime increases.

Verse 7 reads like an epitaph on the grave of an evil man. Rather than being strong in God, he was strong in wickedness.

The last two verses are the testimony of the good man, in this case, the righteous king of Israel. He chooses the green olive tree in God's house to illustrate life, productivity, and peace. Three vows sum up the characteristic attitude of this ancient God-fearer: "I trust," "I will give thanks," "I will hope" (MLB). I recommend this last verse as a pattern for every Christian's outlook.

PSALM 53

Psalms 14 and 53 are almost identical. Only the latter part of Psalm 53:5 varies from Psalm 14, and Psalm 14:6 is not found here. The title to Psalm 53 differs slightly too. It has the additional remarks, "set to Mahalath" and "a Maschil." *Mahalath* is perhaps a hymn tune or a musical instrument. It occurs again only in the title to Psalm 88. *Maschil,* a much more common word, is a kind of song.

No explanation of why there are two copies of the psalm is satisfactory. We must simply understand that here are two redactions of the same work.

In addition to the differences noted above, it is interesting to observe that the name *God* is substituted for LORD (a characteristic feature of Psalms 42–72) in three places (vv. 2, 4, 6), while a fourth occurrence of the divine name in Psalm 14 is in the verse eliminated from Psalm 53. Other variations are even less significant.

While the commentary on Psalm 14 can be read for this psalm, additional remarks are appropriate for verse 5b. It is a picture of judgment—judgment on the enemies of Israel. Because they desired and demanded a decent burial, the scattering of bones may be among the worst threats of punishment. Archaeological finds have substantiated that many ancient peoples had second burials. Shortly after death, the entire body would be interred for a year or more. Only minimal preparation was done to preserve the corpse. Later the bones would be exhumed and put into a smaller casket, ossuary, or bonebox for permanent burial. Sometimes the bones were merely piled in a family cave. The disarray in which some skeletons were found points to such a second entombment.

The scene of Psalm 53:5b is that of God not giving an honorable second burial to His and His people's enemies, who are described in the body of the psalm as very godless. In general, this and Psalm 14 are very gloomy. Only the last verse of each picks us up and makes us glad. With similar aspiration we ought to anticipate the joy of seeing God save and liberate those destined for His kingdom.

PSALM 54

Psalm 54 is a typical short "trouble and trust" song. Its format is that of a prayer but includes complaint to God about enemies, and rejoicing in their anticipated destruction. Several words occur more than once in its seven verses: "God" is twice in the vocative (vv. 1–2) and two other times in addition. "Thy name" occurs in verses 1 and 6. "My soul" appears in verses 3 and 4. There are five synonyms for trouble: two in verse 3, one in verse 5, and two in verse 7. No clear outline appears from noting these features.

According to the title, which comprises two verses in the Hebrew Bible, the setting for this psalm may be found in 1 Samuel 23—a chapter filled with intrigue as it recounts Saul's pursuit of David. David sought to evade Saul by hiding in the woods of Ziph. But the Ziphites were on Saul's side and betrayed David's hideout to jealous and angry King Saul. But, in a fashion similar to old-time radio serials, David was not there when Saul closed in for the kill. He had moved to another desert spot, which Saul in turn surrounded. Only the report of a new Philistine invasion decoyed Saul away, and the relieved David took the opportunity to retrench at En-gedi. The enemies to which David refers in this psalm, therefore, are Saul, his soldiers, and the Ziphite informants.

The opening two verses contain four imperatives which sum up the psalmist's request: "save me," "judge me," "hear," and "give ear." The word "judge" in this context means "to execute justice." David certainly would have won this contest in a court of law. Saul did not have a legal leg to stand on, and both he and David knew it. For that reason only, David pleads for a trial.

Notice once again the appeal to God's name and the parallel, God's strength. To the ancient Semite a name was more than a label or an identification tag; it was the person himself. To invoke a name was to invoke the person. The custom is preserved when we pray in Jesus' name.

Verse 3 delineates the reasons for the prayer. The Ziphites were strangers who for no reason cast their lot with wicked Saul rather than with righteous David. One could forgive Saul's soldiers for being loyal to their leader, but why should strangers who apparently have nothing to lose or gain, show such allegiance? In addition to seeking to kill David, they are also charged with godlessness. Even so today, violent people intent on murder cannot entertain God and His Law in their minds.

If verse 3 is the "trouble" part of this psalm, then verse 4 is the "trust." A *selah* divides this turning point. "Uphold my soul" may perhaps be translated as "sustain my life," the same life that the violent men (v. 3b) sought to destroy. Having said what God would do for him, David continues to tell what God will do to his enemies (v. 5). They will be repaid and, he hopes, destroyed. God's truth or fidelity is not the instrument of their destruction but the reason for it. Because God knows who is guilty or innocent, He can, on the basis of that truth, execute justice.

The last two verses are somewhat of an epilogue. Already anticipating his vindication and his enemies' punishment, David promises to do his duty to God and express his gratitude with offerings. In the light of the discussion on the word "name" above, observe that he gives thanks to God's name, for He is good.

Verse 7 may refer to David's envisioning the answer to this prayer, or it may be a reflection on past deliverances. There is no spiritual therapy like counting blessings and expecting more. The account in 1 Samuel 23 records neither the first nor the last narrow escape David had. If God delivered His child before, will He not do it again? If He has let you see your enemy removed, will He not give you victory over any present or future difficulty?

PSALM 55

The title to Psalm 55 gives no indication of the setting for the composition. We can only guess from the context. Verse 9 may give some indication that the treachery described occurred in an urban context; and verse 13 points out that a close friend turned against the psalmist.

In typical fashion the psalm begins with an invocation to God. After that two-verse introduction there follows complaint in the next three verses. All of the charges are in general terms and could describe any number of troubles David or other biblical saints, or even we, have experienced. The persecution seems to be mostly verbal abuse and threatened, rather than actual, physical harm. As we all know, words can sometimes injure more cruelly than inflicted blows. Whatever the nature of the enemy's attacks, they produce fear, trembling, and horror for the author.

Verses 6–8 probably speak for all of us at one time or another. When things grow bad, the urge to escape becomes much greater. Oh, to be like a bird and fly away from it all! Oh, to be far from the rat race of everyday life and tension to enjoy a cabin in the woods or a cave in the desert! Oh, to be out of the storm and in a safe and quiet shelter! And some Christians' professed love for the Lord's appearance is only a veiled wish for their own disappearance.

Despite the "selah" before verse 8, verse 9 begins a new section. In much the same manner as the psalm began, verse 9 is a prayer followed by complaints in the succeeding verses. It is not as if a new psalm begins, for this section refers to what precedes. The prayer is for destruction of the wicked tongue, that cruel agent which afflicts the psalmist. The prayer also mentions the violence of the city in contrast to the rest and peace available in the wilderness lodge. A description of the wicked city continues (vv. 10–11).

With verse 12 the psalmist starts to focus attention more particularly on his onetime friend, now turned enemy. A traitor is an especially bad enemy, for his enmity is not immediately suspected and certainly not anticipated. He shelters his evil intentions behind your friendship for him. Such treachery must have been perpetrated against the author of this psalm. He reminisces about the days when his friend and he went to God's house together, chatting as they went. But those days are gone forever. That one stab in the back proved what a false friend he was.

Do not mistake the "thou" to be God in verse 13. It is obvious from the grammar of verse 14 that this enemy is not God, though he has been referred to in both the second person pronoun (*you*) and the third person pronoun (*he*).

The balance of the psalm alternates between vindictive prayers for the enemy's destruction and testimonies of God's faithfulness. Here is the record of a man who simultaneously prays for calamity on his foes and blessing on himself, accuses them and defends himself, anticipates their punishment and his own exoneration, testifies to their deceit and his integrity.

The imprecatory verses are 15, 19, and 23. The blessing verses are 16–18, and 22. The prayed-down plagues are as severe as anything elsewhere in the psalms. For instance, note verse 15b, that the wicked might be buried alive; and verse 23b, that they should die before reaching middle age. Verses 20–21 comport with verse 13. It was an old friend who turned against him. The figures of verse 21 are quite vivid. The traitor had a mouth and words like butter and oil but, sword-like, they veiled a heart at war.

On the other hand, the confessions of trust and the notes of praise are as sweet as the complaints were bitter. In spite of the accusations, and beyond the troubles, there is God. And according to verse 16, He will save. Additional thanks for deliverances are in verse 18.

The injunction to us, the modern readers of this ancient literature, is verse 22. This is the lesson the twentieth-century saint can learn from a work such as this. "Cast your burden on the LORD, and He will sustain you; He will never allow the righteous to be shaken" (NASB). The time may come in our lives when a close friend, perhaps even a relative, will turn against us, pull out the carpet, so to speak, and maybe even thirst for our blood. While we pray that such a thing will never happen, let us be prepared to echo the words that close this psalm: "I will trust in Thee."

PSALM 56

Psalm 56 is another in the series of "trouble and trust" psalms, a series extending from Psalm 52 through Psalm 59. It follows the format of others with these various elements: invocation, complaint, supplication, anticipated destruction of enemies, and anticipated bliss and vindication for the psalmist. The order may vary from psalm to psalm, and some features may be repeated or slighted, but generally these themes characterize this type of psalm.

The title is taken with varying degrees of seriousness or authority. Part of the reason is the uncertainty of some of the words, and part because the antiquity of the titles is questionable. Several translations of the tune to which this psalm is set are possible and can be found in modern versions, while the old versions simply transliterate the Hebrew words.

The account of David feigning insanity (1 Sam. 21:10–15) fits the historical note in the title. But, like many other psalms, the content is very unspecific and suits many instances in David's life and the lives of others.

The invocation of this poem is very brief—merely the first stich of verse 1. Immediately the writer launches into his complaint over his enemy, which is sometimes singular and sometimes plural. In fact, the same verb, "swallow," comes in verses 1 and 2. The phrase "daily" (or, "all [the] day long") also appears in these two verses. The verb "fight" also occurs twice. If, indeed, David is the author and it was written on the occasion of his flight from Saul to the inhospitable Philistines, the singular enemy might be the first king of Israel, and the plural enemy the Philistine lords.

From the despair of verse 2 the psalmist turns to the confidence of verse 3. Again, notice the repetition of the words "trust," "in God," and "afraid." Such repetition as occurs in verses 3–4 and in verses 1–2 is typical of ancient Semitic poetry. It does not indicate a small vocabulary but is a device to impress certain concepts on the reader. Reiterating the same words in different phrases is like viewing a jewel from several angles. For instance, verses 3–4 could be summarized: "When I am afraid, I will not be afraid."

The alternate theme of complaint takes the stage in verses 5–6. Once more the expression "every day" (or, "all [the] day long") occurs. These two verses focus on the manner of the attack more than on the simple fact of it. The foe has plotted to ambush the righteous man.

In the middle of verse 7 the complaint gives way to imprecatory prayer. This half verse is the only section of the psalm that can be labeled as prayer against enemies. Complaint and anticipated destruction appear later on. But, unlike some of the psalms, the actual calling down of a curse is relatively brief.

Self-pity is the essence of verse 8. Though there is some question regarding the meaning of "bottle," whether it is a wineskin or simple parchment, the point is clear. God keeps a record of all things, and to that record the psalmist appeals in verse 9. He knows that, on the day the books are opened, God will justify him and condemn his oppressors.

Because verses 10–11 are so similar to verse 4, a hint of the strophic structure of the composition may be present. The answer to the rhetorical question in verse 11 is "nothing." Man can do nothing to the eternal hurt of one who trusts in God. As in several preceding psalms (51:19; 52:9; 54:6) there is the promise to thank and bring offerings for the anticipated deliverance.

A better understanding of Hebrew syntax and the way speech, both ancient and modern, works makes unnecessary the several italicized words in verse 13 (KJV, ASV). A simple interrogative article is attached to the negative, and most accurately it should be translated "No?" or "Isn't it so?" and read with the inflection to indicate the preceding is definitely true. Hence: "You delivered my life from death and my feet from falling. No?"

The psalm closes with a happy benediction which looks forward to a long, godly life. As long as we can see beyond our troubles—those enemies of our souls—to the vindicating, all-righteous God, we will come out spiritually on top. Generally it takes little calculation to see that God's blessings far outweigh the temporal trials that plague us.

PSALM 57

A refrain in verses 5 and 11 divides Psalm 57 into two stanzas or strophes. The first stanza contains prayer and complaint in that order (vv. 1–4). The second stanza contains complaint and promise in that order (vv. 6–10). So there is a rudimentary chiasmus within the total psalm. The composition fits into this series of laments or "trouble and trust" psalms, as we call them.

Again the title focuses on a specific incident (cf. 1 Sam. 22:1), but the generalities in the psalm make it applicable to various episodes in the lives of many different persons. The words transliterated from the Hebrew as *Al-taschith,* mean "destroy not" (see MLB and RSV), and may be cited from Deuteronomy 9:26, where Moses prayed that God would not destroy His people after the incident of the golden calf.

The psalmist is moderate in that he does not get to his complaint for several verses. The first three verses are entirely prayer. Perhaps we could learn from this approach. Which is bigger, our problem or our God? Do we stop to recognize who He is with whom we have to deal before we clutter His audience hall with the trivia of our faithless lives?

The initial supplication, "be merciful," occurs twice (v. 1).

140

Not until verse 5 is there another imperative. Rather, the psalmist asserts his confidence that God will protect and bless. The illustration of verse 1 is of a mother hen comforting and protecting her brood. God does not have wings, but He does provide for our physical and psychological needs.

The last stich of verse 1 and the middle stich of verse 3 only hint at the trouble. Not until the fourth verse do the enemies come into full view. They are like lions. They burn with passion. They have teeth like spears and arrows, and a tongue like a sharp sword. Perhaps no physical harm has yet befallen the writer of this complaint, but the threats are abundant and frightening. Therefore he complains primarily about their teeth and tongues rather than their actual swords and arrows. A benediction closes the first stanza.

The second stanza begins, without hesitation, to outline more of the troubles of this ancient saint. A net was spread and a pit was dug, but the devices produced an unexpected result—the wicked trapped themselves.

Once the initial verse of complaint in this stanza is passed the remainder is praise and promise. From a steadfast heart the psalmist promises to sing God's praise. He summons various musical instruments to assist. Psalm 150 gives more explanation of the musical instruments. We would probably not find such music too pleasing since most of the instruments were percussion and strings. Most likely the music was loud and rhythmic—even shattering.

Verses 9–10 are perfect examples of Hebrew parallelism. The psalmist thinks as high and wide as he can—to the (foreign) nations and peoples, and to the heavens and skies. The refrain of verse 5 closes the work: "Be thou exalted, O God, above the heavens: let thy glory be above all the earth."

PSALM 58

Except for the lack of a historical note, the title to Psalm 58 is identical to the superscriptions of Psalms 57 and 59. Psalm 58 is more caustic in its charges against the wicked than the preceding psalms. It also contains some very difficult Hebrew.

The general outline divides the psalm at verse 6. The first half is a charge against the wicked; the latter half is an imprecatory prayer for their destruction. Evidence of chiasmus is present in the repetition of various words. Concepts of righteousness and justice occur in the first and last verses. The same Hebrew word for wicked appears in verses 3 and 10. Verses 2 and 10 may be linked with the terms "hands" and "feet." Both verses 3 and 8 have the idea of birth in them, though identical Hebrew words are not used. There may be a connection between the snakes of verse 4 and the snail of verse 8, although the latter is one of the questionable words. Lastly, in the middle verse a parallel exists between "teeth" and "fangs" (v. 6, NASB).

The first difficulty arises with the second word (in Hebrew) of the psalm. The King James Version renders it "O congregation"; the American Standard Version, "in silence"; the New American Standard Bible, "O gods"; and the Modern Language Bible, "O you judges." I propose *to them,* although there is no antecedent. The meaning is clear as soon as the second half of the verse is read: "Do you judge the children of men fairly?" (MLB).

The vicious indictment continues through verse 2. Their wickedness takes two steps: first the plot is worked out in their hearts, and then it is executed with their hands.

The psalmist switches to the third person in the next six verses. Though Psalm 51:5 is not part of this series and is in a much different context, it states the same truth.

Verses 4–5 go together and describe the wicked in terms of a venomous serpent. Unlike serpents, which are obedient to their charmers (a word found only once in the Hebrew Bible), they cannot be made to reason or submit. The enemies of the righteous are as untrustworthy and deadly as poisonous reptiles.

The imprecatory prayer begins in verse 6 with two parallel wishes for broken teeth. Perhaps the first teeth belong to the poisonous serpents of the preceding verse (5) and the second teeth belong to the lion of the last half of verse 6. Teeth in particular and other parts of the mouth in general occur in nearly every psalm in this series (cf. Ps. 52:2; 53:4; 55:21; 56:1–2; 57:4; 59:7, 12).

Verses 7–9 are as difficult and uncertain of interpretation as any part of the Psalms. Some words are certain but are in contexts with other words which may be unknown or do not fit well. The number of italicized words in the King James Version gives some indication of the difficulty. Perhaps the biggest problem is our lack of understanding of ancient figures of speech. Whole volumes are given to the study of Semitic curses, and these four or five curses belong among them. Because they are proverb-like, they are difficult to translate or even understand. Think of the difficulty a foreigner must have understanding some of our expressions such as, "He had to eat crow or his name would be mud."

At least there is some consensus on the first half of verse 7. The psalmist wishes the wicked to disappear like water into the sand, an action which the word "melt" could describe. All agree that verse 8 seems to be praying that the wicked will miscarry their babies.

With verse 10 the translation is easier and the point quite clear. When the wicked are punished, the righteous rejoice. The gruesome figure of bathing feet in blood is better tolerated when we remember the age when this poetry was written—an age of bloodshed, violence, physical cruelty, and revenge.

Having been vindicated, the protagonist praises God for His justice. The enemy has received his due and the righteous his reward. Such satisfaction of justice prompts the closing expression, "Verily he is a God that judgeth in the earth."

Christians might well meditate on the conclusion, rather than study the curses. David did not have the beatitudes of the pattern of Jesus' life to follow. We do.

PSALM 59

Psalm 59 is the third *michtam* in a row set to the same tune. It is the last in a series of seven or eight psalms of complaint against enemies, called "trouble and trust" or "lament" psalms.

Again certain themes prevail: prayer for personal deliverance, imprecation on the foes, complaint, description of the enemy, and promises to praise. The verses which focus on the enemy are interwoven with verses of petition to God for the enemy's destruction and the psalmist's deliverance. The verb "defend" ("set me on high," ASV) and the cognate noun "defense" ("high tower," ASV) tie together the latter group of verses (1, 9, 16, 17). Notice also the repetition of verse 6 in verse 14. A *selah* precedes both.

In typical fashion, the psalm begins with four imperatives: "deliver me," "defend me," "deliver me," and "save me." Likewise the foe is described in four ways: "mine enemies," "them that rise up against me," "the workers of iniquity," and "bloody men."

The description of the enemy's activities begins in verse 3 and continues on and off through verse 15. In addition to the complaint, a protest of self-righteousness is present in verses 3–4. The psalmist wants to underscore his enemy's guilt and his own innocence. Such a tactic is all right, providing it is true.

The second half of verse 4 starts another series of demands on God. Two of the requests are antithetically parallel: "awake to help me" and "arise to visit all the heathen." If these two elements are labeled A and C, then the remaining two, B and D, have a militaristic tone: the God of military powers ("hosts") must not have mercy on wicked transgressors.

The first occurrence of the refrain, if we might call it that, comes in verse 6. The picture of a pack of howling, belching dogs roaming the city streets is not a pleasant one, but neither were these enemies very pleasant. With all respect to modern dog lovers, ancient peoples had little use for dogs. Their only contribution was to scavenge refuse and bark at intruders.

Verse 8 is similar to Psalm 2:4.

The halfway point is marked by a note of praise quite similar to the closing verse of the psalm.

Again (v. 11) the cursing of the enemy resumes. If the first word of verse 11 in Hebrew is read differently, it can mean, "O God, slay them" rather than "slay them not."

The complaint of verse 12 centers on the words of the enemy's mouth rather than on their actual deeds. Another series of curses follows, beginning with "consume them" (v. 13) and ending with "let them wander" and "be not satisfied." The "dog" refrain comes at verse 14, and the curses of verse 15 sustain the figure of hungry, roving packs.

A promise and a benediction close the psalm. Elements from earlier verses echo in this optimistic conclusion. The note of mercy ("lovingkindness," NASB) is first struck in verse 10. The high tower ("defence") is in verse 9. "His [God's] strength" also occurs in verse 9. Perhaps the "morning" of verse 16 is in contrast to the "evening" of verses 6 and 14.

All of the psalms in this series, given over to complaints and curses against enemies, end on notes of praise. We all go through times of mental anguish when we wonder if God exists or hears us, or is helping our enemies, and His. We all secretly wish their demise and our own vindication. But let us not stop there. Let us with these ancient psalmists bring our experience to the blessed and hopeful conclusion that ends each of these psalms. Despite circumstances, do not forget, "God is my high tower, the God of my mercy" (ASV).

PSALM 60

In the course of expanding his kingdom, David must have experienced some setbacks. Psalm 60 reads like a national lament over a defeat in battle. The title points to 2 Samuel 8 and 1 Chronicles 18. David conquered the countries mentioned but perhaps suffered some reverses before victory was accomplished. Though the psalm is a lament, it is also a prayer for help and a song of hope. The first half of verse 1 is the same as verse 10a, which may mark the beginning of a new strophe. Verses 5–12 are almost identical to Psalm 108:6–13, with a "selah" at the division point.

Verses 1–4 are the heart of the lament. The defeat in battle is likened to a cosmic catastrophe and blamed on God, who has left their ranks. No reason ever appears why such a reverse should occur, and there is no repentance on the part of the king or the people. Verse 2 describes the calamity in terms of a violent earthquake. Notice that interspersed in the lament are brief petitions for help: "restore us again" (v. 1 ASV) and "heal the breaches" (v. 2 ASV).

As in other passages, God's wrath or discipline is pictured as a drink to be imbibed by the afflicted (cf. Ps. 75:8; Jer. 25:15; Matt. 20:22).

Verse 4 is difficult to interpret in the light of what immediately precedes. The Greek translation gives a sarcastic sense: that the banner ordinarily used to rally to battle is raised for retreat. This is unnecessary if the verse is tied with what follows rather than with what precedes. Despite the present defeat, God has provided a rallying point. That banner is the encouragement of the oracle of hope (vv. 6–8). Its purpose is to deliver the beloved, probably meaning the king, with a play on words, since in Hebrew "David" is from the same root as the word "beloved."

Verses 6–8 and perhaps 9 contain the quotation of God's promise given in His holiness or in His holy sanctuary. As the Owner, He is free to parcel out Shechem and the valley of Succoth. Shechem was the outstanding city in the northern part of the country. The valley referred to may be the Jordan Valley, since Succoth has been tentatively located at a tell north of Jericho. Gilead and Manasseh are in northern Trans-Jordan. Ephraim is a major tribe in the north while Judah is the major tribe in the south, having in its bounds the capital city of Jerusalem. Moab, Edom, and Philistia are neighbors to the east, southeast, and southwest, respectively. The strong city of verse 9 to which either the king or God wishes someone to bring him may be the famous rock city of Petra. The derogatory terms applied to Moab and Edom have several explanations. The shoe-casting (v. 8) may not refer to the refusal of terms, as in Ruth 4:7, but simply to walking over the land, which in this context means invasion. The lamentation resumes (v. 10) with the words that opened the psalm. God has not accompanied the army into battle and this has brought defeat. The last two verses (11–12) are given over to supplication and prayer for victory. Human strength cannot save; only in God is there hope. Though the psalmist complains of being forsaken by God, he is not going to forsake God. He realizes there is no help except in God and that it would be sealing his doom to reject the only avenue of escape and the only source of physical and spiritual salvation.

PSALM 61

A confession of trust and prayer for or by the king comes in Psalm 61. In verses 1–5 the supplicant is "I," but in verses 6–7 the third person is used. Perhaps the king, even David, refers to himself in this detached style (vv. 6–7).

The superscription indicates that the psalm is for or of the chief musician, played perhaps on a stringed instrument called a *Neginah*. It is for, by, or of David. The same preposition precedes the chief musician as precedes David. The enigmatic "selah" divides the work exactly in half, rather than at the point where the object shifts from "me" to "him."

The opening verse is the invocation in a typical synonymous parallelism, with similar verbs ("hear" and "attend unto") and similar direct objects ("my cry" and "my prayer"). Some have inferred from "the end of the earth" that the speaker is in exile in some distant country. On the other hand, the reference to a high rock may indicate a desert exile such as David experienced in his flight from Saul. This verse prompted William O. Cushing to pen the well-known hymn, "Hiding in Thee." The opening lines read:

O safe to the Rock that is higher than I,
My soul in its conflicts and sorrows would fly.

Warrant for such an application is entirely scriptural (cf. Ps. 18:2; 1 Cor. 10:4). The figure is especially vivid to someone who has spent time in a parched, waterless waste. Any rock large enough to offer shade from the scorching sun is welcome. The other noteworthy value of rock is for foundation and that may be the interpretation here as it certainly is in the psalm (v. 2) and in the parable of the wise man who built his house on a rock (Luke 6:48).

From the supplication of verse 2 the psalmist turns to testimony in verses 3–5. God is likened to four varieties of shelters. He is a refuge or fortress; He is a strong tower; He has been a tent for shelter and wings for covering. The tent or tabernacle may allude to the sanctuary of God on earth, or may simply be a figurative term for God's protection. The latter is probably better in this context.

One slight variation of interpretation is available in verse 5. Is it that God has given *to* the psalmist the heritage *of* those who fear His name? Or have *all* God-fearers received the heritage? On either interpretation, the point is that there is some distinct advantage to fearing the Lord, an advantage termed here as an inheritance or a heritage.

The king, who may be the speaker throughout the psalm, is mentioned as the beneficiary of God's blessing of long life (v. 6). Despite his many close calls, David did live to be seventy years old.

Verse 7 can refer to the afterlife. Thus the testimony is twofold: he will live a long life on earth and then forever after in God's presence.

The closing verse (v. 8) contains an interesting contrast between praising God forever and performing vows daily. Sometimes the long view obscures the immediate. It is a fine thing to focus on eternity, but the "here and now" is where and when we should be bearing spiritual fruit.

PSALM 62

A mixture of themes is present in Psalm 62, but the overriding one is trust. Verses 1–2, 5–8, and 11–12 are three groups of assertions or recommendations of faith in God, who will protect and deliver. In fact, verses 1–2 are almost identical to verses 5–6. The remaining verses, 3–4 and 9–10, are complaints about the wicked and warning against wickedness. Grammatically speaking, every person, singular and plural, occurs in the psalm (I, thou, he, us, you, they). Sometimes it is difficult to know whom is being spoken to or about. In verses 1–2 the psalmist confesses to God. In verses 3–4 both the "you" and the "they" refer to enemies. Verses 5–7 are like verses 1–2, but verses 8–10 are exhortations directed to fellow believers. Mainly because of these three verses some call this a didactic or instructional psalm. Finally, the last two verses (11–12) have the psalmist as the subject and God as the object, except for the very first line of verse 11.

As noted in Psalm 39, Jeduthun was an official temple musician (1 Chron. 16:41f.; 25:1). Perhaps he wrote the music to which these words were sung. Again, the title does not help the understanding of the psalm. The terms are quite general and could be the experience of any number of different persons.

The statements are confessions of belief in one God. He is the salvation, the rock, and the high tower (ASV) of the poet. In verse 2 the "greatly" is difficult. Perhaps that modifier should be an adjective with "tower" rather than an adverb with "moved." Hence: "My great high tower; I shall not be moved."

The scene shifts (v. 3) and the remarks are addressed to violent men. Both the leaning wall and the tottering fence may be either the wicked man or the righteous whom he is oppressing. In verse 4, rather than being addressed, they are described as arch-hypocrites and liars.

An appropriate "selah" marks the division between verses 4–5 and 8–9. Another confession of trust begins this section using phrases almost identical with verses 1–2. The words "salvation" and "rock" echo again in verse 7. Verse 8 is still part of the positive section of the psalm, but its format is exhortation. The psalmist's contemporaries, or we, the readers, are urged to trust in God at all times. In form, verses 8 and 10 go together. The former is positive and tells us what to trust in, while the latter is negative and tells us what not to trust in.

Verse 9 intercepts the exhortation with a scathing description of the worthlessness of the wicked depicted by a vivid, everyday scene from ancient commerce. Put the wicked on a balance scale, and up they go for lack of worth. The Hebrew language, interestingly, builds the words for "curse" and "weightlessness" on the same root; "heavy" and "glorify" likewise share a common stem. Evangelists sometimes use this illustration. In one pan is the perfect Godman, Christ Jesus, and in the other the sinner and his meager self-righteousness. The result is that all come short of the glory of God (Rom. 3:23; cf. Dan. 5:27).

Verse 10 urges the saints not to trust in oppression, robbery, and riches. The order in which these appear may be significant. Ill-gotten gain will be of no avail when God weighs our merits.

The two concluding verses (11–12) are a kind of benediction. The "once-twice" sequence is a typical device found elsewhere in the Bible, but with different series of numbers. For "two-three," see Deuteronomy 17:6. For "three-four," see Proverbs 30:18, 21, 29; Amos 1:3, 6, 9, 11, 13; 2:1, 4, 6. For "six-seven," see Proverbs 6:16. The modern English expression is, "If I've heard it once I've heard it a thousand times!" And we have. In capsule form the two major truths of the gospel are summed up in verse 12. God is love, but God will also judge every man. How many times have you heard that? Once? Twice? A thousand times?

PSALM 63

The title to Psalm 63 fits well with the contents. The wilderness of Judea is a "dry and thirsty land where there is no water." And the "king" (v. 11) might well be the psalmist speaking of himself in the third person (cf. Ps. 61:6). The psalm speaks of the aspiration of the believer to be in God's presence. Except for verses 9 and 10 and the last line of 11, no negative note is sounded.

Verse 1 opens with a typical invocation: "O God . . . my God." The verb "to seek early" is related to the noun for "morning" and can be taken with that obvious meaning. This initial confession is a case for morning devotions. Soul and body, he wishes to be in God's presence. Perhaps David was literally in the desert. We may experience dearths of fellowship and droughts of spiritual blessings. The opportunity for fellowship and the privilege of sharing with the gathered church are dearly missed when they are not available. There is no loneliness like that of the Christian in a strange and hostile world, unable to enjoy another believer's presence and comfort.

As in other places in the psalm and elsewhere, the word "sanctuary" may not refer actually to the yet-unbuilt temple but to that retreat where God's holiness is to be found. Verse 2a makes commentators think this an exilic psalm with the speaker yearning to return to the holy city. I prefer the more general interpretation, that the psalmist longs to enjoy God's holiness, power, and glory whether on sacred Mount Zion or in the solitude of En-gedi.

The sentiment of verse 3 is highly exalted. To think of God's covenant fidelity, His loving-kindness, and His unfailing mercy as better than life indicates a spiritual plateau few reach. Paul was on that plateau when he said, "For me to live is Christ, and to die is gain" (Phil. 1:21; cf. Ps. 116:15).

Having said that this life is secondary to enjoying God, David continues to vow that as long as he is alive he will bless God with uplifted hands (v. 4).

Verse 5 stands in contrast to verse 1. Whereas he was thirsty and hungry, here he is full and fat. Notice the metaphors of lips and mouth that pervade this psalm (vv. 3, 5, 11). The word "soul" also ties these two verses together.

Verse 6 also complements verse 1. In verse 1 the speaker seeks God in the morning. In verse 6 he remembers Him in bed and thinks about Him during the night watches. In verse 1 he was in a land parched by the sun; in verse 7 he enjoys the shade under God's wings.

An interesting contrast is found in verse 8. The psalmist cleaves to God and God holds him. There is something in this verse for both positions on the question of the security of the believer. From a human viewpoint we must stick fast to Him, but from God's perspective He holds us in His right hand, the position of favor.

Verse 9 begins the little maledictory section of the psalm. The Hebrew grammar allows the word "destroy" to go with "my soul" or "life," as it is in the standard translations, or to describe the enemies. The latter option would read: "They will be for destruction who seek my soul/life." If this is correct then there are four curses in verses 9 and 10: destruction, dispatch to the underworld, sword, and jackals or foxes. Another promise concludes the psalm (v. 11). Speaking in the third person, the king sees the day when he and all who live in God will rejoice and glory, while all the mouths of the liars will be shut.

PSALM 64

Psalm 64 easily falls into a chiastic outline.

A Prayer for deliverance from wicked *workers* (vv. 1–2)
  B Description of the wicked *tongue* (v. 3)
    C Purpose of the wicked *shooting* (v. 4)
      D Psychology of the wicked (vv. 5–6)
    C´ God *shoots* the wicked (v. 7)
  B´ God confounds their *tongue* (v. 8)
A´ Righteous men enjoy the *work* of God (vv. 9–10)

The italicized words indicate the various paired elements. These are not merely coincidental English translations but represent paired Hebrew words as well. In addition, the word "suddenly" occurs in verses 4 and 7, and "arrows" in verses 3 and 7.

The turning point in the psalm is after verse 6. Up to that point it is a prayer and complaint about secret enemies. From verse 7 on is the anticipating of their condemnation and the vindication of the righteous.

The psalm begins with three words of entreaty: Hear me, preserve me, and hide me. Verses 1–2 are only loosely parallel within themselves. The "fear of the enemy" (v. 1) deserves some comment. Sometimes fear of something or someone can be as destructive as the harm itself. Fear can sap our ability to concentrate, can challenge our faith, and virtually destroy our usefulness. Living under the threat of danger can be more disastrous than the catastrophe itself. Knowing something of this, the psalmist prays for deliverance from such fear. This is a different word from the one rendered "fear" in verses 4 and 9.

The general introduction to the description of the enemy begins with their appellations: wicked plotters and workers of iniquity (v. 2). On the one hand is the private planning session where the wicked plot to overthrow the righteous; then there is the overt execution of that plan, the insurrection (KJV), the tumult (ASV), or the turbulent mob (NEB).

As in other psalms, the focus is first on what the wicked say and then on what they do. So verses 3 and 4 speak of their tongue as a sword and their words as arrows. The adjective "bitter" may mean "poisonous," but the antiquity of poisonous arrows has not been established. Like any assassin, they seek to make the kill privately and at a time when the victim's guard is down, hence suddenly. The word "fear" is the same word as in verse 9 and contains the ideas of reverence, honor, and respect, as well as awesome fear. Naturally, they do not honor their victim.

Verses 5 and 6 are a reconstruction of what goes through the minds of wicked men. The dastardly plot is a corporate venture. They convince themselves that their crime will go undetected and unpunished, a gamble which every criminal takes. In the latter half of verse 6, the Hebrew text has only four words: *and near, a man, and a heart,* and *deep.* Undoubtedly they reflect the context which has to do with secret plotting. Most translations emend the Hebrew text or add words in order to produce a meaningful line.

The *but* at the beginning of verse 7 shows the other side of the coin. They shoot at God's man; now God will shoot back. They plan a sudden attack; God will suddenly wound them. They whet their tongue as a sword; God will make them fall by their own tongue.

Three groups of people react three ways to this phenomenon. God has made their plans backfire, and He has answered prayer and delivered the psalmist. First, all who witness it will run. Second, all men will think and declare God's work with reverent fear. Third, the righteous, those delivered, will rejoice and glory in the refuge that the Lord provides.

When God occasionally chooses to do something extraordinary, and obvious to all men, people react differently. Some ignore it, or run, or wag their heads. Others recognize and perhaps wisely consider it. But only the believers, the upright in heart, rejoice. In which group are you?

PSALM 65

Psalm 65 is a praise psalm which is optimistic, refreshing, positive, and wholesome. No enemies are cursed. No imprecations are prayed down on anyone. No complaints are registered. The first half focuses on God's greatness, while the latter half has an agricultural setting and obviously reflects the happiness that a good harvest brings. Some suggest, and it is grammatically possible, that verse 9 begins a prayer for rain. That explanation is not necessarily better or improved. No outline is discernible in the psalm. Rather, the movement from idea to idea is somewhat like prose. Verses 1–2 are like an invocation. The first line has an interesting expression; the word "wait" is the word "silent," hence, wait in silence. Perhaps the praise is silent until the vows and petitions are made.

Just as our prayers ought to contain an element of confession and a plea for forgiveness, so verse 3 does that in this psalm. "Forgive" here is the word "atone" or "cover," used of the cover of the ark of the covenant, the mercy seat.

Another great theological truth, election, is in verse 4. The verse appears to state exactly what Jesus said in John 6:44 (NIV): "No one can come to me unless the Father who sent me draws him." From the "he" in the first half of verse 4 the psalmist changes to "we," implying that he is among those chosen. These references to the temple may show that the psalm is later than David, who did not live to see the temple which his son Solomon built. Neither the authority of the titles nor the exclusive use of this term for Solomon's temple is a conclusive argument for dating this psalm.

Just as the words "fear" and "awful" in the Bible need reinterpretation, so does "terrible" (v. 5). It is built on the root word for "holy fear" or simply points to those acts of God which prompt our awe and reverence. Because of the reference to the ends of the earth, verse 5 may be Messianic or eschatological. Most occurrences of this kind are definitely futuristic. It is altogether possible that the more enlightened psalmist envisioned the day when God's kingdom would have worldwide subjects. From the Jerusalem point of view the Western Hemisphere would be at the end of the world.

Continuing the praise of God's cosmic deeds, verses 6 and 7 speak of His establishing the mountains and stilling the oceans as well as the people.

Verse 8 easily picks up the thought of the closing line of verse 7, but also echoes verse 5. People in faraway places will react to the evidence that God exists. This natural revelation is apparent morning and evening.

Beginning with verse 9, the focus of the psalm is on God's blessing in the realm of agriculture. A series of nine benign actions carry on through verse 11. From the general statement at the head of the list, "You visit the earth," a progression is evident. God waters, enriches, provides, irrigates, and so forth. The culmination comes when He crowns the year with goodness and, in highly figurative language, makes "your paths drip with fatness" (NASB). Up and down the paths are vegetables and fruits which have spilled off the overloaded wagons.

The exalted speech carries on to the end of the poem. Hills are wrapped in joy. Pastures are clothed with flocks. Valleys are so covered with grain that the actual ground is hidden. The paths, pastures, hills and valleys all shout and sing. It is a picture of abundance but also one of answered prayer and vows performed. Such a small price for such a cornucopia of blessing!

PSALM 66

All the psalms from 51 to 65 have David's name in the title. But just as that may not necessarily mean authorship, so the absence of his name in Psalm 66 may not necessarily mean he was not the author.

Like Psalm 65, Psalm 66 is a praise psalm. We are urged to give glory to the One who has created the world and redeemed His people. Up through verse 12 the terms are you, we, our, and us, while in verses 13–20 the first personal pronouns predominate: I, my, and me. Again, due to the generalities in the psalm, it is impossible to pinpoint the time and place of composition.

A number of imperatives mark the psalm, beginning with, "Make a joyful noise" (v. 1) to, "Come and hear" (v. 16). The opening verses are cosmic and universal. "All the earth" (v. 4) is summoned to praise. Compare verses 1 and 4. Only later in the psalm is God's greatness narrowed to the deliverance of the children of Israel from Egypt (v. 6) and finally to what God did for the psalmist personally (v. 16).

Verses 1–4 overflow with terms for praise: joyful noise, glory, his name, terrible (awesome, NASB), greatness, power, worship, and sing. Several words occur more than once as if to show that the language has been exhausted in his effort to adequately praise God. A somewhat explainable "selah" closes this section.

Beginning with verse 5 the psalmist demonstrates the awe-inspiring works of God first mentioned in verse 3. Verse 6 definitely refers to the Exodus from Egypt. The record of the sea turning to dry land is in Exodus 14:21; the crossing of the Jordan River on foot is in Joshua 3:16. Recounting the events of the Exodus is a common motif in the Bible. Moses did it over and over in Deuteronomy (cf. Deut. 5:15). Psalm 106:9 is just one of many examples of it in the Psalter. And New Testament preachers such as Stephen likewise referred to the Exodus, that archetype of deliverance (Acts 7:36).

Verse 7 is more general but may apply to the events connected with the takeover of the Promised Land. A second "selah" precedes verse 8 which is a charge to bless God. That benediction introduces a somewhat negative introspection which runs to verse 12. Although the beginning of the series (v. 9) and the end (v. 12c) are positive, verses 10–12b are almost a complaint. The total impact is that God has been faithful through thick and thin, through many trials and troubles. Those adversities constitute the middle part of this four-verse section. God refined them like precious metal. Job testified to the same ordeal in Job 23:10. If we translate the verb in verse 10 as "assay" the idea of metal testing comes across better.

The next trial was to be trapped like an animal in a net. The third (v. 11b) was hard work, perhaps slavery. The fourth was war (v. 12a), and then the natural catastrophes of fire and flood (cf. Isa. 43:2).

Finally, and with the important disjunctive conjunction "but" (v. 12), the psalmist declares that God brought us into an abundant place. That inherited wealth prompts generosity in return, as the next verses (13–15) record vows of service and sacrifice.

The psalm has turned more personal in verse 13, but there is no reason to see a new poet or even a major break in the thought. Think about verse 14. How many people make vows when they are in distress, and extravagant promises to God in times of crises, and forget them when life is calm once more! Not so this ancient saint. He looked for the day when prosperity would again be his lot, when his personal storm would be over, and immediately set his accounts right with God. Somehow we think that because we cannot see God, He cannot see us and therefore He will not remember or demand our promissory notes.

A third "selah" introduces the concluding call to praise and testify of received grace. The "come and hear" (v. 16) is similar to the "come and see" (v. 5). The psalmist briefly reiterates in general terms that God has answered prayer. A little lesson on the necessity of confession of sin constitutes verse 18. The older word "regard" isn't as good as the simple Hebrew word meaning "see." This note needs to be resounded since so many public and, presumably, private prayers neglect confession. In fact, this may be the major reason for unanswered prayer. God will forgive sin only when it is confessed.

Apparently there was no known or unconfessed sin in this godly poet. God did hear his prayer. Therefore he utters his concluding *baruch,* "blessed be God," whose steadfast covenant love never fails.

PSALM 67

A simple chiasmus forms the structure of Psalm 67:

A God will bless us (v. 1)
    B God's way on earth (v. 2)
        C Let the peoples praise you (v. 3)
            D Nations joy in God's judgment (v. 4)
        C´ Let the peoples praise you (v. 5)
    B´ Earth yields produce (v. 6)
A´ God will bless us (v. 7)

Verses 3 and 5 are absolutely identical. Verses 1 and 7 have identical forms of the verb "bless," though in English they are translated differently. The word "earth" connects verses 2 and 6, while the middle verse (4) has internal similarities.

Most scholars conclude that this is a harvest song with the Feast of Tabernacles as the appropriate occasion. In particular, verse 6 gives this lead. The verbs of verse 1 can be rendered as prayers, as they are in the King James Version (grammatically speaking, as *jussives*), or as simple futures as in verse 7. Because they can express a wish, some Bible students understand the psalm as a prayer for rain, though that is never expressly stated. The Aaronic benediction of Numbers 6:24–26 is quite similar to verse 1.

In both verses 2 and 7 there are expressions which speak of

the whole world. Usually such terms as "all nations" or "ends of the earth" are Messianic and eschatological, or at least missionary. From the earliest times God had a plan to include in His kingdom subjects from all over the world. The universal nature of the church was not a new idea nor a parenthetical measure in the plan of the ages. Throughout the Psalms and very specifically in such places as Isaiah 49:6, the worldwide spread of the Gospel is anticipated.

Applying verses 1 and 2 to the present, God is merciful and blesses us in order that we might make known His ways in the world and His salvation to all nations. Verse 3 is the result of the conversions of all the people. Let these newly regenerated ones join the chorus of praise. This refrain comes again in verse 5.

The central verse of the psalm (v. 4), ties in very neatly with the preceding and succeeding verses. The "nations" are not only parallel to the "peoples" in verses 3 and 5, but the same nations to whom God's salvation was made known in verse 2 are here praising Him. The word "earth" occurs in verse 4 as well as in verses 2, 6, and 7. These nations are happy to have God as their Judge, not in the sense of Condemner but in the sense of Leader and Vindicator, Sovereign and Justifier.

Verse 6 is the only specific reference to harvest, but since the terminology of the rest of the psalm is so vague, this serves well to reflect the occasion of the psalm. The benediction which closes the song begins in verse 6b, but verse 7 summarizes the two major thrusts. God will bless us. He will be worshiped everywhere.

The questions left to us are: What are we doing with His blessings? Are we keeping them to ourselves? Are we offering only private praise? Or are we telling the world about Jesus? Are we letting the ends of the earth know about the wonderful ways of God, His blessed plan of salvation?

PSALM 68

Psalm 68 is among the most difficult to translate. It has thirteen words in it which occur nowhere else in the Hebrew Bible. It
is difficult to date. Guesses range from a very ancient but updated
ode to the time of the Maccabees. It is difficult to classify. Almost
every kind of literature is found here: praise, thanksgiving, historical reminiscence, complaint, imprecation, and prayer.

The psalm is most like Judges 5 in its style. Basically, it praises
God for past victories. Many of the suggestions center around the
ark of the covenant and its being brought to Jerusalem (2 Sam. 6),
or taken into battle against the Ammonites (2 Sam. 11:11). These
suggestions are in spite of the ark not being mentioned specifically
in the psalm. Either of these occasions comports, however, with
the title which attributes the song to David.

Some Bible students see here a veiled history of Israel beginning
with the Exodus (v. 7) and continuing through the Millennium
(v. 31), including such events as the death of Ahab (v. 23) and
the Passover of Hezekiah (v. 27). Others take the events before
David as historical allusions and the later events as predictions in
order to avoid a later dating and preserve the Davidic authorship.

Probably more technical articles are available on this enigmatic
psalm than any other. Without pursuing the questions of date,
authorship, occasion, and classification any further, turn to the
text itself. Verses 1–2, apart from the opening line, are curses on
the enemy in general. The psalmist prays that their disarray and
dissolution will be like vanishing smoke or melting wax. The
prayer for the righteous (v. 3), on the other hand, is for their
happiness and rejoicing before God.

From the wish form of the verb in verses 1–3 the author turns
to imperatives in verse 4, the only such imperatives until verse 28.

The words "extol" (KJV), or "cast up a highway" (ASV), or "lift up a song" (RSV) use the Hebrew root *salal,* about the only lexicographical cognate for the mysterious "selah" (cf. remarks on Ps. 3).

Many different names for God occur in this psalm. In verse 4c is "YAH," a shortened form of the holy, unpronounced four letters *YHWH.* The full name is in verse 16. "Lord" (*Adonai*) occurs six times. "The God" (*Ha'el*) appears twice. "The Almighty" (*Shaddai*) is in verse 14, and the combinations "God the Lord" and "YAH" or "LORD God" are found in verses 20 and 18, respectively. God is called "King" in verse 24. The most common name, simply "God" (*Elohim*), is used twenty-five times in the Hebrew in these thirty-five verses.

An exalted recitation of God's mighty and merciful deeds begins in verse 5 and continues off and on to the end of the work. Verses 5–6 praise God for His greatness and compassionate concern for lonely orphans, widows, and prisoners. Verses 7–18 echo various triumphs connected with the Exodus from Egypt and the conquest of Canaan. This is very clear from verses 7 and 8, but not so evident from other verses. Psalm 78 (vv. 12ff.) is much more explicit in its review of this great deliverance.

An example of the elliptical form of the poetry in this psalm is in verse 8. It presents a variety of the staircase or progressive parallelism. Read it without the added words:

The earth trembled;
The heavens dropped at God's presence;
This Sinai   at God's presence, the God of Israel.

No one questions the connection of this verse to Exodus 19:18. The "rain" (v. 9) cannot be found in the accounts of the wilderness wanderings, although the word "dropped" (v. 8) may refer to the manna as it does in Psalm 78:24. Because the Hebrew word for "publishers" in verse 11 is feminine, some see the army of publishers of God's news as women (ASV, NASB) Hence the allusions to Miriam (Ex. 15:20), Deborah (Judg. 5:1), or the women who sang at David's victorious return from the Philistines (1 Sam. 18:6). Furthermore, verse 12 may allude to Sisera and Jael (Judg. 4:17 ff.), even as the expression in verse 13 sounds like Judges 5:16a. The Hebrew words are nearly identical in these two passages. Verse 13 introduces the most difficult part of the psalm.

The Revised Standard Version has produced sense by connecting the women at home in verse 12 with those among the sheepfolds ("pots," KJV) in verse 13; and the spoil (v. 12) with the silver and gold of verse 13. Verse 14 continues to spell out the means God used to rout Israel's enemy. The only other mention of Zalmon (v. 14 RSV) in Scripture is Judges 9:48, but it contains no mention of snow. The King James Version translators chose to insert the word "white," thinking that the connection between the scattered kings and the snow was the color. The American Standard Version, Revised Standard Version, Berkeley, and New English Bible make the analogy on the scattering itself. The Jerusalem Bible juggles the verses around, likening the snow to the glittering spoil.

From verses 15 and 16 comes the idea of the ark of the covenant going up to Jerusalem. Because God has chosen to abide in Zion, the other mountains, particularly in Bashaii in northern Trans-Jordan, are envious.

Chariots are ordinarily connected with war and may reflect the ark going into battle (v. 17). We know that such a practice was common (1 Sam. 4:3). Perhaps "Sinai" is elliptical for "the God of Sinai."

Paul's quotation of verse 18 in Ephesians 4:8 has made it

famous. Here it refers to God ascending a mountain, leading away rebellious captives, and accepting the spoils of war. The scene changes in verse 19, which opens with "Blessed be the Lord." The very familiar but italicized words of the King James Version, of course, are not in the original. The meaning might well be that God carries us or our burdens. That He should load us or oppress us is inconsistent with the context. These two verses (19–20) are definitely praise.

Whereas the preceding verses are benediction, verses 20–23 are imprecation. The language is very gory but not unlike the way wars were fought. Because dogs like the enemy's blood (v. 23) and they are referred to in an incident involving King Ahab (1 Kings 22:38), some make that a definite connection. This is not necessary. It merely points to the ignominious death of the foe, and similar occurrences probably took place at every battle.

The setting is more beatific beginning with verse 24. God, perhaps meaning the ark of the covenant, enters the sanctuary in the midst of singing and dancing. Verse 27 notes that one of the smallest, one of the largest, and two of the most distant tribes join in the celebration.

Verses 28–35 are more eschatological than historical. If the psalm is Davidic, then the "temple" (v. 29) was not in existence yet. That and the universal response to God's rule point to a future day. Note that kings bring presents (v. 29), that princes from Egypt and Ethiopia come to worship God (v. 31; cf. Isa. 18:7; 45:14), and that the kingdoms of the earth are urged to sing praise to the Lord (v. 32). The language of verses 30 and 33 also is exalted. Verse 30 beseeches God to rebuke the foreign leaders, pictured here as bulls. Parts of this verse reflect terms in verses 13–14. Several expressions also found in the Ugaritic literature appear in this psalm. One describes the Deity as "him who rides in the heavens" (v. 33 RSV; cf. v. 4; Isa. 19:1).

The praise section continues to the end of the psalm and the kingdoms are urged to ascribe strength to God (v. 34). Next follow three statements regarding God's strength and excellency. As if in a fanfare of praise, the climax is reached as the people confess that the blessed God gives them strength and power.

Though the language is difficult and the thread of logic impossible to follow through this poem, nevertheless it teaches something to the diligent reader. It shows that God can be seen and given glory for His innumerable deeds, great and small. It teaches that any praise or successes we have come from Him and therefore we should give back praise to Him. The very exalted nature of this work points up that we do not yet know everything about the Hebrew language, the culture, or the modes of praise. Let us simply respond with intelligence, humility, sobriety, and reverence to what we do know of them. Blessed be God.

PSALM 69

Psalm 69 is an individual lament. Because several New Testament writers apply verses in it to Christ, the psalm is also Messianic. Apart from the lament portions, the psalm includes prayers for deliverance and imprecations. In fact, the opening line is a prayer, but it is followed immediately by complaints.

Verses 1b–2 picture the psalmist's distress as an overflowing flood. Knowing how little the ancient Israelites had to do with the sea, and that there are no records of their ever swimming, the thought of drowning must have been real indeed. The expression in verse 1 about the water coming to the soul may refer to near drowning, since the word for soul is connected with breath. Some modern translators use the word "neck" (RSV, NEB). No one takes the picture of the flood literally. Rather, the flood of troubles or enemies is clearly in view for the rest of the psalm. These figures appear in the prayer of verses 14 and 15.

The picture changes in verse 3 to that of a man with dried out throat and failing eyes. Perhaps the throat is dry from calling for help and the eyes weary with weeping. Having described himself and his condition, the writer turns in verse 4 to his numerous enemies. With some hyperbole he charges that they that hate him are more than the hairs of his head. Jesus cited this verse in reference to Himself in John 15:25. The charge against the innocent is that he must pay back what he has not taken. This is just the opposite of redemption, which means to purchase back what belongs to you.

In verse 5 the complaint turns to prayer. First comes the confession and protestation of innocence, followed in verse 6 by requests for exoneration for the good people. The two occurrences of "for my sake" are very interesting. If these do refer to Christ then this is His prayer: that we should enjoy boldness and honor.

What the righteous sufferer endured was a result of his obedience and zeal. If he had not been God's man he would not have reaped the unpopularity he did. Verse 8 may have been in John's mind when he spoke the words recorded in John 7:3–5, that even Jesus' brothers did not believe on Him. John 2:17 unquestionably refers to Psalm 69:9. The zeal that Jesus showed when He ran the merchandisers out of the temple was a zeal, a jealousy, for God's house. The temple must be, He was saying, a place of prayer. If the world hates God and His Son then the Christian can expect to be hated too. For, in the terminology of verse 9, those who reproach God will reproach His followers. In Romans 15:3 Paul applies this last half verse to Christians.

The next three verses (10–12) are not specifically mentioned in the New Testament but certainly do depict a righteous man being mocked for his piety. Certain phrases in Job correspond with this psalm. For instance, compare verse 8 with Job 19:13–15 and verse 11 with Job 17:6. Although the New Testament writers never make the connection, certain parallels between the righteous suffering of Job and Christ do exist.

The pendulum of complaint and prayer swings to supplication (v. 13). Generalities introduce the petitions and then turn specifically to a plea for deliverance (vv. 14ff.). Some of the synonyms used for the watery plight of verses 1–2 are repeated in verses 14–15. Although the word Sheol does not appear in this psalm, some commentators believe that this psalm in general, and verse 15 in particular, is a prayer for deliverance from death. It is a moot question.

The prayer section continues through verse 29. Verses 16–18 are still on the lofty level of the devout and patient sufferer. Such choice words as "lovingkindness," "tender mercies," "redeem," and "ransom" (ASV) occur.

In verses 19–20 the theme is one of complaint and self-pity. Instead of comforters, only reproachers can be found; instead of a sympathetic ear only a hostile adversary.

The focus of the charge against the enemy is in verse 21. All four of the gospel writers cite this verse as they record the events at Golgotha (Matt. 27:34, 48; Mark 15:23; Luke 23:36; John 19:28–30). Can anyone doubt that these inspired chroniclers took Psalm 69:21 as Messianic? No records exist of David or any other Old Testament saint suffering this ignominy.

The imprecatory part of the passage encompasses verses 22–28. Several of these curses are cited in the New Testament. Verses 22–23 are used by Paul in Romans 11:9–10. Notice that Paul concurs with the psalm title and ascribes the work to David. Peter quoted verse 25 in Acts 1:20 and applied it to Judas Iscariot. Compare also Jesus' allusion to the verse (Matt. 23:38; Luke 13:35), as He applied this curse to the people of Israel as a whole.

Verse 26 provides an interesting insight into the sovereignty of God. As Isaiah and others indicate (Isa. 53:10), the Messiah's suffering was in God's eternal plan. It was not a mistake, a miscalculation, an accident, a reversal, or a postponement of God's program. Men only crucified Him who was slain before the foundation of the world (1 Peter 1:20; Rev. 13:8).

The last seven verses (30–36) move our attention from the cross to glory. None of these verses are mentioned in the New Testament, but obviously the prayers have been answered and the victory attained. First there is general praise with song and thanksgiving. Then follows the great truth of the New Testament: the sufficiency and efficacy of the substitutionary atonement of Christ. Unlike the often repeated sacrifices of oxen and bulls in the Old Testament, the once for all death of Christ made additional sacrifices and oblations cease (Heb. 9:11–12; 10:9–12).

The psalm continues triumphantly to the end. The meek, the needy, and the despised are all vindicated. Not only do they praise God but also the whole creation joins in the glorious chorus. This is the fulfillment of the prediction of Romans 8:21. The now groaning creation groans because of the Fall but will, on that great day, be released from bondage and join in the song of the redeemed. Such a thought is particularly welcome at this time of ecological concern.

The restored Edenic bliss is especially illustrated by a rebuilt and repopulated Zion, enjoyed and occupied by the believers who love God's name. So a psalm that begins with a drowning man concludes with a renewed planet and a redeemed people.

PSALM 70

Except for a few minor variations, Psalm 70 is identical to Psalm 40:13–17. By itself this psalm is a prayer for help against persecutors. A simple chiastic outline fits these five verses, for verses 1 and 5 have both similar words and sentiments. The interior verses, 2–4, have jussive (wish form) verbs. Verses 2–3 are imprecations on the enemy, while verse 4 is a prayer for God's people.

The title of the psalm has the additional Hebrew word meaning "to bring to remembrance." This may have something to do with the fact that this is a repetition of part of another psalm. There is no good reason to deny David's authorship. The first and most obvious variation from Psalm 40 is in the opening words. Psalm 40:13 has "be pleased" while Psalm 70 has nothing corresponding with that opening plea. Many translations repeat the words "make haste" from the second stich.

Verses 2–3 constitute the curse section. The psalmist puts a curse on those who would put a curse on him. Notice the use of "seek" in verses 2 and 4. The wicked seek the soul of the righteous but the righteous seek God.

The urgency of the situation is reiterated again in verse 5, the echo of verse 1. Not only is "make haste" repeated, but the concluding words are "make no tarrying," or in modern English, "Don't be late." The verb "make haste," incidentally, occurs in the name of Isaiah's son, Maher-shalal-hash-baz (quicken-loot-make haste-plunder). Oh, to find that delicate balance in our prayer life between pious urgency and patient waiting!

PSALM 71

The clue that Psalm 71 is the prayer of an old man comes from verse 9. Since God has been with him from birth (v. 6), he trusts that He will not forsake him now (v. 18). The prayer is comprised of elements of testimony, praise, complaint, and imprecation.

Following an initial declaration of trust, the psalm opens with a series of petitions. In general terms the psalmist prays to be spared shame and invokes God to bow His ear, deliver, rescue, and save him. He calls God his Rock, an epithet used over and over by Moses in Deuteronomy 32. Two characteristics of a rock are applicable to God. First, He is the foundation. And since this word indicates mountain-size rocks, the term implies protection. Notice that Jesus is the Rock in the New Testament (1 Cor. 10:4; cf. Dan. 2:45).

Verses 5–8 recollect the providential care God took of the psalmist from the womb (v. 6), through youth (v. 5), right up to old age (v. 9). Verse 7a can be taken two ways. Either in his affliction, like Job, the psalmist remained faithful and thus was a wonder, or he was always blessed and no harm ever befell him. That would also be a wonder. Nothing in the immediate context points to the first explanation, so the second seems better. Many of God's people can relate amazing deliverances and near-miraculous exploits, while unbelievers show nothing but awe and ignorant wonder. The enemy can understand neither our faith nor the mercy of our God.

Now that the years have taken their toll on the psalmist, he pleads for continued grace (v. 9). Perhaps only now his enemies are forming a coalition against him, as verse 10 indicates. Their words are quoted in verse 11 while the answer of faith is in verse 12. Notice how the foe tries to bring God into his argument and so to sanction his wickedness. Rabshakeh displayed similar arrogance when he tried to convince King Hezekiah of Judah to surrender (Isa. 36:10). He was not the first and he will not be the last to do evil hypocritically in the name of righteousness, to work against God while claiming cooperation with God.

The shame from which he prayed to be spared (v. 1), the psalmist now invokes on his enemies (v. 13). This is the only imprecatory verse in the psalm and it immediately yields to more pleasant, positive praise in the succeeding verses.

A difficult phrase ends verse 15. The Jerusalem Bible (n. 71d.) takes it to be a scribe's comment, "I have not known how to read the letters," on the following word in verse 16. More traditional renderings take it to apply to the numerous righteous acts of God or the innumerable days one will enjoy God's salvation. In this respect the phrase is like Psalm 40:5.

Verses 17–18 again quickly scan the writer's life from youth to gray hairs. He makes the point that, since God has been faithful up to the present, He will continue to bless so that a testimony of His goodness may be passed on to other generations. Verse 20 is one of those rare references in the Old Testament to the resurrection of the dead. To be sure, one might say this is merely hyperbole for temporal troubles, but since the psalmist has described his life from youth to old age, what other deliverance could he anticipate except resurrection from the dead?

The fact that the psalmist speaks of accompanying himself with two varieties of stringed instruments does not prove that he was an accomplished musician or a professional functionary at the temple. The poet is searching for noble terms with which to exalt God. Altogether he says he will do four things: "I . . . will praise . . . sing . . . shout . . . talk" (ASV). Like many "trouble and trust" psalms, this one too ends as if the prayer of the earlier parts is already answered. The psalmist declares that those who sought his hurt have been put to shame. The enemy's confounding (v. 24) may serve as a commentary on verse 7. While the righteous are redeemed and blessed, the wicked are ashamed and confounded.

PSALM 72

The second book in the Psalter ends with Psalm 72. Only this and Psalm 127 are attributed to Solomon in the title. (KJV reads "for Solomon," while the same particle is rendered "of" when used with David.)

Many of the grandiose things said about the king in this psalm are too exalted to refer to an earthly monarch so there is a long Jewish and Christian tradition that this is a Messianic psalm. No New Testament writer, however, ever cites it or applies it to Christ. Three explanations are possible: (1) the psalm is full of hyperbole but applies only to a king such as Solomon and perhaps was written for his coronation; (2) it is Messianic, although ignored by the gospel writers and apostles; (3) it is full of double meanings and is to be read with two individuals in view, Israel's ancient king and Jesus Christ the Lord.

Most of the verbs can be read as wishes, as in the Revised Standard Version or the Anchor Bible. If this is so, then this psalm is primarily a prayer. If the verbs are read as simple futures, Psalm 72 is a predictive psalm. This latter form is used in the King James Version and American Standard Version. Other modern translations such as the Jerusalem Bible and the New English Bible mix the forms.

The first four verses have a strong political or judicial overtone befitting a kingly figure. Several different words for the idea of righteous justice occur here. The appellation, "king's son," in verse 1 fits with the title, since Solomon was both the king and the son of the king.

Throughout the psalm the ministry of this king includes both international functions and social concerns. This very domestic facet of his reign is introduced in verse 2 where he executes justice for the poor. "Judge," of course, does not mean, as it now generally does, "to condemn," but rather "to adjudicate" or "to administer law." Such administration may result in condemnation or vindication. In connection with the poor, it usually involves legal defense leading to protection and exoneration. This theme reappears in verses 4, 12, 13, and 14.

Verse 3 has exalted language but may point to the idyllic situation prevalent during the reign of this earthly king. Rather than the terror which often lurks in the mountains there will be peace. Or the figure may refer symbolically to the crops that grow on mountains and hills. Rather than producing hostile and evil thorns, the harvest will be of peace and righteousness.

The eternal character of this ideal king's reign is like the enduring sun and moon (v. 5). Another illustration of his faithful and beneficent rule occurs in verse 6. Like regular and necessary rain, his benevolence will shower on his subjects.

In verses 7–8 appear some of the terminology that is too exalted for Solomon and fits better with Christ. The several references to peace (*shalom*) link the psalm with Solomon (*Shelo mo*) but might also point to Christ, the Prince of Peace (*Sar Shalom*). It is simply not true that the peace of Solomon outdistanced the moon. Nor did he control the ends of the earth, or even the earth as he knew it. These things are true of Christ, however. The peace He brings endures. He already has subjects of every nation of the world. This will become undeniably evident and more completely fulfilled when He returns.

While verse 9 continues the eschatological and lofty description, verse 10 easily applies to the Solomon of the Old Testament. Second Chronicles 9:21 records the Tarshish tribute, while 1 Kings 10:1 mentions Sheba's contribution. Seba's location is more uncertain than Sheba's. Probably they are both far to the south, since Tarshish is to the north and west.

The psalmist reverts to terminology describing the world-wide reign again in verse 11. Here, too, this is being fulfilled in Christ in a way that only could apply to Solomon by using gross exaggeration.

Verses 12–14 again focus on the immediate social or domestic feature of the administration of this great but humble king. These passages echo in Isaiah 11:2–5; 42:3; 61:1–2; and elsewhere. The last line of verse 14 reminds one of Psalm 116:15, "Precious in the sight of the LORD is the death of his saints."

Just as certain verses would not fit Solomon, so the middle stich of verse 15 does not fit the Messiah. He is not prayed *for* but *to*. This is not a preposition that can mean anything else but "for" or "in behalf of." However, men did bring gold to both Solomon and Jesus (cf. Matt. 2:11).

An idyllic picture of agricultural abundance and expanding population comes in verse 16. The reference to grain growing on the mountaintops may link this verse with verse 3.

Referring to the last of the three promises in this verse, over-population was never given a thought. Large families were an economic blessing and populated cities were a military advantage. Only in recent times have too many people been a problem.

Once more (v. 17) the eternality of this king's reign is stressed. That all nations should be blessed in him definitely sounds like Genesis 12:3 and 22:18, where a similar promise was given to Abraham. An appropriate and blessed benediction concludes the psalm and this second book of the Psalter. The first line at least is like Zacharias' benediction in Luke 1:68. Interestingly, God's name occurs only in the first and last verses of this psalm. A double "Amen" brings to a close the body of the psalm.

Verse 20, appended to the psalm, indicates this to be the end of David's prayers. Perhaps this psalm was a prayer by him for Solomon as well as for his greater Son. David's name continues to occur in psalm titles (e.g., 86, 101, 103), but perhaps they cannot be called prayers and so this postscript is correct.

PSALM 73

The third book of the Psalter opens with a series of psalms attributed to Asaph (Pss. 73–83). Perhaps he was the author. Perhaps they were written under his administration of the music program at the Jerusalem sanctuary (cf. 1 Chron. 15:19 and the remarks on Ps. 50). Maybe these titles only refer to a style of psalm.

Like Psalm 37, this psalm is in the wisdom category. The psalmist raises the old question: Why do the wicked prosper and the righteous suffer? In a manner similar to the preacher in Ecclesiastes he sketches a picture and produces an argument that shows the futility of being good. But verse 17 brings an abrupt change. He lifts his eyes toward God and begins to put things in the perspective of eternity. He considers the end of the wicked and reverses his opinion of the whole matter, concluding that righteousness does pay and crime does not.

The psalm begins on a note of praise but immediately changes to a note of despair and discouragement. Verse 2 anticipates the conclusion to the psalm by stating that the psalmist nearly fell for the common argument that wealth proves one's righteousness and God's blessing while sickness and poverty are evidence of evil and God's displeasure. The line of argument proceeds from verses 3–16, where this pained but imperceptive protagonist confesses that he cannot figure out life. In the course of this half of the psalm are enumerated the many benefits the wicked enjoy. First, they are prosperous (v. 3). Second, they do not suffer long and painful illness before they die. They enjoy full strength until their dying day (v. 4). Third, they have no troubles, a general term lumping all the things that make life burdensome (v. 5).

While surfeited with these temporal fortunes, the wicked continue in pride and violence. Notice the figures the poet uses to attach these attributes to the ungodly; pride is like a necklace and violence a garment. A description of their attitude continues to the summary in verse 12. With glutted appetites (v. 7) they brag of the evil and scoff at the righteous (v. 8). They shoot off their mouths toward heaven and earth (v. 9).

Interpreters differ on the meaning of verse 10. It is best to understand that the followers of the wicked stay with him and drink with him, or drink up everything he says. Their words are quoted in verse 11, and they are a blasphemous denial of God's omniscience. Little do they realize what this psalmist is later to realize: that God is aware of their sins and will ultimately judge them. Verse 12 sums up the superficial assessment of the wicked. Not only are they evil, but also while they loaf they still get rich. Psalm 37 spoke to this attitude much earlier with its opening words: "Don't fret over evildoers."

Beginning with verse 13, the psalmist focuses on the futility of good behavior. He says what we might often think: that it is of no use to have a clean heart and washed hands. He sees no immediate benefit to obedience. In fact, he suffers the opposite: daily plagues and chastening (v. 14).

The light begins to dawn (v. 15) when the righteous sage realizes that he has an obligation to his children. He would be untrue to that trust if he let this psalm end here. Surely he could not recommend to his sons a God who is not basically just or who does not know all things. Surely he could not suggest wickedness as a way of life. Certainly what he has said in the verses above is incomplete. The coin must have another side; there must be a different perspective on life. Perhaps a visit to the sanctuary will provide the missing insight into this painful problem.

So in verse 17 the whole psalm changes character and the true wisdom nature of this poem becomes evident. From God's point of view the wicked men look different, dramatically different, diametrically opposite, in fact. Their latter end, eternity, and other weighty spiritual considerations produce a different assessment.

Whereas this ancient saint had almost slipped into the trap of wickedness (v. 2), he now realizes that it is the wicked who stand on slippery ground. And so through verse 20 the imminent and sudden overthrow of the wicked is described. "In a moment . . . utterly . . . like a dream when one awakes . . ." (NASB, RSV) and all the phantasies are gone, so will their fortunes evaporate.

Verses 21–22 record the bitter self-castigation of the psalmist. He confesses his ignorance and shortsightedness, his carnality and faithlessness. From these expressions of regret-filled unworthiness he turns to sound faith and confidence, through to the end of the psalm. He even confesses his hope to see God (v. 24), an end quite different from that of the wicked man. Verse 25 is a favorite of many of God's people and in times of crisis or discouragement can be the balm it was to this pensive poet.

Only verse 27 interrupts the felicitous picture in this half of the psalm. There, as in many other psalms, note is made of the accomplished judgment of the wicked. But rather than close on such a negative observation, verse 28 once more underscores the essential good that comes from casting one's lot with God, making Him a refuge, and putting faith in the Lord Yahweh.

PSALM 74

Psalm 74 is a community lament. Most commentators agree that the occasion was the destruction of the temple by the forces of

Nebuchadnezzar in 586 BC. He, then, is the madman of verse 22 (foolish man, KJV). The translation "synagogues" (v. 8) in some of the older versions has misled readers of the English Bible. The same Hebrew word is rendered "congregation" ("assembly," ASV) in verse 4. Most scholars agree that the synagogue had not begun before the exile. Others view the day of composition as later than the exile. Verse 9 is the primary clue: "There is no more any prophet." Actually, Haggai and Zechariah preached to the returned exiles.

Several rhetorical questions mark this as a lament. Notice the "why" (vv. 1, 11) and "how long" (vv. 9–10). Compare Psalms 10:1; 22:1; 44:23–24; 79:10; 80:12; and 88:14 for the former expression, and Psalms 80:4; 90:13; and 94:3 for the latter.

This psalm begins on a most discouraging note. Verses 2–3 are a prayer asking God to take note of the destruction of His people and His holy city Zion. Notice there is no repentance here. On the one hand, the psalmist appeals to God's redemption and election of Israel; on the other hand, to what the enemy has done to the sanctuary. The expression at the beginning of verse 3 means to make one's way or to pick one's steps, as the disheveled ruins would necessitate. From verses 4–8 the psalmist elaborates on the last half of verse 3 (ASV): "all the evil that the enemy hath done." The record of Nebuchadnezzar's destruction is in 2 Kings 25:8–21, but this account is more explicit. The first offensive move was to violate the temple's precincts, an area where no Gentiles had ever come. Verses 5–6 relate how the enemy destroyed the woodwork with axes and hatchets. After reducing the edifices to kindling, they set them on fire, along with all the other places of worship in the land (vv. 7–8).

As verse 1 of this section contained two questions, so the close has three questions (vv. 10–11).

Verses 12–17 contain praise to God for His power displayed

in nature. The language is very exalted, cosmic, even apocalyptic. After a general introductory statement (v. 12) His victory over the sea creatures is stated. Some students of Ancient Near Eastern culture see here the Lord's superiority over pagan gods personified as the sea, the dragons, and the mysterious leviathan. Whether that is convincing, these verses point out God's dominion and power.

Verse 15 may allude to the Red Sea and Jordan River crossings (Josh. 2:10; 3:13), or perhaps to Moses when he struck the water-laden rock (Ex. 17:5–6). The events of verses 16–17 predate even the Exodus, and the creation seems to be in view (Gen. 1:14–18).

Having reminded God—not that He needed reminding of former demonstrations of power and redemptive exploits—the psalmist returns to the problem at hand. He commences with a prayer for deliverance (v. 18). His first point is the blasphemy of insulting pagans. His second point is the frailty and helplessness of the defeated Israelites (v. 19). His third point is the covenant (v. 20). Since God promises, He must fulfill. Since He vowed, He must make good. At least on this occasion the psalmist viewed the covenant as unconditional.

The prayer continues to the end of the psalm with rephrasings of the points already made. Verse 21 is like verse 19 in that it speaks of the oppression of the people of God. This ancient intercessor employs the classic for-Your-name's-sake argument in the latter half of verse 21. He implies that if God does not save His people, His honor will be clouded. Although God ultimately will answer the prayer, it is probably not for this reason.

The last two verses (22–23) are like verse 18, reiterating the charges against the heathen conqueror. The psalmist is saying, in effect: "God, answer those blasphemous fools! Don't let them have the last word! Speak for Yourself!"

On these rather bitter notes the psalm ends. To this day God's people pray that God will stem the volley of reproach that rises continually from a world of war and woe.

PSALM 75

Because of its first verse and last two verses (9–10), Psalm 75 is in the category of praise or thanksgiving psalms. However, the central part speaks of God's judgment of the wicked, and some of those verses are in the first person. Hence, verses 2–6 are like an oracle delivered by a priest or prophet. It is impossible to set the occasion for this psalm's composition. The title is similar to that of Psalms 57–59 but attributed to Asaph rather than to David. The Hebrew words in the title or their translation, "destroy not," probably indicate a well-known tune. In no way does it agree with the contents, which are somewhat maledictory.

Verse 1 is introductory and, although the general point is obvious, the wording is open to several possibilities. No unnecessary words, in fact only eight Hebrew words, are used. Three times that many are used to convey the same meaning in the King James Version, for instance. The simplest, most word-for-word translation is as good as any others:

We are thankful to you;
God, we are thankful.
Your name is near,
Your wonders declare.

Remembering that "name" is tantamount to "person," the third line is readily understandable and fits nicely with the fourth. Proof of God's presence in the universe is His working of wonders.

The oracle or first-person section runs from verses 2–4, but includes the words of verses 5–6. With verse 7 God is spoken of in the third person again. The thrust of the oracle is that God is the Judge who rebukes the proud. Different translations of verse 2 are easily available. With verse 3 it serves to introduce the rebuke of verses 4–6. The psalmist sketches a quick picture of God's power. He is the One who dissolves or shakes the earth and also the One who stabilizes its pillars. A somewhat appropriate "selah" closes this scene.

The quotation continues with an attack on the arrogant or foolish (v. 4). The command not to lift up the horn is interesting. That term appears four times in this short psalm. Here as elsewhere it is a symbol of strength or pride. Compare its use (Deut. 33:17; 1 Kings 22:11; Amos 6:13; Zech. 1: 18–21). Lifting the horns and speaking with a stiff neck are in parallel in verse 5 and not without reason, since for the horns to be lifted up the neck must be stiff. This is an unusual unmixed metaphor.

As verse 4 was cosmic in its scope so verse 6 encompasses all the world. The part about lifting up is difficult to connect with the rest of the verses and, again, many variant translations are available. The translation of the Jerusalem Bible may correctly fill in this elliptical verse. It reads: "Not from the east, nor from the west, not from the desert, nor from the mountains." This is not a complete sentence and may therefore be the introduction of verse 7 or the conclusion of verse 5.

God is Judge everywhere, putting down and setting up, to use the phrases of verse 7. Undoubtedly the psalmist uses the words "lift up" here and in verses 4, 5, and 10 (ASV) intentionally. First there is the command to the boastful not to lift up their horn; then the statement that God is the ultimate "lifter up" or "putter down." At the end of the psalm the prediction or testimony comes that God lifts up the horns of the righteous.

The figure of the cup of judgment fills verse 8. This theme

of drinking God's wrath appears elsewhere in the Bible (cf. Job 21:20; Isa. 51:17; Jer. 25:15; Hab. 2:16). The symbol is particularly meaningful since Jesus used it when He spoke of taking the sins of the world on Himself (Matt. 20:22; 26:39; John 18:11).

The psalmist concludes his composition with words of praise (vv.9–10). So the psalm ends as it began, with praise. Then the figure of the horn is taken from verses 4–5 and used to sum up judgment. Psalm 1 closed in a similar manner with judgment for the wicked and vindication for the righteous.

PSALM 76

A singer in Israel uses Psalm 76 to vocalize God's greatness, especially in the light of a particular victory. Of course the author cannot be the Asaph of 1 Chronicles 15:19 if the jubilation here is over the defeat of Sennacherib's army in 701 BC. Perhaps it is Asaph's family or school or style. The Greek translation of the Old Testament adds the words "regarding the Assyrian" to the title. If there is truth to that addition then the possibility of the psalm pointing to that occasion in the life of King Hezekiah is all the more likely.

Both 2 Kings 18:13–19:37 and Isaiah 36–37 record the attack on Judah by the Assyrian king, Sennacherib. That threat to Jerusalem ended when the angel of the Lord struck down 185,000 enemy soldiers in one night and Sennacherib retreated to his capital in Nineveh on the upper Euphrates. The last verse of both historical accounts records the assassination of the king by his sons during his devotions in the house of his pagan god, Nisroch.

Archaeologists have uncovered verification of this biblical account. Though the famous Prisms of Sennacherib on display in Chicago and London (both originals by Sennacherib) report the siege of Jerusalem, they carefully avoid claiming destruction of the holy city or the surrender of its king. The mysterious death of the Assyrian king is alluded to in the Rassam Cylinder where Ashurbanipal tells how he punished the murderers of his grandfather, Sennacherib. The ancient historian Eusebius concurs with the Bible's account of the assassination.

With this background the psalm is more meaningful. Four different terms for the Holy Land and the holy city appear in verses 1–2. Note the parallels. "Salem" is a shortened form of Jerusalem (cf. Gen. 14:18. The first part of the city name simply means "city" while "salem" means "peace.") These two unusual names (Zion and Salem) for the capital city may have been chosen to point up its holiness, antiquity, spirituality, and significance. This is not an ordinary city, not merely the seat of government, but the very place and the only place on earth where God chose to have His name dwell. "Tabernacle," as noted earlier, indicates temporal quartering. "Booths," to give another translation, were shack-like structures hastily put together in the field at harvest time to protect the workers in the heat of the day. The word for "dwelling place" is used elsewhere of the lion's den or lair. The choice of this word may point to the lion-like protection God will give His favorite city.

Verse 3 is a minimal poetic report of what God did. The language is elliptical, and the phraseology may differ from translation to translation, but the sense is apparent. God destroyed the weapons of war employed against His people. A "selah" ends this first of four three-verse stanzas. Notice that each of the four stanzas begins with a note of praise and ends with some specific feature of deliverance. Hence verses 1, 4, 7, and 10 are similar. Another "selah" would be appropriate after verse 6, according to this outline.

The figure of mountains of prey is difficult to interpret unless it is a reference to the amount of equipment abandoned by the

fleeing army of Sennacherib (cf. 2 Kings 19:35–36). This interpretation is supported by what follows in verse 4. The continuing
account of the enemy sleeping (v. 5b) comports with the accounts
in 2 Kings and Isaiah that the Lord's angel struck down the enemy
at night. Most of them never woke up from the sleep of death that
fateful night. Verse 6 elaborates on verse 5 by stating that even
the chariots (or perhaps the riders) and horses were cast into a
deep sleep. This is a different word for sleep than used above and
indicates a torpor or sleep from which it is difficult or impossible
to wake.

The third stanza (vv. 7–9) lacks the particulars in the first two
stanzas. Rather, the focus is on the awe-inspiring God Himself.
In view of the unusual defeat and consequent withdrawal of the
surviving enemy, God is to be feared. The question involving who
may "stand" in verse 7 may hark back to the incident when all the
enemy were sleeping, not standing.

This deliverance of God's people was not merely a natural
catastrophe or a military coincidence. It was planned by God and
the sentence was issued from heaven. Neither Hezekiah nor his
men had to raise a finger. They simply stood back and witnessed
God's judgment on the enemy. Incidentally, Herodotus, another
ancient historian, mentions Sennacherib retreating from an invasion into Egypt when field mice swept his camp and ate the strings
from the bows and the straps from the shields in one night. Some
connect this account with the biblical record by assuming that the
rodents also carried a highly contagious and fatal plague. Verse 10
is the best-known verse of the psalm. After one reads again the
words of the arrogant and blasphemous Rabshakeh delivering the
message of his equally boastful and profane king, this verse is all
the more meaningful. The world would hardly know of these two
men if it were not that God chose to record them in the Bible for

His glory. They meant it for disgrace and shame, but God meant it for His own praise.

With verse 11 comes a command to the readers of this psalm. Having seen the justice and power of God, we are urged to bow and pay our vows to the "LORD your God." If the first half of verse 11 refers to the immediate city of Jerusalem, then the latter half refers to the surrounding country. If the first half refers to the people of Israel in particular, the latter half refers to the surrounding nations.

The last verse (12) summarizes the reasons God should be feared. He has and He will cut off the spirit of princes. That idiom might be paraphrased to say: "He brings the lies of monarchs to an end." That He did in 701 BC, and He will do so again, for He is the terror-inspiring God.

PSALM 77

Part of Psalm 77 reads like an individual lament, but beginning with verse 11 and especially from verse 17 on, it has the characteristics of a hymn. Notice the number of first person singular pronouns and the negative nature of the verbs in the opening verses: "I cried . . . I complained . . . I am . . . troubled." The latter part of the psalm is quite exultant and positive. The best explanation for this abrupt change is that the psalmist himself had a change of heart. Verses 11–12 hint at this. From the depths of despair he determines to count his blessings, turn his eyes on the Lord, and exercise the power of positive thinking.

In typical lamentation style the psalm opens with a groan. Although the two lines in English appear unbalanced, this is a fine example of a progressive parallel outlined as ABC, ABD. A word-for-word rendering would be:

My voice to God and I cry out.
My voice to God and he hears me.

Having stressed the intensity of the outcry, he proceeds to assert its unceasing nature. "In the day . . . in the night" are the main words of verse 2. That verse actually has four stichs, the last two connected with negative ideas. "My hand" ("sore," KJV) must be understood as the subject of the rare verb "ceased not" (KJV), or "slacked not" (ASV), or "without wearying" (RSV).

In verse 11 it is the remembering that brings this complaint to praise, but in verse 3 remembering only brings the psalmist to despair. As elsewhere, "spirit" may simply mean "breath," so here he speaks of physical as well as psychological exhaustion.

The three "selahs" in this psalm divide the poem somewhat symmetrically. One occurs at the end of verse 3. Again at the end of the complaint section there is one (v. 9). Halfway through the praise section it occurs again (v. 15). Hence the psalm is divided roughly into three parts by the "selahs," once verse 3 has been reached. (Verses 16–17 could easily have been made three verses on the basis of the number of ideas, then the division would have been even more symmetrical.)

The thought pattern does not change in verse 4, but the psalmist continues in his dejected manner, putting the blame on God. Once more he tries reflecting on the past (vv. 5–6), but such an effort only produces more despair. Unlike the therapy such introspection and recollection will produce later in the psalm, its only fruit here is the plaguing question, the problem of evil.

From time to time God's present-day children may ask the same questions as are in verses 7–9. They are not bad questions nor out of order. But they are incomplete. Never does the psalmist, and seldom does the modern saint, entertain the old-fashioned but wholesome guilt feeling. As long as God's Law shall stand and as long as man shall break it, guilt will be a part of life. Not to admit guilt is a far more serious psychological and spiritual problem than suffering from too many guilt feelings.

The answer to the first five questions in verses 7–9 is "no." The answer to the last one (v. 9b) is "yes." It is not true that the Lord will cast off forever or that He has forgotten to be gracious. But the truth is He may be angry—angry with His people's national sins and with this psalmist's personal uncleanness.

Some scholars put this psalm in the exilic period by assuming the captivity was the supreme reason for any lament. Others, because of the archaic language, particularly of the latter part, put it in the united kingdom period or earlier.

The tune begins to change with verse 10, a verse that by itself is difficult to translate and understand. The use of italics in the older versions indicates that. Newer translations understand the Hebrew root for "years" to be the verb "change," which is altogether possible. It helps to clarify the meaning since it provides a predicate for the second half of the verse. Whatever the exact meaning of verse 10, most likely it is in agreement with the next two verses (11–12) which speak of reflecting on God's mighty deeds. Only this time such musing and recalling buoy up this sinking soul and cheer him, as well as us.

Verses 13–15 sketch God's power in general terms. He is holy. He is great. He is a Worker of wonders. He is strong. The climax and the purpose for all this power is the redemption of His people, who were the children of Jacob and Joseph in the original Exodus. After all, is not this God's great plan of the ages: to redeem a people unto Himself? All else works to this end: the creation, the Exodus, the monarchy, the offices of priest and prophets. They serve His people, prefigure Christ and His work, and blend like a symphony orchestra playing the great work of redemption.

The five concluding verses (16–20) elegantly describe the opening of the Red Sea for the children of Israel to pass through. This poet adds to the account thunder, lightning, and rain, but is certain to give God all the honor. When the waters saw God they shook. The lightning bolts are God's arrows. The thunder is His voice; the dry seabed is His path; the rescued are His people.

Altogether it is an uplifting record. It exalts God and encourages the downhearted. As spiritual physicians, let us prescribe the tonic of praise, the kind of review of God's mighty acts of redemption, such as is in verses 16–20.

PSALM 78

The second longest in the Psalter, Psalm 78 is a didactic psalm. Verses 1–8 make the reason for this classification very plain with numerous injunctions to recite the history of Israel and to teach it to the children. The lessons of history fill the rest of the psalm to verse 72. By and large the poem is depressing, for only the bad behavior of the people is noted. The most outstanding example of disobedience is the departure of the ten northern tribes in the civil war which followed the death of Solomon in 922 BC (cf. Isa. 7:17). Verses 9–11 and 67 cite this unfortunate historical development.

This psalm is like Deuteronomy in repeating the history through the wilderness wanderings (cf. Deut. 1–3). Because of this, some scholars say that Psalm 78 was used on occasions of national festivals, particularly the Day of Atonement. Moved to contrition by the rehearsal of the historical failures, the people would be ready to pledge renewed allegiance to the God of their fathers.

In verses 1–2 the psalmist writes in the first personal singular but changes to the plural in verse 3. Verse 4 states an interesting principle almost unique to Israel among ancient peoples. They made no effort to cover up the sins of their forefathers. Reconstructing the history of the countries surrounding Israel is very difficult because they rarely record some of the most significant events such as military defeats, paying of vassalage taxes, and the ignominious deaths of esteemed kings. God, in His Word, never whitewashes His heroes. All the patriarchs and prophets have their sins recorded. Perhaps God is subtly underscoring the truth that all men have sinned and come short of the glory of God, even great men such as Abraham, Moses, and David. The righteousness of God and our desperate need for Christ's atoning death stand out all the more strikingly against this black background.

Verses 7–8 sum up the introduction and the purpose for the psalm. The first reason is to evoke faith in a powerful God (v. 7). The second is to warn against backsliding and apostasy (v. 8).

Although the historical sections of the psalm (vv. 9–72) seem to stress the infidelity of Ephraim, representing the northern tribes, the story really starts with their bad attitude back in Egypt (vv. 9–12). The first marked estrangement between the north and the south is the intertribal battles recorded in Judges 20 and 21. Perhaps verse 9 refers to those days in particular.

Verse 12 begins the record of God's wonder-working against the Egyptians prior to the Exodus. Zoan, Egypt, of verse 12 still exists with the name San in the northeastern part of the Nile delta. Tanis is another name for it.

From the famous ten plagues the psalmist moves to the crossing of the Red Sea, using terminology from Exodus 15:8. Then follows the record of the pillars of cloud and fire, and the miracle of water from the rock (vv. 14–16).

The account of God's faithful doings is interrupted by the account of the people's unfaithfulness (vv. 17–18). This alternation of themes persists through the psalm and points to the two lessons the children were to learn from their parents: God's love and power, and man's sin.

Next come the manna and the quails (vv. 24–30), but these too the wandering Israelites abused and so earned the displeasure of God (v. 31). Even the slaying of some Israelites failed to teach obedience to the survivors. Like the unstable waves of the sea or the constantly rising or receding tide, the devotion of the redeemed went up and down, both historically and in this song. Verse 33 marks a low point, but after judgment, their allegiance went up (vv. 34–35). However, the purity of that devotion lapsed again into deceit and falsehood (v. 36). So the history alternates between fidelity and apostasy. In between these shifting attitudes is the careful balance of the mercy and the justice of God.

By verse 43 the psalmist is repeating himself. Notice how similar the terms of verses 12 and 43 are. But in this latter section he spends more time detailing the plagues of blood, flies, frogs, and other insects and diseases. Any cross-reference Bible will lead to Moses' accounts of these momentous events.

Verse 53 (like v. 13) recounts the crossing of the sea. But in the next verses the children of Israel are already through the forty years of wilderness wandering and on the border of Canaan. Whereas the first account (vv. 11–41) quickly dispenses with the plagues and focuses on the desert rebellions, the second account (vv. 42–54) explains the plagues but hastens through the rest of the Exodus.

Beginning with verse 55, the conquest of Palestine is in view with the book of Joshua as the historical backdrop. Now, rather than God providing the necessities of life—manna, water, direction—He provides victory over enemies. But again God's people are ungrateful, unfaithful, and undeserving. The arch sin of idolatry appears in verse 58. This wicked practice of the Canaanites was adopted by the people of the living, invisible God. Among the stratagems God used to bring back His people was to let the ark of the covenant be captured by the Philistines (v. 61). The record of this disciplinary tragedy is found in 1 Samuel 4:11.

General terms describe the havoc that prevailed as a result of God's abandoning His people (v. 62). Then in due time, God went to the aid of Israel, reversed their defeats, and once more defended them against their godless enemies (vv. 65–66).

The year 922 BC dates the events of verses 67–68. At the death of Solomon the northern tribes abandoned their allegiance to Jerusalem and made their own independent and impious way. The psalmist describes that split in terms of God's rejecting Joseph (for his two sons, Ephraim and Manasseh, were the forebears of the larger, more influential tribes in the north) and choosing Judah, the major southern tribe, and the area where Jerusalem is located.

The record goes in reverse from verses 68–72, for verse 69 points to the building of the temple of Solomon, which was prior to the events of verse 68. Then verse 70 backs up to the choice of David as king. And on that note exalting David, the psalm rather abruptly ends. The psalm could not have been written especially for David's coronation for, as pointed out above, it reflects very definitely the civil war of 922 BC.

The similarity of the conclusions to Psalms 77–78 is remarkable. One ends with Moses and Aaron shepherding the flock of Israel; the other with David doing the same thing. Notice, in this final connection, the concluding verses of Psalm 79.

The lessons of Psalm 78 are as old as man. Sin has separated us from God. Though He is merciful He is also just. Though we deserve punishment, He has given grace instead. Let us not be spiritual boors like the wandering Israelites or rebellious ingrates like the tribes of Ephraim.

PSALM 79

Psalm 79 is a national lament sprinkled with heavy doses of malediction. On the one hand, the people grieve over their defeat and on the other they pray down God's curses on the enemy. A certain ambivalence characterizes this psalm. Sometimes it reflects a noble belief in the sovereignty of God; elsewhere the logic is purely human. For instance, verse 8 makes it sound as if this defeat is part of God's purpose, His holy wrath on ancestral sins. Yet the opening verses admit no such divine direction to the recent catastrophe.

Jerusalem fell to the armies of Babylonia about 600 BC. Against the backdrop of that dread calamity this psalm begins. The prose record of this tragedy is in 2 Kings 25:8–21, while the Book of Lamentations is entirely devoted to it.

The opening word of Psalm 79 is an invocation, a plea that God would hear this solemn complaint. The first abomination the heathen committed was to trespass into the sacred precincts of the temple, thus profaning the earthly house of God. From that initial complaint this psalm moves on to describe the wreckage and bloodshed within the city in general. The word "heaps" at the end of verse 1 is the plural of the Hebrew *Ai,* the name of the city destroyed by Joshua after the fall of Jericho.

Among the important things in an ancient Semite's life was the hope for a decent and honorable burial. Verses 2–3 describe the indecency with which the dead of Jerusalem were treated. So here and elsewhere the ultimate ignominy, the postmortem punishment, was to be left unburied. Compare the taunt song against the king of Babylon in Isaiah 14:19, and the thrust of Psalm 53:5 and Amos 2:1.

The lament turns slightly at verse 4 and becomes more of a complaint. The psalmist is working around to the for-Your-name's-sake argument. The defeat of the holy city has brought shame directly on the people of Israel and indirectly on their God. That logic introduces the plaintive question in verse 5. These rhetorical questions are typical of the psalms of lamentation, both personal and communal (cf. Ps. 13:1; 74:1; 85:5; 89:46).

With verse 6 begins the imprecatory section. Somewhere the penitent and grieving spirit of the early part of the psalm yields to bitter invective. The verbs no longer describe what has happened to God's people but command God to punish their enemies. Notice that verse 6 is the prayer and verse 7 the reason. Then verse 8a is another prayer and verse 8b the reason. Verse 6 is a prayer *against* the enemies, while verse 8 is a prayer *for* themselves.

For the sake of God's name, for His holy reputation, the psalmist prays for help, salvation, deliverance, and expiation (v. 9). The argument is expanded and explained (v. 10). Imagining what the unbelievers might say, he pleads for blood vengeance on the murderous enemy.

The imagery of verse 11 is very vivid. One can see the captured Jerusalemites languishing in a stinking Babylonian dungeon. A modern paraphrase of the last part of the verse might call these sufferers the ones on death row.

In these latter verses the pendulum swings back and forth between prayer for self and a curse on the enemy. Verse 12 is another pair of maledictions.

But the psalm ends on the more positive note of praise and testimony. Verse 13 is a promise of praise anticipating the answers to the prayers and complaints in the body of this psalm.

PSALM 80

Addressing God as the Shepherd of Israel in verse 1 of Psalm 80 closely connects it with the preceding psalm, which ends on a similar pastoral note. This psalm, however, is more of a national prayer for restoration than a communal lament. Because Israel, Joseph, Ephraim, Benjamin, and Manasseh are mentioned in verses 1–2, the psalm probably belongs to the Northern Kingdom and may reflect its captivity in 722 BC. Epithets for the Southern Kingdom such as Judah, Jerusalem, Zion, or David do not occur.

The superscription offers little help in determining the occasion of composition. Some Bible translations give the meaning of the Hebrew words transliterated in the older versions. *Shoshannim* means "lilies" and *Eduth* means "testimonies." The Greek translation of the Old Testament (the Septuagint) adds to the title the words, "concerning Assyria," which supports the suggestion that the psalm has to do with the fall of Samaria to the forces of Assyria (2 Kings 17:6).

A refrain occurs four times with slight alteration, dividing the psalm into stanzas of unequal length. Verses 3, 7, 14, and 19 are like a chorus to the verses that precede them. The key word might be translated either "restore us" or "turn us" or "bring us back" (from captivity), except in verse 14 where a different form of the verb demands that God Himself turn. The same verbal root is the "restore" of Psalm 23:3 and the "convert" of Psalm 51:13.

The first stanza (vv. 1–2) is basically an invocation. God is urged to listen, wake up, go to work, and save His people. Among the titles given to God is "You that sit on the cherubs." This expression appears in 1 Samuel 4:4, 2 Samuel 6:2, and Psalm 99:1 and echoes Exodus 25:22, which describes the interior furnishings of the Holy of Holies.

Ephraim and Manasseh are the two sons of Joseph and the largest and most influential of the ten northern tribes. Benjamin is also important, being on the border of Judah and having within its boundaries the sanctuary city of Bethel. Remember that Joseph and Benjamin were the two favorite sons of Jacob and the only children of his first-chosen wife, Rachel.

The second stanza is more typically a lament and hence is not unlike Psalm 79. Notice the "how long" question (v. 4) and the theme of the ridiculing heathen and the damaged reputation (v. 6). The expression "angry" (v. 4) is literally "to fume" or "to smoke" (cf. Ps. 74:1).

The third stanza is in parabolic form. Israel is like a vine brought out of Egypt in the Exodus and transplanted in Canaan (cf. Hos. 9:10). Just as Isaiah in his fifth chapter used the same figure, so here many horticultural details appear to fill up the picture. The difference between this account and Isaiah's is that the great prophet gives the reason for the vine's rejection but the psalmist does not. Although many of the details answer to fact in the expansion of Israel, the main point is that the vine is God's, for His glory, for His use, even His to destroy. The river of verse 11 is the Euphrates, which marked the northeastern-most extremity of Israel's expansion (cf. Gen. 15:18; Josh. 1:4; 2 Sam. 8:3; 1 Chron. 5:9; 2 Chron. 9:26).

The fourth stanza continues the imagery of the vine. Whereas verses 12–13 speak of the invasion of the garden by wild animals, meaning the attack of a foreign enemy, verse 16 speaks of its utter ruin by fire and pillage. Verses 14–15 go together as a prayer that continues in verse 17, except that the symbol of the vine is discontinued at that point. The psalmist continues the prayer for restoration through the end of the psalm, repeating the refrain in the last verse.

PSALM 81

Verse 3 of Psalm 81 indicates that this song was used on the occasion of one of the three annual religious festivals in Israel.

Because of the mention of Joseph in verse 5, some scholars say that it was written in the north during the period of the separate kingdom of Israel (922–722 BC).

The psalm divides into two parts, with the break at verse 5. Exhortations to praise and the occasion of the psalm fill the first four and one-half verses. Beginning with *I* at the end of verse 5 and continuing to the end of the psalm, the poem is in oracular form. That is, the psalmist writes as if God were speaking. Notice the first person singular pronouns which, in the context, must be God and not man speaking. Like Psalm 8, this psalm is set to the "Gittith." No certain sense can be made of the expression, although some connect it with a person or event of the town of Gath. Five imperative verbs enjoining the people to celebrate the feast mark the opening three verses. In this respect the psalm is in the praise category and is very much like Psalm 111 and onward, only this psalm has no "hallelujah" in it.

More is said in Psalm 150 about the musical instruments. For now, note what they are and imagine the sound they might produce. The stringed instruments were strummed, not played with a bow. The timbrel is a small drum. The trumpet (v. 3) may or may not have been part of the orchestra. Numbers 10:10 states that the trumpet should summon the worshipers, much as it will summon the dead and the living believers at the rapture (1 Thess. 4:16).

Since they were on a lunar calendar, the festivals coincided with the moon phases. So the new moon is the first of the month. The parallel word in verse 3 occurs only this one time in the Bible. The King James Version uses "the time appointed," while most modern versions use "new moon."

The statute and ordinance to which the psalmist refers in verses 4–5 are in Exodus 23:14–19 and other places where these liturgical details are spelled out. Although some argue for the Feast of Tabernacles, verse 5 points rather to the Passover feast. The psalm is more concerned with the deliverance from Egypt than with thanksgiving for an abundant harvest.

Some question arises as to the division of the psalm. Verse 5b was put in the latter part, but some would include that line with the former. If that is so, then the psalmist and not God speaks in verse 5b. He is confessing that he hears an unknown language, the language of God. In the other interpretation, God is speaking and declaring that He hears a foreign language, perhaps the Egyptian of His people's oppressors. Yet another minor question arises as to whether this is a language He does not know or the language of a people He does not know, that is, know in the sense of election and love. God only hears those who belong to Him and who come in Jesus' name.

All commentators argue that at least by verse 6 the oracle has begun, and these are the words of God as He recites His mighty acts on behalf of Israel. Verse 6 refers to the labor forced on the Israelites by the Egyptians.

As the psalmist traces the Exodus he passes quickly to the wilderness trials which tested the wanderers' mettle. Especially did the showdown at Meribah, recorded in Exodus 17:6–7, serve to establish Israel's absolute dependence on their delivering God. A "selah" closes this section. Verse 7 introduces God's exhortation to the people. Usually in these psalms man seeks God's ear, but the reverse is true in verse 8. The uniqueness of Israel's religion was its tenet of absolute monotheism, a truth introduced here, as it is in Deuteronomy 6:4, with a summons to attention.

Then verse 9 states in negative terms the most basic of the Ten Commandments. With the prohibition the psalmist recites again that most notable deliverance, the intervention into history which molded Israel into a nation, the Exodus from Egypt. The

Passover celebration, to this day, focuses on the varied facets of that archetypal deliverance.

Having begun to recount the Exodus again, the psalm takes another negative turn in verse 11. From there to the end there is a logical development of ideas, ending positively with promises of abundance. Here is the development of ideas: God delivered His people (v. 10). They did not appreciate it but rebelled (v. 11). So God abandoned them to their own wills (v. 12). He wished they would return and obey (v. 13). If they would, God would punish their enemies (vv. 14–15) and bless them with the finest food (v. 16).

These few verses are a commentary on the lives of some Christians. Despite all that God has done to save us, we ignore Him. Though His only begotten Son gave His life, we refuse to yield our lives to His service. We also have the deaf ear, the stubborn heart, and the selfish counsel that characterized His people of old. How God wishes we would not grieve His Spirit! How He loves to bless us by eliminating our troubles and giving us spiritual wheat and honey! How He would feed and satisfy us! But we do not listen or walk in His ways. Or do we?

PSALM 82

Psalm 82 easily falls into an outline which is roughly chiastic.

A Statement that God is the Judge (v. 1)
  B Statement of God the Judge (vv. 2–4)
  B′ Judgment by the psalmist (vv. 5–7)
A′ Prayer of the psalmist that God would judge (v. 8)

Whether verses 5–7 are the words of God or of the psalmist is the only question about this outline. That God, the Most

High, is spoken of in the third person in verse 6 supports the suggested outline.

An even more major question is: Who are the gods of verses 1 and 6? Are they pagan deities or are they corrupt political figures? The Hebrew word *elohim* is used occasionally for human beings, as in Exodus 21:6. In John 10:34 Jesus cites verse 6 and applies it to the Jews who were about to stone Him for blasphemy.

Whether those among whom God judges are the heathen gods or local legislators, the point is that God is the Judge. Quite clearly, they are guilty of the abuses noted in the following verses. Verses 2–4 certainly fit better with the explanation that the gods are men, but verse 5 could easily describe dumb idols.

The crimes to be judged are generally in the area of social injustice. This theme is prominent in many of the prophets, especially Amos. Notice the number of times forms of the word "judge" occur in this psalm (vv. 1, 2, 3, 8). Because wicked men twist justice, God will judge them. The second charge (v. 2b) is tantamount to bribe-taking. These crooked elders gave preferential treatment to the rich and influential, while the weak, the orphans, the oppressed, and the destitute could hardly hope for a fair deal.

Verses 2–4 can be understood as the quotation of God's sentence against the gods. This interpretation is based on the use of the pronouns "you" and "them" (vv. 2, 4). With verse 5 the defendants are "they" not "you," so perhaps the speaker is the psalmist commenting on God's sentence. However, some argue that verse 5 describes the oppressed victims and not the abusive leaders.

Like Psalm 8, something of the dignity of man is asserted in verse 6. Because they are superior to the majority, better is expected of them. But since they sin they will die (v. 7). The last verse is partly prayer, partly prediction. Notice the word "fall" (v. 7) and its opposite, "arise" (v. 8). Such plays on pairs of words are these ancient authors' poetical devices. Since rhyme and meter are all but absent, other characteristics mark their poetry. The prayer consists of two petitions: arise and judge. The prediction reflects the prophetic overtone of the whole poem in that God will inherit the nations. Since "nations" and "Gentiles" translate the same Hebrew word, this dimly anticipates the New Testament era when non-Jews will be part of God's kingdom.

PSALM 83

Psalm 83 is a complaint and a prayer of cursing. After one verse of invocation, seven verses of complaint follow. A "selah" closes that section. Then verses 9–17 constitute a series of maledictions, or imprecations, both big words for curses. The final verse (v. 18) gives the purpose for the curse, namely, to establish God's reputation.

As few other psalms, this one is filled with geographical and historical allusions which show at least that the author was a good student of the past. Not all of the places can be connected with recorded hostilities, but enough are clear to be impressive.

Three urgent pleas mark the summons to God in the opening verse. There is nothing of the flowery, exuberant address here. Nor are any of the particles of entreaty such as "please" present. It is a short verse, for the agonizing sufferer wants to get immediately to his subject.

Verses 2–8 simply recite the abuses in general terms. This section subdivides at verse 6, where the offending and offensive nations are specifically named. Each of the verses (2–5) contains two accusations against the warring heathen. Notice that the psalmist begins by calling them God's enemies, and later he comes around to telling what evil they intended against Israel.

As many can testify, one's closest enemies can be relatives or former friends. Protestant denominations and splits within them testify to this. So in ancient times the children of Isaac were constantly at war with the children of Ishmael. Though both were descended from Abraham, the Edomites and the Israelites lived too close together to ever be friends. Also, note the children of Hagar (v. 6), the handmaid of Sarah and the mother of this hostile tribe living in Moab (cf. 1 Chron. 5:10).

Gebal is a city north of Beirut and hence north of Tyre on the Mediterranean coast (cf. Josh. 13:5; Ezek. 27:9). It is also called Byblos. Ammon is well known even to modern times since it serves as the capital of the Hashemite Kingdom of Jordan. However, Amalek is not a place but a people, roving nomads from the deserts east of the Jordan River (1 Sam. 15:2).

Philistia is the enemy mentioned often in the times of the judges and the monarchy. Although Tyre was on good terms with Israel in the time of Solomon, the later prophets pronounce words of judgment on it (cf. Ezek. 27:3ff.; Amos 1:9ff.). Assyria, the giant that finally toppled the Northern Kingdom, is last in the list, having joined with the children of Lot. Remember that Lot was a nephew of Abraham and became the patriarch of a desert tribe.

The second major section of this psalm is marked by verbs of command. The curses are in typically Semitic style. Note especially the picturesque style of verses 13–16. At the top of the list is a plea to make these enumerated enemies like Midian. Gideon thoroughly routed the Midianites in the Esdralon Valley (Judg. 7). Barak and Deborah won over Jabin, king of Razor and his general Sisera, at the river Kishon (Judg. 4–5). Endor (v. 10) is near the river Kishon, but was not mentioned in the record of the Book of Judges. Oreb and Zeeb were Midianite princes whom Gideon's men killed at the end of a chase after the battle which at first was fought with only trumpets and torches. Zebah and Zalmunna are two other Midianite kings whom Gideon killed (Judg. 8:21).

The citing of names stops (v. 13) and in its place begins a vivid and imaginative way to word curses. Above, the prayer was that the enemy would be like former victims; now the prayer is that they will be like certain useless by-products, dust, and stubble. Then the psalmist wants God to be like a consuming fire and destroy them like a burning forest. The next image (v. 15) is that God will blast them as in a storm. The conclusion may begin with verse 16 because of the purpose clause inserted at the end of that verse. The reason for all this damnation is that God might be glorified, a purpose that is the essence of verse 18 as well.

It is hard to keep the glory of God in focus when overcome by anger. We ought to appeal to these imprecatory psalms most cautiously in order to avoid abusing the privilege of prayer and doing exactly what unbelievers do when they ask God to damn someone or something. If there is any other way we can make people know that God alone is the Most High above all the earth, then let us take it.

PSALM 84

Like the psalms of ascent (120–134), Psalm 84 was probably sung by pilgrims making their way to one of the annual festivals in Jerusalem. The many rhymed versions of the psalm set to various tunes have contributed to its popularity. Here is the first stanza of one version:

O Lord of Hosts, how lovely
    The place where thou dost dwell!
Thy tabernacles holy
    In pleasantness excel.
My soul is longing, fainting, Jehovah's courts to see;
    My heart and flesh are crying,

O living God, for thee.

AUTHOR UNKNOWN

Many lovely pictures fill the psalm and speak both of the springtime of the year and the springtime in the believer's heart. But the devotion expressed here is rarely seen among Christians, who have the benefit of a fuller revelation and a clearer picture of what God has done for them through Christ Jesus.

Verse 1 sets the scene: a meditation on the glories and beauties of God's house. Then the psalmist puts into beautiful words (vv. 2–3) his own longing to be where God is. Having said it matter-of-factly and yet movingly (v. 2), he compares his experience to a bird finding a safe and suitable place to call home. Verse 3 does not speak of birds in the temple but of contented pilgrims arriving at the sanctuary.

Verses 4–5 form a pair of beatific expressions describing the believer. In the former the worshiper is in God's house; in the latter his strength is *in* God while *in* his heart are the ways of God.

One of the routes to Jerusalem may be described in verse 6. The "ways" of the preceding verse prompted a reference to this incident or way station. "Baca" means "weeping" or "balsam trees" and may refer to an approach to Jerusalem from the west. The weeping may be for joy, or a highly stylized reference to rain, hinting that the occasion may be in the fall when the showers begin.

The psalm may be divided into three stanzas of four verses each, with a "selah" marking the division points. On that arrangement, verses 1–4 describe the psalmist's personal devotion; verses 5–8 depict the pilgrimage itself; and verses 9–12 form yet another expression of devotion. Notice the expression "LORD of hosts" (vv. 1, 3, 8, 12).

Verses 8–9 are actually prayers. The first is personal, the second for the anointed. Some would say this "messiah" is the king, others the high priest, and still others a reference to Christ. Another option is that the psalmist himself is an anointed functionary and this is a personal prayer, though it is in the third person. When one remembers that the Korahites were the gatekeepers of the temple (1 Chron. 26:1), this interpretation is especially fitting in the light of verse 10. This well-known verse is self-explanatory. One could only wish that it were the conviction of more of God's children. Words of praise and exaltation fill verse 11 and then a benediction concludes the psalm. The word "blessed" occurs three times in the psalm, once in each stanza. It is not the usual Hebrew word for bless, the one used of God, but a broader word meaning "happy," a condition invariably brought on by close communion with God. The word opens Psalm 1 and is found at the close of Psalm 2. Blessed is the man that trusts in God!

PSALM 85

Based on the forms of the verbs, Psalm 85 is in three parts. Verses 1–3 are praise and testimony of what God has done. Verses 4–7 are prayers mostly in the form of questions. Verses 8–13 are like an oracle predicting the bliss that will come upon his people. It is possible to read verses 1–3 as questions or as imperatives, thus making the first section essentially the same as the second, namely, prayer.

Mention of the captivity in verse 1 points to a post-exilic origin of this psalm. So do the later allusions to Isaiah and Zechariah. On the other hand, that may be merely a general term for trouble even as the psalm is full of unspecifics regarding sin and blessing.

Verses 1–3 consist of a series of six statements of what God has done. All are unspecific, but all are positive and evocative of thanksgiving. In a sense the logic is in reverse. First God must turn from His wrath (v. 3). This paves the way for the forgiveness of sins (v. 2) and in turn results in the return from captivity. The necessary item which must be understood is the repentance of the people.

Verse 4 begins the prayer section. Apparently some new cause for broken fellowship has arisen, and to this unspecified sin this psalm is directed.

Various uses of the root "turn" occur throughout this psalm. It describes the return from captivity (v. 1, "captivity" itself is built from the same root); God's change of attitude (v. 3); our conversion (v. 4); our requickening (v. 6); and our possible backsliding (v. 8). This flexible verb also characterizes Psalm 80.

Question marks distinguish the style in verses 5–6. They are rhetorical questions with the understood answer in the negative. The psalmist hopes that God's anger will not last indefinitely. He prays that God's people will not go unrevived or unrejoicing. Positive imperatives, as in verse 4, reappear in verse 7 to conclude this supplication section.

Verse 8 introduces what amounts to an oracle or prediction. It is a benevolent pronouncement with the anticipated accomplishment of bringing peace and instruction to the people. The content of the prospect is in verses 9–13. Certain expressions are like Isaiah (32:17; 45:8; 46:13) and Zechariah (2:5; 8:12; 9:10). The language is exalted with certain attributes or attitudes personified. Note the words "salvation, glory, mercy, truth, righteousness and peace" and what they do in verses 9–11. It is a beautiful picture, although hard to recreate visually. The source of all these blessings finally is mentioned in verse 12, which is a kind of summary note. "The LORD will give what is good" (NASB, RSV). Some would see here merely rain and subsequent agricultural abundance, but the tenor of the psalm is more exalted and prophetic.

All the virtues of verses 9–11 belong to and come from God.

He alone is the Possessor and Giver of righteousness, salvation, truth, mercy, and peace.

PSALM 86

Psalm 86 is a prayer of David, stated in the superscription. The contents support such a classification. The only evidence against this identification is the statement at the end of Psalm 72 that there the prayers of David are ended. However, there are many reasons to believe that the psalms are not in chronological order. Psalm 72 may be the latest in time, though far from the end of the Psalter.

Although the psalm is primarily a prayer, verses 8–13 constitute a hymn of praise in the middle of the psalm. The first prayer section (vv. 1–7) is positive, general, and optimistic. The second prayer section (vv. 14–17) is somewhat negative with its complaints about the enemy.

The psalm opens with a request for a hearing. The second half of verse 1 gives a reason why God should answer. Several times over this motif occurs: "Do this because . . ." (vv. 1, 2, 3, 4, 7). In verse 1 the psalmist says he is poor and needy; in verse 2 he is godly and believing, and in verses 3 and 4 he is importunate. The petitions themselves are rather general: "preserve, save, have mercy, and make joyful."

Just one note on the choice of terms. The word "holy" (KJV) or "godly" (ASV, RSV) in verse 2 is built on the same root as the "merciful" (v. 3 KJV), "lovingkindness" (v. 5 ASV), or "steadfast love" (v. 5 RSV). It is the Hebrew word *ḥeseḏ*, and Hasidic (pious) Jews use it to label themselves. Many English words are necessary to give all the shades of meaning, but basically it denotes faithfulness to promises. Just as God's covenant fidelity endures forever (Ps. 136), so this ancient intercessor claims he has broken no vows but unswervingly maintained his devotion and trust.

One reason for the general terms used in this psalm by God's inspiring Spirit is to allow believers to use the psalms through centuries of changing circumstances. If people and places, events and times were too specific it might detract from an easy and immediately relevant application. Any Christian can quote this prayer and supply his own particulars as to troubles and wishes.

Verses 8–12 form a praise section (v. 11 is a petition for assistance in praise). Verse 8 is a strong monotheistic statement. The second half of the verse is difficult, as various translations will indicate by their divergence of opinion. Again, the shortest and most literal is as easily understood as those encumbered with verbiage: "There is nothing like your works."

Verse 9 may be messianic insofar as it speaks of Gentiles (nations) coming to God. The frequent recurrence of this theme of the worldwide extension of God's kingdom in the Psalms should be no surprise since this is the book most often quoted in the New Testament.

The ideas of God's oneness and His wondrous works are reversed (v. 10) from what they were (v. 8). The hymn concludes with a promise of wholehearted, everlasting praise for deliverance from spiritual death.

The last four verses of the psalm are a mixture of complaint and prayer but include no imprecations. Verse 14 describes the evil intentions of the king's enemies. Notice the psalmist's diagnosis: their bad attitude comes from lack of God-consciousness. We might be more understanding and less vindictive if we saw those who hate us as spiritually lost men and as potentials for evangelism. Verse 15 may even be viewed as a prayer for the enemy as well as for the psalmist. The foes are again in view in the last verse (v. 17). Despite the hope that they will be shamed, there is still the prayer that they will recognize it is God doing good for the one who prays. Another probing question a Christian might ask himself: Why do I want God to do good for me? For personal comfort? Or for a testimony to unbelievers? Perhaps God would do more if we had His glory as our chief purpose.

PSALM 87

Psalm 87 exalts Jerusalem, poetically called Zion, and the privilege of being one of its citizens. The holy city is best known as Jerusalem, but in many psalms the exalted name Zion occurs. Generally, spiritual aspects or concepts of that significant city are in view when this poetic name is used. A popular anthem is based on verse 3, but again the songwriter chose to call the city Zion rather than Jerusalem.

Verses 1–3 describe the city and God's love for it. The next three (4–6) speak of the cosmopolitan makeup of the worshipers there. The last verse, although difficult and elliptical, describes the program at Zion.

Verse 1, though very brief (because the title is considered the first half of the verse in the Hebrew Bible), makes the point that Jerusalem is located, by God's choice, in a high and separated or holy place. The psalmist goes on to state in verse 2 that it is loved more than any other city in the country. To cite the gates of the city is to use the part for the whole, a device used frequently in Hebrew literature. Then follows the well-known verse 3. Read Psalms 122, 125, 132, 133 and elsewhere to see some of the glorious things spoken of the city of God. Grandest of all descriptions is that given by John in Revelation of the New Jerusalem coming down from heaven (Rev. 21:10–22:5).

Verses 4–6 are somewhat prophetic in that the worldwide acceptance of the gospel is in view. The most hated enemies of the

Jews are seen making their way to worship at Jerusalem. "Rahab" is a poetic term for Egypt, that archenemy to the southwest (cf. Isa. 30:7), and Babylon is the enemy to the northeast. Philistia and Tyre are geographically closer. Remember that Goliath was a Philistine, as were the enemies of Samson. The Philistines captured the ark of the covenant and later killed Saul and Jonathan. The mention of Tyre is reminiscent of the Messianic psalm (45:12). Ethiopia (Heb., *Cush*) is essentially the same as it is today, but at the time this psalm was written it had ascendancy over Egypt.

Just as the gospel was for Jews first and then for Gentiles, so, in this psalm, no citizenship is superior to Zion and no birthplace more noble than Jerusalem. Often Jews make the best Christians. A "selah" ends this section as one did verse 3.

The last verse allows several translations. A literal but unintelligible rendering is: "And songs (or singers), like dances (or dancers), all my fountains are in you." If the first two elements are reversed and a copulative added, the verse makes good sense. I suggest: "Like dances and songs, all my fountains are in you." The King James Version follows the Greek rather than the Hebrew in translating "players on instruments."

Another question focuses on the "you" in verse 7. Is that the city of the Lord? Primarily it is the city, the source or fountain of the songs and dances. But of course the city is nothing without God. So the church building is nothing without the Lord of the church. Where are our fountains?

PSALM 88

Among the personal laments, Psalm 88 is one of the most discouraged and pathetic. It is the poetic groan of a man in extreme agony. Since he has no clear understanding of the afterlife, he is terror-stricken by the unknown. By contrast, Christian believers have no reason to fear the grave, and several reasons to welcome death, the chief one being their union with Christ.

The elaborate title demands some explanation. "Song," "Psalm," and "Maschil" (poem) all occur at the beginning to describe the work. Despite the frequent use of these various words, it is still impossible to consistently differentiate between them. Note that it is by or for the sons of Korah, the chief musician, and a certain Heman. Perhaps here is a good place to apply the theory that some of the psalm titles are not superscriptions to what follows but subscriptions to the preceding. Perhaps the part about the sons of Korah belongs with Psalm 87 and is in agreement with the superscription to that psalm. Two uncertain words, transliterated in the older version as "Mahalath Leannoth," come after the chief musician. The first looks like the word "dance" (cf. Ps. 87:7), while the second is like the word "to answer." Both words, however, may be rendered, as in the Jerusalem Bible, "in sickness or suffering." Such an interpretation fits well with the contents of this depressing psalm. Ezrahite means "native born" and may refer to a non-Hebrew or original Canaanite.

No outline is readily evident in Psalm 88. Rather, there is a stream of prayer-like complaints centered on the themes of being forsaken by God and man, sickness, and imminent death.

Verses 1–2 form the invocation and address to God. Several modern translations unnecessarily change the meaning of the opening line from a suitably literal, "God of my salvation" to a prayer, "I call for help" (RSV, NEB). Even a second-best translation involving less emendation of the Hebrew text would read simply, "Save me."

Verse 3 begins the recital of the psalmist's problems, most of which speak of his nearness to death. This psalm is unique in having so many different words for grave and related concepts: the Hebrew *sheol* (grave, or hell) (v. 3); "pit" (v. 4); "the dead" (vv. 5, 10); and "the grave" (v. 5)(not the same Hebrew word *sheol*; cf. v. 11); verse 6 has "pit" again with the adjective "lowest" plus "dark places" (cf. v. 18) and "deeps"; verse 11 has "Destruction" (Heb., *abaddon* as in Rev. 9:11); in verse 12 is an alternate form of the word "dark" and the poignant epithet, "the land of forgetfulness" (ASV).

The only hint at the reason for the trouble is in verses 7 and 16, but even then the specific cause is not given. The psalmist assumes that God is angry with him, but he arrives at no reason for that anger. Not all misfortune is judgment; it may be discipline or simply for God's glory. And certainly the God of all the earth will do right. The divine attributes of justice and mercy are obscured in this work.

A rather definite disbelief in the life after death or resurrection shows in verses 10–12. From the wording of the six questions in those verses the expected answers are "no." On the other hand, the poet may be like the preacher of the Book of Ecclesiastes who spells out the unbelieving position in detail and later presents his own conviction. In this case, verse 13 contains a glimmer of hope. "In the morning" may very well mean "after death," not merely the next day. That ray of hope is quickly snuffed out, however, by the continuing despondency of the rest of the psalm. Verse 14 contains two more discouragingly pessimistic questions. Then, to the end of the psalm, more complaints are directed Godward. In fact, the unpacified plaintiff begins to repeat himself. Note the similarity of verse 17 to 7, and of 18 to 8.

If the standard translation of verse 1a is correct, then let us meditate on that truth as well as on the truth of verse 13. But the Lord knows that the sentiment of the whole psalm sometimes best describes his wayward, shortsighted, impenitent, insensitive, and faithless children.

PSALM 89

Psalm 89 is concerned with the Lord's covenant with David. Some of the promises of the middle section do not fit David himself but admirably suit the most notable Descendant in his dynasty, the Lord Jesus Christ. In Christ are fulfilled all the glorious promises to this ancient and godly monarch. Here is an outline of the psalm.

Introduction (vv. 1–2)
Restatement of the Davidic covenant (vv. 3–4)
Hymn to the Creator (vv. 5–18)
Promise to David (vv. 19–37)
Lamentation (vv. 38–45)
Reproaches by the nations (vv. 46–51)
Benediction (v. 52)

Without question the speaker of verses 1–2 is not the speaker of verses 3–4. In the introduction, the psalmist, perhaps the Ethan mentioned in the title (cf. 1 Kings 4:31), prefaces the psalm with words of praise for God's loving-kindness and faithfulness. The words "mercy" and "faithfulness" occur in verses 1 and 2.

Originally the covenant made to David came through the prophet Nathan, as recorded in 2 Samuel 7:12–17 (cf. Luke 1:33). The seed, of course, is the offspring, Christ being the ultimate Occupant of that throne. A "selah" appropriately concludes this little section even as other "selah's" occur at verses 37, 45, and 48.

Various allusions to creation power and sovereignty over the cosmos fill the hymn (vv. 5–18). Only at its end (vv. 15–18) is there something about God's human subjects, those on whose behalf His power is exercised. Notice the repetition of the themes

213

of loving-kindness and faithfulness (vv. 8, 14).

The main part of the psalm (vv. 19–37) includes a number of eulogies and promises to David and his dynasty. In exalted language David is lauded (v. 19). The Hebrew root for "anointed" in verses 20, 38, and 51 is the same used for "Messiah." Among the promises are those of military success (vv. 22–23) and territorial expansion (v. 25). The king's piety is noted (v. 26).

With verse 27, the terminology becomes even more exalted. One suspects that the description fits only David's "greater Son." David was not the firstborn, but rather the last-born son of Jesse. Jesus was the only born Son of God. Other superlatives such as highest (v. 27b, ASV, RSV) and the statement regarding the eternality of the reign are more descriptive of Christ and His kingdom than of David. Strangely, no New Testament writer quotes this psalm and applies it to Christ, except perhaps for an allusion in Revelation 1:5–7.

Notice again the ideas of loving-kindness, covenant fidelity, and never-failing faithfulness in this section (vv. 28, 33, 34). The promises of the covenant are repeated in verses 35–37, with special stress on God's integrity in giving the covenant and on the everlasting quality of it.

Verses 38–45 almost seem foreign to the genre of the psalm. Lamentation-like, the psalmist looks at the discouraging present. He sees a kingdom which reflects only dimly the glorious past. Some commentators say the psalm was written during Solomon's reign, some during the divided kingdom period, and others during the exile. Judging from these verses alone, the situation is very bad. God is angry with His anointed (v. 38). His crown has been desecrated (v. 39). The buildings and bushes of the capital city are in ruins (v. 40), and the kingdom is at the disposal of murderous enemies (vv. 41–43). All that was beautiful and cherished has turned to shame (vv. 44–45).

The concluding prayer (vv. 46–51) is largely negative and complaining. It sounds like the plea of an exile. The covenant to David is remembered and appealed to (v. 49), not only in the historical past but also in the early part of this psalm. Bitterly the psalm closes with a view of the enemies of God shaming God's servants.

Book III within the Psalter closes with Psalm 89:52. The benediction applies to the entire book and not merely to this psalm.

PSALM 90

"A prayer of Moses the man of God" is the title of Psalm 90. Most scholars agree that the archaic nature of the psalm's vocabulary and grammar support its early composition.

Psalm 90 ranks high on the list of well-known favorites. It is particularly fitting for funerals since the major teaching is the brevity and uncertainty of human life in contrast to God's eternal existence. Moses may be anticipating life after death in God's presence (vv. 3, 14). The general and elusive nature of most poetry disallows any certainty. "In the morning" (v. 6) may simply be the next day, or it may mean the day after death.

Evident in verses 1–2 is a beautiful chiasmus. Notice in the outline of these verses how the poet reverses direction in the middle and repeats himself with synonyms.

A Lord
  B You have been our dwelling place
    C From generation to generation
      D Before the mountains
        E Were brought forth
        E´ Or you formed
      D´ The earth and the world
    C´ From everlasting to everlasting
  B´ You are
A´ God

Having opened the psalm with this general statement of God's eternal nature, Moses then notes His sovereignty over the fortunes of men (v. 3). The words "turn" and "return" translate the same Hebrew verb for what is an obvious play on words (cf. v. 13). The verse may be speaking of death and resurrection. God turns man back to dust or slime (ANCHOR), but one day He will command him to rise. Some men will sleep for thousands of years and others for but a few days. With God both spans of time are equally brief. Peter cited verse 4 when he spoke of the immanency of the return of Christ (2 Peter 3:8).

Then the focus of the psalm moves from the eternality of God to the finitude of man (vv. 5–6). Reflecting on the short life of desert grass, Moses likens man to the green blanket that thinly veils the sand for a brief period after a rare but abundant rainfall.

Verses 7–9 and 11 connect the shortness of human life to the anger of God. The implication is that if men did not sin they would live longer, maybe forever.

Perhaps the most frequently quoted verse is 10. In Hebrew, numbers are written the same as in modern English. It says seventy years and eighty years. In 1611 when the King James Version was translated, "score" was used for twenty, but that is not a literal translation of the original. The psalmist was remarkably accurate in putting at seventy the average age at death. Actually, only in modern Western countries has such a high average been achieved. And often those ten years from seventy to eighty are sad and hard because of decreasing strength and failing health.

The point made throughout the psalm is epitomized in verse 12. From this reflection on God's eternality and man's brevity comes the lesson: Learn to number your days. This is an excellent prayer text for the lessons of self-discipline and goal-oriented living. But how few do it!

The application of the prayer of Moses, the man of God, continues (v. 13) with a second imperative: "Return, O Lord." The overtones of a lament echo in the words "How long?" But this request is against the background of all that precedes, especially the anger-provoking sins of God's people.

A flicker of belief in the afterlife may be seen in verse 14, depending on the meaning of the poetic terms. Even if Moses does not understand the resurrection, this verse at least expresses his desire for a long and happy earthly life.

Verse 15 is an interesting contrast. Moses asks that, for every day of affliction and for every year that witnesses evil, God give occasions to rejoice in their stead. This is especially meaningful in the light of the 400 years of oppression in Egypt and the forty years of agony in the desert of Sinai. Those who accept Christ later in life often testify that the few recent years of peace with God are worth more than all their pre-Christian decades.

The three sentiments of verses 16–17a express the truth of Romans 6:13b. Moses prays that God's work, glory, and pleasure might be evident not only to the people but also through them as well. Naomi, the feminine name meaning "pleasantness," is the root word behind the term "beauty" or "favor" (v. 17 ASV, RSV).

The psalm concludes with two almost identical phrases. It is a fine example of Hebrew repetition done here for stress and to seal the prayer of this ancient interceding sage.

PSALM 91

Although Psalm 90 ranks high on the list of popular psalms, Psalm 91 is loved by even more people. It speaks of the security of trusting in God. Verses 1–2 constitute the introduction, while the central part of the psalm (vv. 3–13) speaks of the individual dangers from which the believer is protected. The last three verses (14–16) are a series of promises from God, who speaks in the first person.

Modern versions recast the first two verses in several different ways to overcome the difficulty of the changing persons. All these solutions are possible by adjusting the vowels of the Hebrew text, which were not part of the inspired original. So the New American Standard Bible has, "He who dwells." The Revised Standard Version and others have at the beginning of verse 2, "will say to the LORD, 'My refuge. . .'" This confusion of speaker and addressee is not uncommon in Hebrew poetry. The overall teaching is not obscured by any of the translations. The truth is that whether you, I, or he, meaning the king or some other believer, dwells in the secret place of the Most High, we can say of the Lord, "He is my refuge and my fortress."

These two opening verses include four different names for the Deity: Most High (Heb., *Elyon*), Almighty (Heb., *Shaddai*), LORD (Heb., *Yahweh*), and God (Heb., *Elohim*). Like most of the Old Testament, the psalm is written by someone with experience in desert life. The figures of secret place and shadow are particularly vivid against that background. In the desert you can see for miles, and a hiding place is hard to find. To the desert traveler the sun is his fiercest foe and a shady spot a most desired friend. God is such a shade as well as a military defense.

For the next eleven verses there is no inconsistency between speaker and addressee. The poet assures the believer of God's everlasting vigil over His people. Some Bible students understand this psalm to be written for and about the king of Israel, David. No superscription so limits the application.

The enemies against which God provides protection are of several sorts. The militaristic terms (vv. 4b, 5, 7) suggest protection in battle. Several phrases seem to refer to disease or plague (vv. 3b, 6, 10). Then there are the natural calamities, snakes and lions (v. 13), and finally the ever-present possibility of harmful accidents (vv. 3, 5b, 11, 12). Some interpreters see this explanation as too literal, and would rather understand the various ills as descriptions of human enemies. The first threat is the bird-catcher's trap, the plain meaning of the poetic "snare of the fowler." Although no record exists of anyone using such a device to catch men, it is quite possible. The next enemy on the list is the deadly pestilence. Immediately the plagues of Egypt come to mind, especially since Moses recorded how his people were spared the worst of them (Ex. 8:22).

Verse 4 interrupts the catalog of catastrophes by reasserting the sentiments of verse 1. God is pictured zoomorphically as a mother bird sheltering her chicks. No one says God has wings and feathers! The second image is reminiscent of the catalog of armor in Ephesians 6:14–17.

The point of verses 5–6 is not the terror or the arrow (which, incidentally, like the Hebrew are a nice pair of almost rhymed words), but that God cares for us night and day, in darkness and at noon. God never sleeps, and His watch is constant even when

His servants sleep and cannot be consciously praying for safety.

Many military veterans have quoted verse 7, and such an application is entirely in order. However, it can have a much wider application, including deliverance from plague and other natural disasters as well as manmade ones. My wife and I think of this promise as we reflect on the hundreds of thousands of accident-free miles we have traveled. Of course, this is not to say unequivocally that everyone who has accidents or suffers disease is getting his just reward for wickedness.

Verse 9, like verse 4, is an interruption in the list of threats to life and safety. The "my" on "refuge" is difficult and translators have squirmed in various directions to make this verse fit the context. The King James Version added words to ease the situation. Others, such as the Revised Standard Version have simply changed the possessive pronoun to "your." Ugaritic studies have now shown that this latter option is possible since in that language the words for "my" and "thy" are often identical. Notice too that two of the titles for God from verses 1–2 are reused here.

Again (v. 10) the motif of protection from plague appears. A connecting particle joins verse 10 with the reasons found in verses 11–12. These are well-known verses because Satan cited them when he tempted Jesus in the wilderness. Also this is about the closest thing to a proof text for the belief in guardian angels. Two kinds of lions and two varieties of snakes conclude the list of threats in this psalm. Ultimate authority or victory is pictured as stepping on the vanquished. So the Messiah will tread on His enemies according to Isaiah 63:3 and Hebrews 2:8 (citing Ps. 8:6).

Beginning with verse 14, God speaks to His faithful one, mentioning all the things He will do for him. Because the believer loves and knows God, God will repay him with this eightfold reward. He will deliver him and set him on high (v. 14). He will answer him, be with him in trouble, deliver him (translating a different Hebrew word than is in v. 14), and honor him (v. 15). He will give him a long earthly life plus salvation (v. 16). The last term implies everlasting life, the best and most enduring of all God's good gifts. But these blessings come only because the recipient knows and loves God. Both these requirements need underscoring since both are loaded with meaning far beyond their normal, modern use.

PSALM 92

Several outlines could be fitted to Psalm 92, but the one which divides the psalm into three parts as follows is preferred.

Hymn to the Lord (vv. 1–5)
Judgment on the foolish wicked (vv. 6–9)
Personal testimony to God's goodness to His people (vv. 10–15)

The sections are very closely related, with a flow of ideas from one to the next. For instance, verse 5 ends on the note of the incomprehensibility of God's thoughts, and verse 6 takes up with the inability of the fool to understand. Or, verse 9 speaks of the destruction of the wicked, while verse 10 is the other side of that coin, the vindication of the righteous.

Taken as a whole, Psalm 92 falls in the category of a hymn. The title supports this classification: "A Psalm, a Song for the Sabbath day" (NASB). Verses 1–4 are grammatically connected. It is good to do three things: to thank, to sing, and to show. In turn, we should show two things: God's daily loving-kindness and His nightly faithfulness. This demonstration should be accompanied by three musical instruments: a ten-stringed device, the psaltery, and the harp. Finally, the reason for this injunction to praise comes in verse 4, which is connected to the preceding verse with the key word "because" or "for." So this long sentence begins and ends with God's holy name.

Verses 4b–5 are exclamations about God's great works, with the Hebrew author using two different words for the three occurrences of the word "works."

As this section ends focusing on the incomprehensibility of God's thought, so the next begins with the finite understanding of a senseless and foolish mortal.

Verse 7 outlines the quick growth, the brief life, and the sudden death of evil men. Then, after the benediction-like interruption (v. 8), they perish and are scattered. Though verse 8 breaks the idea flow from verses 7–9, it is not altogether unrelated. As the wicked are destroyed forever (v. 7) so the Lord is on high forever (v. 8). The grass springs up (v. 7), but God is on high (v. 8).

The psalmist's personal testimony begins at verse 10. Notice the personal pronouns (vv. 10, 11, 15). The interior verses of this section (12–14) speak more objectively of the success and fruitfulness of God's people.

This closing section contains a rich combination of very interesting figures or analogies. First is the confession of ox-like strength. Horns, then as now, are symbols of strength. The next figure is of anointing with oil. No liturgical or sacerdotal sense is necessary here. This is but a token of luxury of leisure comparable to a hot bath or a soft chair. The imagery speaks of God's supply of strength and joy (cf. Ps. 104:15).

The next verse (11) is a bit of what the Germans call *schadenfreude,* meaning "happiness at the grief of others." To see the enemy fall is a cause for joy.

An extended simile fills verses 12–14. First is the simple statement that the righteous are like palms or cedars, two of the stateliest trees in the Near East. According to the next verse, they are planted and grow in the temple of the Lord, meaning of course that in the house of God, the church, if you please, is found spiritual nourishment and holy maturity. Finally, though old, they are, like any good tree, very alive and productive.

The last verse uses yet another figure. God is a rock for shelter, defense, and stability. Unlike the workers of iniquity who have no righteousness, in God there is no unrighteousness. Can that be said of His people?

PSALM 93

Psalm 93 is a short hymn exalting God's power over the raging sea. Verses 1–2 form the first thrust and the initial statement about God's majestic reign and everlasting strength. Verses 3–4 describe the roaring sea, and verse 5 concludes the poem with a reflection on God's perfections of truth and holiness.

Within the hymn are several fine illustrations of the features of Semitic poetry. Note the repetition of "is clothed" or "robed" (v. 1). In the original Hebrew these two identical words are back to back in the middle of the verse. The word "established" connects verses 1 and 2. Next is an excellent illustration of a staircase or progressive parallelism (v. 3). The scheme is ABC, ABD, ABE. Set up in poetry it might look like this:

> The floods have lifted up
> > O LORD
> The floods have lifted up
> > their voice;
> The floods lift up
> > their waves.

Verse 4 is not too dissimilar in its arrangement. Notice also that both verses 3 and 4 (ASV) contain the word "voice." Additional plays on words might be seen in verses 4–5 with "waters" (*mayim*), "sea" (*yam*), and "evermore" (*yamim*).

The poet who penned Psalm 93 offers a picture of a great and trustworthy Sovereign. Because of the connection between the words "reign" or "is king" (NEB) and "the LORD" (v. 1), some interpreters see here an enthronement festival where belief in God's rule over the created world was annually reasserted. Others see a foreshadowing of the Messiah where God the Father makes God the Son King (cf. Ps. 2:6; 110:1). Still other commentators understand this as a song celebrating God's victory over the chaotic forces at the time of the creation. The girding then reflects the ancient sport of belt-wrestling (cf. Job 38:3).

No hint of polytheism is present, however. God is presented as the absolute Sovereign partaking of eternity while the created cosmos does not. God alone is everlasting. He made the world.

The ancient Israelites were not friendly with the sea. Even their directions were named so that north was to the left, south right, and west or the Mediterranean behind. Palestine has no natural harbors. Seagoing Hebrews were the exception to the rule. So the mysterious power and unharnessable might of the roaring ocean are all the more fearsome against this background. Their only hope was that God was stronger than the sea, higher than the waves, and more everlasting than the tides.

Having touched on God's glory, majesty, eternity, and power over the mightiest thing in creation, the sea, the psalmist concludes this hymn by asserting the truthfulness of God's word and His holiness. This climax to the song is also the conclusion to the argument. If God is stronger than anything He made, will He not be truthful? If He is greater than the sea, will He not be holy?

The very last line is a strong, affirmative answer to those implied questions. Yes, the LORD is and will be so forever.

PSALM 94

Several themes are prominent in Psalm 94. The most common is lament over the present success of the wicked and the misfortune of the good. Also present are the motifs of prayer for vengeance, imprecation, trust, and praise. The very title given to God in the opening verse sets the tenor of the entire psalm. He is the God of vengeance. Verses 1–2 constitute the invocation. God is summoned to take His seat at the bar of holy justice and render to the proud their just rewards. The first lamentation part of the psalm is in verses 3–7.

The characteristic question, "How long?" prefaces this series of complaints. The charges against the wicked vary from general accusations regarding their success (v. 3) to specific sins and attitudes. In summary, their wrongs boil down to violence and pride; violence in oppression and murder (vv. 5–6), pride in boasting (v. 4), and insult (v. 7).

It is clearly against the background of verse 7 that verse 8 admonishes the wicked to wise up and get smart. Notice the device of the rhetorical questions through this psalm (vv. 3, 8, 9, 10, 16, 20).

In a sense the questions are really answers. So verses 9–10 are the answers to the sorry picture painted in verses 4–7. Yes, God can hear. Yes, He can see. Yes, He will discipline and correct. For God not only hears their words and sees their actions but also even knows their thoughts. Then verse 11b serves as a sort of postscript: "By the way, those thoughts are vain."

Though verses 12–13 are like a benediction of a different sort than the preceding, they nevertheless are connected by the key words "chasten" and "teach."

Through verse 15 the felicitous state of the vindicated righteous is described. Among the benefits of a chastened and God-taught man are rest and the assurance of not being forsaken. Couched in verse 13 is also the joy of seeing the wicked fall into his grave. The promise of verse 15 makes better sense when read with verse 20, where the wicked have control of the courts and decree unjust laws to their own benefit. But justice again returns to the control of the righteous (v. 15).

The questions of verse 16 introduce the first part of the psalmist's testimony (vv. 17–19). The questions and the complaint of verses 20–21 introduce the second part of that personal testimony (v. 22). But even those words of praise are colored by complaint and vindictiveness. His God is the God who rises against evildoers and stands in opposition to workers of iniquity. God is the high tower (ASV) and rock of refuge from those bloody men who conspire to kill him. The sentiments of verses 17–19 are very tender. Here is a picture of a man on intimate terms with his Lord. He understands that just as God knows the inward thoughts of unrighteous men (v. 11), so God knows his personal integrity. Although at the end of the psalm the righteous are vindicated, it is on a somewhat negative note. Three separate statements of judgment constitute the closing verse (v. 23) and focus (as did v. 1) on God the Avenger. The same God offers both refuge and revenge. Which do we deserve? Which do we have?

PSALM 95

Psalm 95 has two distinct parts. Verses 1–7a are praise, while verses 7b–11 are exhortation. The first part can be subdivided into two strophes, with the break after verse 5. Notice how both verses 1 and 6 begin with the admonition, "come." Then both verses 3 and 7 start with a "for" and give the reason the worshiper should come. The latter part of the psalm is familiar to Christians because it appears in Hebrews 3:7b–11 verbatim (cf. also Heb. 3:15; 4:3–4, 7). An additional connection to the New Testament may be the mention of God the rock (v. 1b). Paul identified that wilderness rock from which water miraculously came as Christ (1 Cor. 10:4).

The first part of the psalm is a fine call to worship and is often used for that liturgical purpose. Although it is not evident in any English translation, the two words for "let us sing" and "let us make a joyful noise" sound alike in Hebrew.

Elsewhere God is called a rock (e.g., Deut. 32:4, 15, 18, 30, 31). Because of the historical connection later in the psalm to the events of Exodus 17, that epithet was chosen. The term was carefully selected from several available synonyms. Just as Jesus (Matt. 16:18) was careful to distinguish between small stones and a solid rock suitable for a building's foundation (cf. NASB marg. notes), so this word is almost parallel with mountain, crag, or natural fortress. From where this is written the Continental Divide is in view. Geologists who have analyzed these mountains say that some are solid granite and weigh billions of tons. Such is the nature of our God: immovable, impregnable, immense, unshakable, everlasting. "I will lift up mine eyes unto the mountains" (Ps. 121:1 ASV).

Verses 3–5 are a hymn, perhaps one of the "psalms" we are urged to bring (v. 2b). According to the opening statements, Yahweh is a great God, a great King, and is over all gods. This is not a confession of polytheism or even henotheism. But, in the light of the following verses, it is tantamount to a denial of any superhuman force besides God.

Two pairs of extremes make up verses 4–5. First, God is in

control of the deep places of the earth, meaning the graves, the sea bottoms, or the valleys. Next, He is the Owner of the mountaintops. To the Palestinian the highest point was 9,232-foot Mount Hermon; the lowest, the surface of the Dead Sea, was almost 1,300 feet below the level of the Mediterranean. Explorers have found no deeper hole, but they have found the Himalayas rising more than 29,000 feet above the level of the ocean beach. Both extremes are made and controlled by God. The second contrasted areas are the sea and the dry land (v. 5).

The second strophe (vv. 6–7) is briefer than the former but contains the same basic elements: command to worship and a reason for praise. As verses 3–7 spoke of God's transcendence and control of the cosmic, so verse 7 speaks of His immanence and His rule over His people.

The expression "hand" in verse 7 may be a highly poetic term for field, which would be parallel with pasture (cf. Jer. 6:3 where the Hebrew word for "hand" was rendered "place" as early as 1611; Job 1:14, where all translate it "beside"). With verse 7b, the tenor of the psalm changes from worship to warning. Some Bibles give the Hebrew names of the two places while others translate the words. The episodes referred to are recorded in Exodus 17 and Numbers 20 (cf. Deut. 6:16; 33:8; Ps. 81:7; 106:32). The wandering Israelites complained about the lack of water, and Moses brought it from the rock at God's command. Verses 8–11 are the words of God to His people, both ancient (here in Ps. 95) and modern (Heb. 3–4).

The psalm ends on an unhappy note, but perhaps this is to impress on the reader God's demand for absolute obedience. No words of comfort insulate the end of the believer from the intended sting of discipline. No opportunity is made available to let the mind shift to neutral and so forget these strong words of warning. For the inspired interpretation of these events read the message of the apostle in Hebrews 3–4. "Let us, therefore, make every effort to enter that rest, so that no one will fall by following their example of disobedience" (Heb. 4:11 NIV).

PSALM 96

Another edition of Psalm 96 appears in 1 Chronicles 16:23–33. According to that context the work was commissioned by David and executed by the sons of Asaph. It is a fine example of a worship hymn. The thirteen verses divide neatly into four parts: verses 1–3 constitute a summons to praise; verses 4–6 assert God's uniqueness; verses 7–10 exhort to service; and verses 11–13 enjoin all creation to rejoice.

Verses 1–3 contain several imperative verbs. Three times the command "sing" occurs. The words "shew forth," incidentally, sound like the word "sing" in Hebrew. The worldwide scope of the psalm is noted as early as verse 3 where the saints are urged to spread the word of God's glorious works. Verses such as 3 are the missionary mandates of the Old Testament. Ancient Israel, like the modern church, had the divinely given obligation to tell. And like the Great Commission (Mark 16:15), the specific command is to preach. The success of the mission is God's business.

In Psalm 95 the pattern was "come, sing, for" (Ps. 95:1, 3, 6–7). Psalm 96 has an echo of that theme. The "for" occurs in verses 4, 5, and 13. "For great is the LORD. . . . For all the gods of the peoples are idols [nothings]" (RSV). Again, this is not a confession of imperfect monotheism but a denial that other gods exist. True, they exist as statues, but statues are mere wood or stone, not deity. The Hebrew language words for foolishness, vanity, emptiness, and evil constantly overlap in meaning.

God is everything idols are not. He is to be feared (v. 4). He created (v. 5). He is worthy of honor and majesty since He possesses strength and beauty (v. 6).

The psalmist returns to imperatives again (vv. 7–10). Just as the command to sing is three times over in the opening part of the psalm, so the command to bring or give occurs three times (vv. 7–8). An expression at the beginning of verse 9 is difficult. The King James Version has "in the beauty of holiness," while the New English Bible has "in the splendor of holiness." Most others have something like "in holy array." The Hebrew allows both meanings as well as others such as "with the beauty of holiness," meaning a pure heart or a guileless attitude. Compare verse 6 with Psalm 29:2, where a similar expression occurs.

As the close of the first section (v. 3) had a missionary injunction, so the last verse in this section (v. 10) commissions the worshipers to be evangelists also. It is a three-point message that we are to bear according to verse 10: Tell everybody God reigns, He created and sustains the world, and He will judge it with fairness in the end. Verse 2b contains the additional necessary part of the good news: "Show forth his salvation from day to day" (ASV).

The verbs of verses 11–12 are technically not imperatives but do serve as commands to the heavens, earth, sea, and fields. This sub-human, inanimate creation is to join the song of praise. The creation was cursed in the Fall (Gen 3:17–18). It shall be delivered in the end (Rom. 8:20–22). So why should it not rejoice, exult and sing?

At the end comes the reason why all creation should praise God. In a beautiful staircase-type parallelism the truth is underscored. God is coming to judge the people of the world with righteousness and truth.

PSALM 97

Psalm 97 is a hymn devoted to the Lord's power and dominion. Its first half especially is loaded with prophetic terms and apocalyptic language. Most Bible students agree that a major break comes after verse 6 and a minor one after verse 9. Verses 1–6 describe God in His cosmic rule. Verses 7–9 picture the true worshipers' glee when image worshipers are put to shame. The last three verses (10–12) focus on the vindication and preservation of the righteous.

The psalm opens with a command to the earth and the distant islands or coastlands to rejoice. This follows the opening statement and the reason why they should be glad: the Lord is King. Note that a similar command closes the psalm (v. 12a).

Verse 2 and on is an extended theophany. God is described in terms of nature. The first line of verse 2 may hark back to the revelation of God on Mount Sinai. Righteousness and justice are concretized and made the foundation of His throne. That throne is actually not material either, but a way to attribute sovereignty and dominion to God.

Verses 3–4 may go together since they both refer to light. However, verse 3 may speak specifically of the pillar of fire that led the wandering Israelites through the desert, and the lightning (v. 4) to the manifestation on the mountain. Or, the fire (v. 3) may be the one that devoured Nadab and Abihu from their presumption (Lev. 10:2), and the lightning (v. 4) any storm which evokes the fear of God.

Melting mountains, a familiar figure in the Old Testament (cf. Amos 9:5; Mic. 1:4; Nah. 1:5), may describe an earthquake, a landslide, a volcanic eruption, or a terrific rainstorm. This section concludes with a statement on the universality of general revelation. It is not unlike Psalm 19:1. An anti-idolatry polemic appears (v. 7) in the form of a fervid wish that all idol-worshipers be put to shame. The second order is that all gods worship the true God. "Gods" may mean false deities or simply human leaders. Either explanation would fit here. The Greek translation has "angels." Verse 8 depicts the true worshipers rejoicing over God's judgment on the false. Then verse 9 forms a benediction to this little series of events and ties in with verse 7 on the note of God's superiority to other things that people worship.

The last three verses take up the theme of the bliss (v. 8) of the enlightened righteous. Actually, verse 10 begins with an exhortation to hate evil. The second two stichs of that verse probably refer directly to the preservation from evil and deliverance from its power.

The light and gladness of verses 11–12 were probably chosen to reflect those same words in the opening verses of the psalm. These ancient inspired writers were conscious of style and form. They knew they were writing poetry and this often-used device occurs again here. As verse 10 had opened with a command, so verse 12 ends with one. Here it is to give thanks at every remembrance of God's holiness. The Jerusalem Bible translation of this exhortation is quote worthy: "Remember his holiness, and praise him!"

PSALM 98

Psalm 98 is very similar to Psalm 96, with opening lines that are identical. Verse 7 is the same as 96:11; and the last verse like 96:13.

A happy psalm, it enjoins us to rejoice in God's manifold goodnesses. His triumphs are described generally in verses 1–3. Verses 4–6 contain a volley of praise, while the last three (7–9) show the whole creation accompanying the victory of God at the end of the world.

The new song contains references to old triumphs. First and most comprehensive is the statement that the Lord has done marvelous things. Perhaps all the plagues of Egypt are in the psalmist's mind. Then, more specifically, He saved by His right hand and His holy arm, both interesting metaphors. This may refer to the Exodus miracles of the Red Sea, the destruction of Sihon and Og, and attendant wonders. The publication of God's saving and vindicating power is stressed (v. 2). Together with verse 3, this is the Evangel of the Old Testament. The Good News was that God existed and that He has saved His people. The additional New Testament message is that we may join His people by receiving Christ, His Son.

A second exhortation to praise comes in verse 4 and is repeated (v. 6). Various strummed and blown musical instruments are to be employed in this holy rejoicing before King Yahweh. Even inanimate creation is summoned in verses 7–8 to participate in this song. In highly imaginative style the roaring seas, the clapping waves, and the singing hills are a part of this symphony.

The climax is God coming to judge the world (v. 9). Involved in that administration of justice will be reward for the righteous and the condemnation of the wicked. In this happy psalm, however, no mention is made of the wicked. The psalm merely closes on the high note of anticipating God's equitable court at the end times.

PSALM 99

Psalm 99 is one more in this short series of praise psalms (95–100). In this one, particular stress is laid on the holiness of God (vv. 3, 5, 9). Some divide the psalm on the basis of the occurrence of the word "holy." Three stanzas then are broken after verses 3 and 5. Others make just verse 5 the one major break since verses 5 and 9 are almost identical. Note the progression from God's transcendence and unreachability in verses 1–3, through His dealings with the nation as a whole (v. 4), to His special relationship of revelation through Moses, Aaron, and Samuel (vv. 6–8).

Verse 1 sets the regal tone that prevails through this psalm. The Lord is King. He sits on His throne between the cherubim, a word lifted right from the Hebrew because our language cannot translate it. They were the attendants of the ark of the covenant, covering the seat on that sacred box with outstretched wings (Ex. 37:7–9).

After two more statements about God's greatness (v. 2) the order comes (v. 3) to all peoples that they should praise this holy God. Though holiness is a rather unknown and difficult-to-define quality to most modern people, it had a real message to these ancient Semites who used it. The basic sense is separation. As it applies to God, it means He is separate from sin, sinners, imperfection of any kind, guilt, and even from the bad attitudes of prejudice, pride, and presumption. God is free from these many forms of vice, and He commands us to be the same.

"The king's strength" may be an epithet for God (v. 4). God loves justice. In the rest of the verse God is addressed in the second person. Verse 5 brings another command to worship (cf. v. 3) and also ends with "he is holy."

In the last stanza the subject is God's revealing Himself to men. Moses, Aaron, and Samuel had a unique privilege to communicate with God. But through the testimonies and statutes we all can hear God's will. Again, verse 8, like verse 4, addresses God as "you." This is direct praise of God's justice and mercy.

The psalm concludes with a third verse of admonition to praise. Rather than ending with a simple "He is holy," the last line spells out God's name more fully. The LORD our God is separate from the world locally (v. 2). He is separated from its injustice (v. 4) and gives revelation rather than needing to receive it. He is holy.

PSALM 100

The fitting title to Psalm 100 indicates it is a psalm of thanksgiving or is to accompany a thank offering. It was probably sung by worshipers making their way into the temple.

The psalm is very familiar, especially because of William Kethe's 1561 paraphrase set to the tune, "The Old Hundredth" by Louis Bourgeois.

> All people that on earth do dwell,
>> Sing to the Lord with cheerful voice;
> Him serve with fear, his praise forthtell,
>> Come ye before him and rejoice.
>
> The Lord ye know is God indeed;
>> Without our aid he did us make;
> We are his folk, he doth us feed,
>> And for his sheep he doth us take.
>
> O enter then his gates with praise,
>> Approach with joy his courts unto;
> Praise, laud, and bless his Name always,
>> For it is seemly so to do.
>
> For why? the Lord our God is good,
>> His mercy is for ever sure;
> His truth at all times firmly stood,
>> And shall from age to age endure.

Most of the verb forms are commands. The worshipers are charged to make a joyful noise, serve, come with singing, know, enter with praise, give thanks, and bless.

The psalm is universal. All lands are summoned to come and

worship the Lord. God's loving-kindness is "for ever" to "all generations." The vocative (v. 1) may be all the earth rather than
"all . . . lands." "Make a joyful noise" is a heavy translation for
one Hebrew word. The suggestions of some modern translations
convey the crispness of the command: "acclaim" (NEB; JB) or
"hail" (ANCHOR).

The psalmist is careful that the joy of worship be tempered with
adequate reverence for the object of worship. So verse 3 serves to
remind us of God's creative power and absolute sovereignty over
us. But to do so, he chooses the figure of a shepherd and sheep, one
of the more tender illustrations of His concern and care.

If any outline fits Psalm 100 it is A B A′ B′. Verses 1–2 (the
A in the outline) contain a series of three commands. So does
verse 4 (the A′). Verse 3b (the B) has two statements regarding
our finitude and dependence, while verse 5 (the B′) mentions
the everlastingness of God's attributes of love, mercy, and truth.

Verse 3 contains a problem. The written Hebrew has, "and not
we ourselves" (KJV). The Hebrew read by the scribes was "and we
are his" (RSV, et al.). Both make good sense and there is no certain
way to resolve the problem.

Altogether this is a most pleasant hymn with which to conclude this second volume of comments on the Psalms. At Psalm
51 the never-failing covenant fidelity (Heb., *ḥeseḏ*) of God was
in view (Ps. 51:1). And here at the end that same comprehensive
attribute is left for our comfort and admonition.

> For the LORD is good;
> His *ḥeseḏ* lasts forever,
> And his faithfulness for all generations.

PSALMS 101–150:
SONGS OF
DISCIPLESHIP

....

This is the third and concluding part of observations on the Hebrew Psalter. I trust that these remarks will deepen the appreciation of Scripture and of this portion of the Psalms in particular.

Though there are many unanswered questions in the Psalms—questions of language, custom, theology—it is hard to miss the main lessons. The Psalms, like all other Scripture, are for our teaching, rebuke, correction, and training in righteousness, so that we may be thoroughly equipped for every good work (see 2 Tim. 3:16–17).

Many of the remarks are of a technical nature, but many are of a devotional nature too. Scholarship ought not be divorced from piety. Obviously, not every word or even every verse can receive comment in an endeavor of this scope, but perhaps what is included will whet the appetite for even more concentrated Bible study.

As in the first one hundred psalms, these last fifty evidence great variety. We find here psalms that expose the innermost feelings of God's ancient people. Some of the psalms may lead to tears; others should evoke profound joy. Different psalms are for different moods. If you know what the themes of the psalms are, you can select one to meet your spiritual need: "Rejoice with them that do rejoice, and weep with them that weep" (Rom. 12:15).

This group of psalms has an above-average number of public or liturgical works. So think of standing before the tabernacle in the days of David or in the temple precincts in later years. Imagine worshiping with believers of a bygone era. Put yourself in the ensemble or in the chorus as it lifted its praise to God who lived then, who is alive today, and who will live forevermore. In other words, enter into the sweet spirit of praise, join the anthem of exaltation, and let the hymnbook of ancient Israel become part of your spontaneous worship of God your Savior.

PSALM 101

Psalm 101 may fall into the category of wisdom psalms or royal psalms. Many of its sentiments reflect the teaching of Proverbs. Compare verse 4 with Proverbs 11:20, verse 5b with Proverbs 6:17, and verse 7 with Proverbs 25:5.

The title states that it is a psalm of David. If one reads the eight verses of the psalm with a king in mind, it sounds like a code of royal ethical behavior. The psalm takes the form of a protestation of integrity, justice, and piety. The things the king is *for*, as well as the things he is *against*, receive equal emphasis. He is for wisdom, perfection, and faith; he is against baseness, perversity, evil, slander, pride, and deceit. Every verse and every stich within each verse, except for the last, contain the pronouns *me* or *my*.

The opening two verses strike a positive note in general terms, with the twin virtues of covenant faithfulness (Heb. ḥeseḏ) and justice as the first words in the Hebrew text.

The only problem in the psalm is the explanation of the question in the middle of verse 2: "When will you come to me?" (JB). If the reading and translation are correct, it may be a rhetorical way of expressing the wish, "Please, Lord, be with me."

The poem continues in verses 3–5 with claims of innocence. David resists any identification with evil deeds or wicked people. Not only is he pure, but he does not look with approval on sin (v. 3a), and he hates those who commit such things (v. 3b). The word "know" in verse 4, as in other places it occurs, has a very broad meaning. It includes cognizance, experience, intimate participation, and even love.

Verse 6 turns once more to the positive side of things. Whereas in verse 3 David would not set his eyes on anything base, in verse 6 he says he would set them on the faithful people of the land. From the end of verse 6 through verse 7 the psalm reads like the hiring policy at David's palace. Those who serve must walk in a perfect way, must not be deceitful or tell lies. In a broader sense, the entire nation was the household of the king. Perhaps this policy is a general outline of the judicial system in ancient Israel. This last observation is supported by verse 8, which expands the coverage of this justice to include the city of the LORD, Jerusalem, and the land, Israel. The expression "morning by morning" (ASV) points to the regular meeting sessions of the court.

The modern believer, of course, is not on David's throne, but he is responsible for applying these standards to his own life. Verse 3 warns us to keep only pure scenes before our eyes. Verse 5 states the fact that talking evil behind a neighbor's back is abhorrent to God. Verse 7 demands that we be absolutely honest. Verse 8 reminds us to examine our lives daily for sins and to destroy them before they destroy us.

Only as we meet these requirements and seek to conform our

lives to the tenets of Psalm 101 can we sing of God's loving-kindness and justice, and behave wisely in a perfect way (vv. 1–2).

PSALM 102

Psalm 102 divides easily into three parts: verses 1–11 record the believer's complaint, verses 12–22 contain praise to God for His mercy to Zion, and verses 23–28 meditate on the brevity of human life and the eternality of God.

The opening third of this psalm describes in as desperate terms as may be found anywhere the plight of the man who feels cursed by God. Affliction is not seen as punishment for sin or as chastening for righteousness' sake but, rather, is without a reason. Although the afflicted appeals to God's mercy, there is no hint of repentance.

After the initial two verses, which are a prayer for mercy, there follows a catalog of unpleasantries. In highly poetic style the author of this psalm describes his lack of appetite (v. 4), the quick passage of his brief years (vv. 3, 11), his malnutrition (v. 5), his loneliness (vv. 6–7), his abuse by enemies (v. 8), and his sadness (v. 9). The imagery is quite rich. Note for instance brevity of life compared to smoke (v. 3) and grass (v. 11), solitude compared to the habits of the pelican, owl, and sparrow (vv. 6–7), and food and drink compared to ashes and tears (v. 9).

The first and third sections of this psalm go well together with the focus on fast-approaching death. Compare verses 3 and 11 with verses 23 and 24. The middle section fits with the last section by emphasizing God's eternality. Notice verse 12 and verses 25–27.

Verses 12–22 are not so much a prayer for deliverance of Zion as an anticipation of that deliverance. This ancient poet is sure that just as God is eternal and sovereign so will He see to the preservation of His holy city. These verses are the only clue to the date of the work. Apparently Jerusalem is under siege, already destroyed, or its people are exiled.

The expression at the end of verse 13 is similar to Isaiah 61:2 (MLB), "The year of the LORD's favor." In due time, when He has all circumstances ready and at the most propitious moment, God will act. That time had arrived, according to verse 13, and so God's restoration of Zion will have the greatest apologetic value. Unbelieving nations and foreign powers will have to notice that there is a God who acts on behalf of His people. Those who have been destitute can use these blessed facts for their own encouragement, for the persuasion of outsiders, and for strengthening that heritage of faith for their descendants. The psalm builds almost to eschatological proportions at verse 22, where we see people of all races and languages, realms and ages, gathered to serve the King of kings.

The third part of the psalm, verses 23–28, is familiar because Hebrews 1:10–12 is a quotation of verses 25–27. Both here and in Hebrews the everlasting nature of the godhead is in view. Naturally, with the limited revelation available in Old Testament times, one thinks of God the Father in these verses, but the author of Hebrews ascribes them to God the Son, the Lord Jesus Christ. He participated in the creation (v. 25), He lives forever (v. 27), and He is unchangeable (v. 26). Together with John 1:3, verse 25 is one of the best for showing that Christ was active at the genesis of the world. This whole third section is spoken by a man aware of approaching death, but full of assurance in the everlasting God. Though his days are short and his strength failing, he knows God who is the opposite of all human frailty. Though we are like old garments and withering grass, our God is the Creator, the Sustainer, and the immutable Lord of heaven and earth.

PSALM 103

"Bless the LORD, O my soul" both begins and ends this well-known psalm. Other verses within it are familiar and beloved also. Verse 10 reads:

> He hath not dealt with us after our sins;
>> nor rewarded us according to our iniquities.

And verse 13:

> Like as a father pitieth his children,
>> so the LORD pitieth them that fear him.

Some people are confused by the word "bless." God blesses us and we are told to bless God. "How can we be God's benefactor?" they rightly ask. The answer is to be found in the broader meaning of the Hebrew word which lies behind the translation. It is correctly rendered by the word "bless," but it means both to get good things from God and to give good things back to God. One of the few things we are in any position to return to God is praise; hence in this psalm and elsewhere "bless" means "praise."

Even more interesting is the root from which the Hebrew word comes. The same root letters are in the noun "knee" and hence the related verb is "kneel." Ancient blessings between fathers and sons and between sovereigns and subjects were made with the latter kneeling at the knee of the former. Hence "to bless" may mean "to kneel" as well as "to bestow divine gifts."

This psalm does have evidence of plan in it. Not only the same words of injunction both open and close the psalm but there is a loose chiastic structure. Note the following proposed outline:

A Admonition to personal praise (vv. 1–5)
　　B God's being and doings (vv. 6–14)
　　　　C Man's being (vv. 15–16)
　　B′ God's being and doings (vv. 17–19)
A′ Admonition to universal praise (vv. 20–22)

The first section is composed of the admonition to praise the Lord *who* does such and such. There are five relative clauses which describe all the things God did and does, things which we ought not to forget. He forgives all our sin. This is our first and most desperate need in terms of His demands and our inability. He heals all our diseases. If we might spiritualize here, He cures us of the fatal cancer of sin. He redeems us from destruction. He saves us forever. He repossesses us from His enemy and the enemy of our souls. He crowns us with loving-kindness and tender mercy. Then He satisfies our desires with good things. By this time our desires are His desires and He delights so to bless us. Without these daily provisions our lives would be impossible.

The section on God's being and doings is an abbreviated list of God's attributes in poetic form. Verse 6 speaks of His justice, verse 8 of His mercy, verse 11 of His love, and verse 14 of His omniscience. In addition, verse 7 speaks of His revelation to Moses and the people of Israel.

This is a blessed psalm not only because of the admonition to "bless the LORD" at its beginning and end, but also because there is almost nothing of God's anger or punishment in it. It is for God's redeemed people, and its truths neither apply to the unregenerate nor may be appropriated by them. The second section on God's doings makes this distinction. Verse 17 indicates that His loving-kindness, His covenant love, is for those who fear and reverence Him. Man, though finite and temporal, may have a blessed, everlasting heritage through membership in God's family, "to such as keep his covenant, and to those that remember his commandments to do them" (v. 18).

The closing section exhorts the whole creation, heaven and earth, to praise God. His mighty angels, who have the privilege of seeing Him firsthand as well as we, the works of His hands, are enjoined to bless Him. Verses 20 and 21 are probably addressed to those heavenly creatures under the terms "angels," "hosts," and "ministers." Each reader, however, is under the same orders when he reads the last words of this blessed psalm: "Bless the LORD, O my soul."

PSALM 104

Psalm 104, like Psalm 103, begins and ends with the words, "Bless the LORD, O my soul." The outline of Psalm 104, however, is not as discernible as the one in the psalm which precedes it. These thirty-five verses constitute a majestic hymn of praise to God, especially for His creative and sustaining power.

In a very general way, the psalm follows the order of creation in Genesis. The light of Genesis 1:3 appears in verse 2. The cover of water and the subsequent appearance of the dry land (Gen. 1:2, 9) correspond to verses 6 and 7. The growth of the herbs and grass (Gen. 1:11–12) appears in verse 14, and the daily and monthly divisions of Genesis 1:14–18 receive mention in verse 20.

The New American Bible offers this broad outline for Psalm 104:

The marvels of atmosphere and sky (vv. 1–4)
of the dry land and ocean (vv. 5–9)
of the streams and fields that give drink and food to man, beast, and bird (vv. 10–18)

of the sun and moon with the activities of day and night
(vv. 19–23)
of the manifold life in the mighty sea (vv. 24–26)
The Lord governs and sustains all His creatures (vv. 27–30)
God's omnipotence and sanctity (vv. 31–35)

The language is very lofty and picturesque throughout. From the beginning this psalm illustrates the Hebrew penchant for describing concepts and relationships in concrete terms. Note in verse 1 how God is clothed with honor and majesty. In verse 2 He is dressed in light. According to verse 3, He rides on the clouds and walks on the wind.

Verse 4 is quoted in Hebrews 1:7, where the writer is arguing for the superiority of Christ over angels. "Angel" and "messenger" are alternate translations of the same Hebrew and Greek words. In Psalm 104 they are wind and fire, which serve God. In Hebrews, Christ is over them in the ranks of superhuman beings.

Job 38:9–11 somewhat parallels verses 5–7, especially as the waters are viewed as a garment for the earth and as God has set boundaries for the oceans.

From the cosmic descriptions of God's creative activity (vv. 1–9), the psalmist begins at verse 10 to examine the more mundane and everyday features of His providence. Not only is God responsible for seas, winds, and clouds, but He also provides food and drink for all animal life. A certain orderliness characterizes the earth, with all its natural processes moving like clockwork to the benefit of all. So trees are for birds (v. 17), mountains are for goats (v. 18), and all are to enjoy the grass and herb (v. 14) watered by rivers and springs (v. 10), which ultimately get their water from the sky, God's chambers (v. 13).

Verse 15 is a beautiful and well-known reference to the three basic crops of the ancient Palestinian: grapes, olives, and grain. These supplied his three basic commodities: wine, oil, and bread (cf. Deut. 24:19–21). Oil had several uses: for cooking, to make perfumed lotions, to combat skin dryness, as medicine, and to fuel lamps.

Just as in verses 17 and 18 certain animals lived in certain places, so in verses 20–22 different animals have special times to hunt and hide. Man too fits into this elaborate scheme by being a daytime worker (v. 23).

Verse 24 is a kind of doxology inserted at a point where the psalmist seems overwhelmed by the intricacies and magnificence of God's wise operations.

After two verses relating to activities in and on the seas, God's provision of food for all is once more emphasized (vv. 27–28). Just as God is in control of life, so death comes to all creatures (v. 29). This too is part of His sovereign design for the world.

The concluding five verses of the psalm read like a prayer with several jussives ("let" forms expressing mild commands). The worshiper wishes himself to be constantly and everlastingly praising God. As in Psalm 19:14, he prays that his thoughts, as well, might be sweet and hence acceptable to God (v. 34).

Only verse 35 has a negative note, although the ancient servant of God probably would not agree. God is glorified, he would protest, both by blessing the righteous and by cursing the wicked. Not to punish the sinner would be unjust. So, coupled with all the lovely thoughts of verses 31–35 is the imprecation against the enemies of God. But even in this the poet enjoins his soul once more to bless the Lord.

PSALM 105

Psalm 105 is like Psalm 78 in that they both recite the history of Israel. As Psalm 104 speaks of the history and operation of the creation, so Psalm 105 praises God for His faithfulness to the Abrahamic covenant in giving the Israelites the Promised Land. The story goes from the father of the faithful to the occupation of Canaan.

For purposes of study, the psalm's forty-five verses divide into several pericopes. Verses 1–6 are a general invitation to praise, indicating that perhaps this composition was for some festival. God's faithful keeping of the Abrahamic covenant is the theme of verses 7–11. Verses 12–15 briefly speak of the wanderings of the patriarchs. Then the life of Joseph is summarized (vv. 16–22). The next three verses capsulize the 400 years in Egypt. Verses 26–36 speak of Moses and the Egyptian plagues. Then the Exodus and the forty years of wanderings come into view (vv. 37–42). The final three verses summarize the whole poem and end on a note of praise to God for bringing His people into the Promised Land.

If the "praise the LORD" (Heb., *hallelujah*) at the end of Psalm 104 goes at the beginning of Psalm 105, as the Vulgate translation of the Old Testament indicates, then this psalm both begins and ends with the same words. (It would also make the opening and closing words of Psalm 104 match more perfectly.)

In 1 Chronicles 16:8–22 are found the first fifteen verses of Psalm 105. Other comparisons exist between verse 36 and Psalm 78:51; verse 39 and 78:14; and verse 40 and 78:24. A series of imperatives opens the psalm. Note the injunctions to give thanks, call, make known, sing, praise, talk, glory, rejoice, seek, and remember (vv. 1–5). This psalm especially emphasizes a note of remembrance. We are to remember (v. 5) that God has not forgotten His covenant

(v. 8). As the historical section begins with that idea, so it ends the same way. Verse 42 states once more that He remembered His holy word and Abraham His servant.

The essence of the promise is in verse 11: "Unto thee will I give the land of Canaan." Then the body of the psalm traces the events from Abraham, who first received that promise, to its fulfillment under Joshua (v. 44). The only major events left out are those connected with Mount Sinai and the giving of the Law. However, Moses and the Law do receive passing mention in verses 26 and 45.

As is the case elsewhere, even in the New Testament, the picture is drawn to show the people as weak and God as strong. So in verses 12–17, the people of Abraham are few and homeless. They are moved by hunger only to prove that it is God who sustains and protects them.

It is interesting that the patriarchs are called "anointed" ones and "prophets" in verse 15. Although they wrote no Bible books, they were, in their time, the chosen spokesmen for the living God.

Joseph receives unusual emphasis with details added, such as the chains of verse 18, which are not mentioned in the Genesis account. Again, note how the strength of God is made perfect through the weakness of man; in fact, God's righteousness overrules the wickedness of men.

The psalmist is committed to the sovereignty of God, as verse 25 indicates. It was not that the Egyptians merely turned against the Israelites, but God was responsible for this hatred toward His people. But remember the larger picture: God wanted to fulfill His promise and that could not be done as long as they were welcome and prosperous in Egypt.

The plagues listed in verses 28–36 are not in the same order as in the book of Exodus (chaps. 7–12). In fact, the murrain

(Ex. 9:3) and boils (Ex. 9:9) are not mentioned in Psalm 105, but rather the breaking down of vines and trees (v. 33), which is excluded from the Exodus account.

The many events of the wanderings are passed over quickly with only the pillars of fire and cloud (Ex. 13:21–22), quails (Ex. 16:13), manna (Ex. 16:14–16), and water from the rock (Ex. 17:1–7) receiving mention. These, of course, are the great positive things God did for them. The next psalm, 106, gives much more emphasis to the bad behavior of the Israelites, but this psalm underscores instead the fidelity of God.

An almost humorous note penetrates at verse 38 where the psalmist records that Egypt was glad to see Israel leave. The summary verses consummate the account and also give, as it were, a moral to the story. The deliverance itself, as well as the recounting of it, has a purpose. That purpose is to make God's people keep His statutes and laws. The whole duty of man is to obey and praise the Lord.

PSALM 106

With Psalm 106 the fourth book within the Psalter comes to a close. Verse 48 of the psalm is a kind of doxology or benediction very similar to the phrases that end the other divisions (cf. Pss. 41:13, 72:18–19, 89:52, and 150:6). Also note that a hallelujah opens and closes the psalm.

Praise, prayer, and confession are the categories into which this, another historical psalm, falls. By far the majority of verses recount the ingratitude, infidelity, and undependability of the Israelite forefathers. So, while the psalm coincides with the preceding ones, being replete with scriptural allusions and historical illustrations, the emphasis is on the depravity of God's people rather than on His covenant faithfulness.

The opening verse is the same as 1 Chronicles 16:34 and Psalm 107:1 and 136:1, and is similar to many other verses sprinkled throughout the Psalms. It introduces the first five verses which, with the last two, are the only ones outside the review of the calamitous disobediences of the ancient Hebrews.

Although verse 6 has the pronoun "we," the rest of the psalm talks about "them"—the fathers who left Egypt, rebelled all through the desert wanderings, and eventually reaped their harvest of faithlessness in the exile (v. 46).

The account begins with the actual Exodus from Egypt. And, just as Exodus 14:11–12 records, the people were rebellious even on the Egyptian shore of the Red Sea. At that early point they began questioning Moses directly and God indirectly. But God took away their doubts by the mighty miracle of the dried-up sea, which at the same time destroyed the enemy. Only after that did the redeemed believe God and praise Him (Ex. 15:1–21).

This order of events points up the basic carnality and infidelity of the people. They were the kind who would not believe unless they could see. They were the sort who could be convinced only by the most extravagant and obvious of miracles. They walked by sight and not by faith.

The episode alluded to in verses 13–15 is most likely the incident at the waters of Marah, which follows immediately after the songs of Moses and Miriam in Exodus 15. Again, note how quickly the Israelites forgot God's deliverance and started thinking of their own problems. As a result of their bitter complaint God "gave them their request; but sent leanness into their soul." This is a frightening indictment on these children of God who thought mainly of their comfort and never saw themselves as actors in God's drama of redemption. This is a very easy verse to apply to modern Western Christianity because in every community of believers there are satisfied bodies hosting starving souls; wealthy purses and impoverished hearts.

The events of Numbers 16 are the background of verses 16–18. Korah, Dathan, and Abiram arrogantly challenged the authority of Moses and Aaron and paid for their insolence with their lives.

But while in verse 16 Aaron is called a saint or holy one (a person "set apart" by and for God), referring to his office as high priest, he was the one mainly responsible for the golden calf, the next episode cited in Psalm 106 (vv. 19–23). Exodus 32 records the tragic turn of events which led the nation to the very brink of extinction. Only the intercession of Moses moved God to spare them.

When the twelve spies were sent to investigate Canaan (Num. 13), the people accepted the majority's pessimistic report and chose not to obey God and attack (Num. 14). That is the backdrop of verse 24.

Baal-peor (v. 28) was a Moabite deity which attracted worship from the Israelites, according to Numbers 25:3. Naturally, this syncretism angered the Lord and He was about to annihilate them when Phinehas, Aaron's grandson, intervened after 24,000 had died from the divinely sent plague.

Again the people angered God, this time at Meribah (vv. 32–33). Numbers 20:2–13 provides the details of this unfortunate act of unbelief on the part of the Israelites. The last example of little faith and disregard of God's will the psalmist chose is from Judges 1. Over and over in that chapter, one reads that this or that tribe did not drive out the inhabitants of the areas they were to possess. In addition, they intermarried and they adulterated their worship of Yahweh with idolatry. They even adopted the abominable practices of the heathen, such as child sacrifice (v. 38), which were outright transgressions of God's written Law. All this compounded the anger of God against them until ultimately He judged them with the Babylonian captivity (vv. 41–43).

Yet even in that most dreadful of punishments God was faithful to His covenant. According to verses 44 and 45, He heard their cry and reversed Himself, as His great mercy would demand.

Against this bleak background, the patient and enduring love of God shines clearly and brightly. And to that love the psalmist appeals when he prays in verse 47 (NASB), "Save us, O LORD our God, and gather us from among the nations."

God's people were little different in Babylon than they were in Egypt. And they are little different now than they were 3,000 years ago. They still question God at other Meribahs; they substitute new Baals; they fail to muster for His marching orders. But though we are like ancient Israel, God is as gracious and full of pity now as He was then. His ear is still open to the penitent's cry, and His hand is ready to help the feeble of knee. He is the God blessed from everlasting to everlasting. Amen and hallelujah!

PSALM 107

Book V within the Psalms begins with number 107. This division, however, marks no break in the style of the Psalms. Like the ones immediately preceding, Psalm 107 is a praise psalm probably written after the exile for one of the annual festivals. Verse 3 pictures devotees streaming in from all directions, while the balance of the psalm features various hardships brought on by the dispersion. From each affliction God delivers the faithful.

The opening three verses are a kind of introductory summons to praise. Then follow four stanzas, each dealing with a different kind of trouble. Verses 4–9 are about starving in the desert, verses 10–16 speak of imprisonment, verses 17–22 deal generally with sickness, and verses 23–32 describe the perils of sea travel. The last section, verses 33–43, constitutes a hymn of praise to God for His provisions which meet His people's needs.

Like Psalm 106:1 or 136:1, the opening words are typical of the Psalms. The word "covenant love," translated "mercy" (KJV, ANCHOR), "lovingkindness" (ASV), and "steadfast love" (RSV), also appears in the refrains of verses 8, 15, 21, 31, and 43, the concluding verse of the psalm. Verse 2 is often quoted as an encouragement to witness. That is precisely its meaning here as well. Those worshipers gathered from around the Mediterranean were invited to share their testimonies of God's mercy and redemption.

The first category of hardship was desert wandering accompanied by hunger and thirst. In view of the fact that hundreds of miles of trackless wasteland separate Palestine from Babylonia and Assyria, some exiles may have suffered these very things journeying either as captives or pilgrims from one land to the other. Verse 6, like verses 13, 19, and 28 in the other stanzas, records their cry to God for help. God heard that cry and spared them. Then verse 8, with its wish form of the verb, urges men to praise God for His love and wonders (cf. vv. 15, 21, 31). To that refrain is added the reason for praise. It relates directly to the deliverance. According to verse 9, men should praise God because He fills and satisfies the hungry.

The second category of hardship is incarceration. The "shadow of death" found here in verses 10 and 14 is the same as that in Psalm 23:4. This confinement may refer to the actual treatment of captives by the Babylonian and Assyrian soldiers. However, the psalmist gives a spiritual reason for this particular punishment. They brought on this affliction through their rebellion against God and their scorn for His words (v. 11). Again, they cry for help and God spares them. It is interesting to note that spiritual salvation is often described as release from prison. In this connection compare Isaiah 42:7; 61:1; Psalm 102:20; Luke 1:79; 4:18; 13:16; and 1 Peter 3:19.

Charles Wesley put it beautifully in his hymn, "And Can It Be That I Should Gain":

> Long my imprisoned spirit lay,
>> Fast bound in sin and nature's night;
> Thine eye diffused a quickening ray,
>> I woke, the dungeon flamed with light:
> My chains fell off, my heart was free,
>> I rose, went forth, and followed thee.

Verses 17 to 23 describe those with some debilitating disease which ruined their appetites. Healing for the malady is the "word" of God (v. 20). This may mean that God dispatched a specific order in response to their prayer, or that the Bible in general has the cure for the sin-sick soul.

"They that go down to the sea in ships" are the subjects of the last category (vv. 23–32). Throughout the Old Testament the Hebrews had little to do with the ocean. But though places such as Greece are connected by land to the Middle East, overland travel was virtually impossible because of international hostilities, lack of roads, danger of robbery, and general inconvenience. So God's people put to sea and exposed themselves to another set of difficulties and dangers. This, the longest of the four stanzas within this poem, describes a frightening, divinely sent storm and the resultant troubles for the sailors (vv. 25–27).

Once more the endangered prayed and once more the all merciful God heard and saved. This theme too has occasioned gospel songs and testimonies of salvation, for example, "Ship Ahoy!" "Let the Lower Lights Be Burning," and "Jesus, Savior, Pilot Me."

The hymn at the close of Psalm 107 makes use of a series of contrasts. Note in verse 33 that God replaces deserts with rivers. Then verse 34 has the opposite. But verse 35 reverses the figures once more. Verses 36–38 describe the fortunes of the blessed, while verses 41 and 42 again underscore the benefits which come to the upright.

Verse 43 is a general conclusion to the poem and an exhortation to weigh and consider the varieties of God's faithful covenant love.

PSALM 108

Except for minor variations, the entirety of Psalm 108 is found elsewhere. The first five verses are nearly identical to Psalm 57:7–11 and the last seven verses are almost the same as Psalm 60:5–12. It is impossible to say which verses were written first. More comments than those found here appear under Psalms 57 and 60.

The brief title, "A Song, a Psalm of David," introduces this psalm. Three psalms in a row, beginning with this one, have ascriptions to David. Both Psalms 57 and 60 were ascribed to him, but with longer titles giving the occasions for the compositions.

The smaller opening portion (vv. 1–5) is purely praise. The psalmist testifies to his determination to sing and praise. Because of the reference to musical instruments, he may be leading a small orchestra or accompanying himself.

The parallelism is used rather strictly in verses 3 to 5. Note the synonymous pairs: give thanks-sing praises; peoples-nations; mercy-truth; heavens-skies; O God-Your glory.

Though this appears as a composite psalm, the two parts fit together very well. The opening Hebrew word translated "that" in verse 6 is, in fact, a kind of conjunction to introduce a resultant clause.

The word for "beloved" is essentially the same as the proper name David. To what extent David might have reminded God of the meaning of his name is just a guess.

This latter section is more of a prayer for military victory than praise. The title and context of Psalm 60 makes this even clearer. Apparently Israel had lost a battle and the people blamed themselves for faithlessness. This section of Psalm 60 records God's words of threat against Israel's nearby foes. Actually, these words do not occur outside these two psalms. Gilead, Manasseh, and Ephraim all refer to the northern tribes, while Judah was the major tribe in the south. Moab and Edom were perennially hostile neighbors to the southeast, while Philistia constantly harassed Israel from the southwest.

Verses 11–13 are respectively complaint, prayer, and hope. To be cast off is to be abandoned to the enemy. If God should leave the army it cannot help but lose the battle, so the prayer is both a petition for help and a confession that no man can save. Although somewhat vengeful, the statement of faith in verse 13 speaks of profound conviction. The Jerusalem Bible paraphrase is worth noting: "With God among us, we shall fight like heroes."

PSALM 109

Psalm 109 illustrates the imprecatory psalms. Verses 6–19 are a series of curses invoked on an enemy. The opening five verses and the closing twelve frame this central section with the complaints, praises, and prayers of the psalmist.

One big question mark hangs over this psalm. Are the curses in verses 6–19 the words of David against his enemy or the words of the enemy against David? The first alternative is the more popular one. The translators of the Berkeley Bible even eliminate the option by adding the words "I pray" to verse 6. That way it certainly sounds like David's curse on his adversaries.

Several verses offer hints that the second alternative is correct. Verses 3 and 4 both mention the fact that the wicked have been accusing the righteous. So this may be the introduction to the long curse section. Also verse 20 mentions how the adversaries speak evil against the psalmist. Verse 28 has "Let them curse," which is exactly what they have been doing in the major part of the psalm.

If this latter interpretation is correct, then another problem is solved. The man of God is not as cruel, vengeful, and even caustic as it first appeared. These curses are not his words but his enemy's. The only imprecations coming directly from the God-fearer are the two relatively mild ones of verse 29. On the other hand, David and other Old Testament saints were not above heaping curses on their foes. Psalms 69, 137, and 143 all contain unabashed imprecations.

The entire psalm has overtones of a court scene. The plaintiff is the psalmist and gathered around to accuse him are false witnesses (v. 3), a corrupt jury (v. 5), and a judge open to bribery (vv. 6–7). Under those circumstances the righteous man has only one source of help: God. So the opening words of the psalm are a desperate prayer that God, the key Witness against the trumped-up charges, will speak up. Notice that one facet of the complaint is the assertion of personal innocence. And not only that, but while they hated, he loved; while they cursed, he prayed (vv. 4–5). Think of Jesus' words in Matthew 5:44, "Pray for them which despitefully use you."

The central portion of the psalm (vv. 6–19) contains some of the most vituperative, invective, and vitriolic vengeance found anywhere in Scripture. The word pictures are vivid and cruel. Verses 6 and 7 describe the legal process of accusation. The King James Version and the Anchor Bible both transliterate the Hebrew word for "accuser" into the proper name "Satan." The latter version reads in the first line, "Evil One," thus making it too a title for the enemy of all righteous men. The root for the word "accuse" (Heb., *satan*) occurs also in verses 4, 20, and 29 ("adversaries" in KJV and ASV).

The next curse is a wish for the adversaries' death (v. 8). The latter half of this verse, along with Psalm 69:25, is cited in Acts 1:20 in connection with Judas Iscariot's suicide. The consequences of such an early death would mean a widowed wife, fatherless children, and a destitute situation for all.

Verses 11 and 12 expand on that theme of financial stress which verse 10 introduced. The prayer is that the creditors will demand and extract in payment all his savings and that strangers will enjoy the things he worked for so long.

The maledictions of verses 12 and 13 continue even to the dead man's offspring (picking up the theme of vv. 9–10). He wishes for them, as well, to die so that there will be no memory of the cursed man after one brief generation. This evil wish shows something of how some ancient people thought of life after death. They believed that a man lives only in the minds of those who work at remembering him (cf. v. 15). It certainly is a sub-Christian view, but it is still maintained by many modern Jews, especially of the reformed movement.

Verses 14 and 15, on the other hand, envision a divine judgment after death. The curser prays that the man might also be charged with his parents' sins (cf. Num. 14:18).

The curse wishes break off at verse 16 for three verses in order to enumerate the reasons for the charges. This man, be he the psalmist's enemy in the usual interpretation, or the psalmist in the interpretation I favor, is charged rightly or wrongly with unkindness, cruelty, murder, and cursing. The imagery of verse 18 may relate to the water ordeal of Numbers 5:22.

The final verse in this section, 19, reverts to the jussive or wish form of the verb to wrap up the victim in the very curses with which he chose to clothe himself.

The third major part of the psalm begins with verse 20. No one questions that these words are the psalmist's and not a quotation of someone else. He and not the wicked accuser is more likely to appear to the Lord. So verse 20 is the transition from the imprecations to the complaints. Verse 21 is a prayer with typical "riders" on it to help make God feel His responsibility. This ancient saint tacks on the "for Your name's sake" argument (AMP) and the phrase "in the goodness of thy unfailing love" (NEB). What can God do but respond positively!

Protestations of helplessness fill verses 22 through 25. Count the first person pronouns there: I am weak. I am needy. I am like a shadow or a locust. My heart is sick. My knees are weak. My body is gaunt.

The words of this suffering servant in verse 25 find an echo in the crucifixion accounts of Matthew (27:39) and Mark (15:29). At that scene also men shook their heads at the accused.

Verse 28 might be a good thought to keep in mind when one is personally vilified. It predates considerably the words of Jesus in Matthew 5:44 and Luke 6:28 and the injunction of Paul in Romans 12:14. Our Lord said, "Bless them that curse you," and the apostle Paul said, "Bless, and curse not."

As noted above, verse 29 may be the only real imprecation from the mouth of the psalmist. By comparison with verses 6–19 it is kind, but notice that the same figure of a garment is used (cf. vv. 18–19).

The final two verses are praise and assertion. Just as Psalm 108 closed with an expressed confidence in the ultimate justice of God, so this one ends on a note of assurance that the virtuous will be acquitted and exonerated because of a just God who stands by the side of the accused. Observe how many of the terms in the opening verses are repeated at the close: mouth, praise, stand, right hand, and condemn. At the beginning it was a kind of kangaroo court, but in the end the Judge of all the earth effects justice.

PSALM 110

Psalm 110 is the most popular of the Messianic psalms. Quotations from it and allusions to it occur more than twenty times in the New Testament. This is remarkable in view of its seven brief verses. Jesus Himself used the first verse to prove His deity (Matt. 22:44; Mark 12:36; Luke 20:42–43). Peter cited it in Acts 2:34 when he preached at Pentecost, and the author of Hebrews quoted it at 1:13. In addition, the concept of Christ sitting at the right hand of God appears many times (Matt. 26:64; Mark 14:62; 16:19; Luke 22:69; Eph. 1:20; Col 3:1; Heb. 1:3; 8:1; 10:12; 12:2; and 1 Peter 3:22).

Also the idea of the enemies being a footstool occurs in 1 Corinthians 15:25; Ephesians 1:22; and Hebrews 10:13.

The Hebrews author quotes and refers to verse 4 as well. (See Heb. 5:6, 10; 6:20; 7:11, 15, 17, 21.) These inspired comments by Christ and the apostles should be adequate to guarantee the Messianic character of this psalm.

As to its structure, Psalm 110 also proves intriguing. There is a parallel between verses 1 and 5, 2 and 6, 3 and 7. Notice the words "right hand" in the first pair; the synonyms, "enemies," "nations," and "countries," in the second pair; and the ideas of moisture, "dew" and "brook," in the third pair (ASV).

Furthermore, note that verses 1 and 7 speak of opposites, "feet" and "head," while verses 3 and 5 both mention the day God goes to war. "Day of Your power" is in verse 3 and "day of His wrath" in verse 5 (NASB).

All this leaves the middle verse, 4, unconnected. This statement certainly is the apex of the psalm. While verse 1 may speak of the royal prerogatives of the Messiah, verse 4 states His priestly office and lineage.

Despite the usual English translations, the verb "said" in verse 1 really represents a much stronger action such as oracle or divine pronouncement (cf. JB and ANCHOR). Therefore, it balances well with the strong thought of verse 4a: "The LORD hath sworn, and will not repent."

Now let us examine the composition verse by verse. The title ascribes the psalm to David, and the words of Christ in Matthew 22:44 agree to this. The fact that David wrote it is part of the argument. How can the Messiah be merely David's son if David himself called Him "Lord"?

Most English versions note when God's proper Hebrew name is used by spelling LORD with all capital letters. The American Standard Version renders the name "Jehovah" and the Jerusalem Bible, "Yahweh." Unless this distinction is clear, verse 1 makes little sense. But here God the Father is addressing God the Son and granting Him the honored position on the right hand.

So far the poem could be a royal psalm, since David the king did enjoy certain privileges as God's favorite earthly monarch. The vowels in the Hebrew expression for "my lord," which the Jewish scribes put in, indicate a human title, but the inspired consonantal text would allow either human or divine.

Verse 2 speaks of the Lord delegating authority to the Son. From Zion, the poetic name for Jerusalem, Christ's rule will go out and ultimately bring even His enemies into submission. Philippians 2:10–11 comes to mind, that every knee shall bow to the name of Jesus and every tongue shall confess that Jesus Christ is Lord. This verse also echoes Psalm 2:9, which speaks of the Messiah's conquest of all unsubmissive powers.

The first half of verse 3 shows Christ's army ready and willing to fight on the chosen day. The Revised Standard Version, the Jerusalem Bible, and other versions, together with several Hebrew manuscripts use the phrase "on the holy mountains" instead of "in holy array" (ASV), or the like. The two words would be very similar in the original language. The holy mountains then would be the hills around Jerusalem, including Mount Zion.

Difficult indeed is the last half of verse 3. The words are all readable but the figure of speech is strange. The phrase may refer to the vigor and virility of the conquering Messiah. The high point of the psalm is verse 4. God the Father puts Himself under an irrevocable oath that the Messiah is indeed a Priest. He is not a Levitical priest but a Melchizedek Priest. In the Epistle to the Hebrews much is made of this unique analogy between Christ and the ancient king of Salem. Genesis 14 is the record on which this verse is based. After routing a Mesopotamian coalition, Abraham gave a tithe to this otherwise unknown king-priest, Melchizedek. The point of chapters 5 to 7 of the book of Hebrews is that Christ is of a superior, more ancient line of priests. As royalty He is from the tribe of Judah (Heb. 7:14), but as a priest He is not from the tribe of Levi (Heb. 7:11–13). Melchizedek preceded Levi just as Christ is a Priest distinct from and better than the Levites (Heb. 7:22–24).

Verse 5 begins the anticlimax in the second half of the chiastic outline of this psalm. Many of the elements in verses 5–7 reflect or echo words and ideas in the first half of David's composition. A minor problem exists in the opening line. The Berkeley and New American Standard Bibles solve it by reading the divine name (YHWH) "Lord" instead of the usual "Lord." The question is: Is this God the Father or the Son? If He is the Father how can He be at the right hand of the Son, since verse 1 showed it the other way around? If He is the Son, then there is a change of addressee. Up till now the "you" (or "thou") has referred to the Son, not the Father. The former explanation is preferable, that it is God the Father at the right hand of the Son (despite the logistics problem) helping Him win in the day of battle.

In verse 6 is a description of the judging-destroying process. Again, all the words are clear, but how to put them together has been a problem for all Bible students. A casual glance at several modern versions will show the different possibilities. Whatever the exact meaning is, the general thrust of the passage is Christ's victory over His foes.

If the interpretation of other verses has been in doubt, the last one certainly is obscure. All the Hebrew words appear to be intact, but to make sense of the picture or figure of speech is very hard. Since verse 7 has some structural connection with verse 3b, the phrases might refer to the victorious Hero refreshing Himself after the heat of the battle has passed.

Altogether this is a most fascinating, interesting, and important psalm. Though it is short and despite its difficulties, it deserves much study, especially because the New Testament writers used it so extensively to argue the case for the kingship and high priesthood of the Lord Jesus Christ.

PSALM 111

After the initial hallelujah (Hebrew for "Praise the LORD"), Psalm 111 is a perfect alphabetic acrostic. Each of the twenty-two lines (two in each verse except verses 9 and 10, which have three each) begins with the successive letter of the Hebrew alphabet. Some Bibles list these Hebrew letters at Psalm 119, the most outstanding of the acrostics in the Psalter. Other alphabetic acrostics are Psalms 9 and 10 together, 25, 34, 37, 112, and 145.

In addition to Psalms 111 and 119, several sections outside the book of Psalms also follow an acrostic pattern. They are Proverbs 31:10–31; Lamentations 1, 2, 3, and 4; and Nahum 1. Since there are twenty-two letters in the Hebrew alphabet, note how many of these passages have multiples of twenty-two in the number of their lines.

Psalms 111 and 112 represent the simplest system with just one line for each letter. Lamentations 4 has two lines for each letter, Lamentations 1, 2, and 3 have three lines for each letter, and Psalm 119 has eight lines for each letter.

It may be that the author of this psalm was so concerned with his alphabetic scheme that he did not work too hard on the contiguity of the whole. In general it is a praise psalm, but there are no specific references to people, places, or times, so the occasion for its composition is unknown. From a grammatical point of view the Hebrew word order is often unusual. The effort to fit the poem into the acrostic system has undoubtedly occasioned this.

The psalmist mostly speaks of praising God for His many benefits to His people. The only "I" is at verse 1. Otherwise all the attention is on what God has done.

The first adjectives are very general: the works of the Lord are great and desirable (v. 2). With verses 3 and 4 (RSV) more specific terms appear: honor, majesty, righteousness, grace, and mercy. Even more specificity comes with verse 5: God gives food and remembers His covenant. Although some commentators see this as a reference to the manna in the wilderness, it is an unusual word with the basic meaning of "victim" or "prey." Perhaps verse 5a is to be understood with verse 6b, so that the prey is the land of Canaan which God gave to Israel.

If there is any division to the psalm, it comes between verses

5 and 6. There are broad comparisons between the two halves of the work. Note the linking words "the congregation" and "his people" (vv. 1, 6); "the works of the LORD" and "the works of his hands" (vv. 2, 7); "forever" (vv. 3, 8); "his covenant" (vv. 5, 9); and "fear" (vv. 5, 10). The items for praise continue through the second half of the psalm in most general terms. Proverbs 1:7 and 9:10 reflect the opening line of verse 10: "The fear of the LORD is the beginning of wisdom."

PSALM 112

Like Psalm 111, Psalm 112 is an alphabetic acrostic. And like Psalm 111 it has its twenty-two lines in ten verses (the last two verses using the last six letters of the Hebrew alphabet). Both psalms begin with a hallelujah. For these reasons, plus many other similarities in vocabulary, most Bible students attribute these two poems to the same inspired, although anonymous, author.

Whereas Psalm 111 was a hymn of praise to God for His goodness, Psalm 112 speaks of the blessed way of life the godly man has. Several of the virtues attributed to God in Psalm 111 describe the righteous man in Psalm 112. Note righteousness (111:3; 112:3), grace and mercy (111:4; 112:4), and honor (111:3; 112:9).

There is also a connection between the last verse of Psalm 111 and the opening one of this psalm. Blessed is that man who fears the LORD because he has begun to be wise. Also note that idea in Psalm 111:5. The word "command" also ties 111:9 to 112:1.

With verse 1b we have an answer to the question: What does it mean to fear God? It means to delight to obey His commandments. The "commandments" are not limited to the famous ten or even to the legal portions of the Old Testament, but to all teaching about God. Psalm 119 is an extended treatment of the same theme.

Verse 2 begins a list of the benefits that accrue to such a good man. Most of the success is measured in rather materialistic terms, but the authors of the psalms did not have the teaching of Christ to guide them. They operated under the belief that the good are rewarded with money and health while the wicked suffer shame and sickness. We know that wealth can be counted in ways other than money and that blessings come in many unostentatious forms.

The miscellaneous thoughts continue, hitting on certain traits and characteristics of the good man. Like God, he is gracious, merciful, and righteous—three of the communicable attributes (v. 4b). The attitude of generosity comes up in both verses 5 and 9. Incidentally, Paul cites verse 9 in 2 Corinthians 9:9.

A good reputation, even after death, was a coveted thing. Verses 2 and 6 mention that. Note also that verses 3 and 9 end on the same theme.

Because this saintly believer fears the Lord (v. 1), he will not be afraid of bad news (v. 7) or have a fearful heart (v. 8). The exact meaning of verse 8b is uncertain. Most translations either add a word such as "his desire" (KJV, ASV, RSV) or strengthen the word "see" into "gloat over" (NEB) or "he looks with satisfaction on his adversaries" (NASB). The Berkeley Version, however, avoids both these solutions by simply reading: "He will be joyful and unafraid, while he looks upon his adversaries." Perhaps a comment is in order about the "horn" of verse 9. This meaningful word has a much broader sense than its usual connotation. It not only represents that bony growth on an animal's head which is occasionally made into a musical instrument, but in the Bible it also stands for strength (Dan. 8:3–9), fertility (Isa. 5:1), or supernatural office (Ex. 34:29).

The foes who were mentioned in verse 8 are the entire subject of verse 10. Because of their envy of God's blessing on the righteous, they grieve, curse themselves, and despair. The terms the psalmist chose, especially "gnash with his teeth," were probably common ways to express this almost neurotic surrender of hope. In order not to end up in that wretched psychological state, we need to revere the Lord and find joy in His Word.

PSALM 113

As part of the Jewish liturgy for Passover, Psalms 113–18 are sung. This may be the "hymn" that Jesus and His disciples sang after the Last Supper (Matt. 26:30). Notice that Psalm 113 both begins and ends with a hallelujah or "Praise the LORD." The Greek translation, however, which several modern versions follow, puts the latter hallelujah at the beginning of Psalm 114. This is also done in Psalms 115, 116, and 117 so that all the psalms in the group from 111 to 118, with the exception of 115, begin with hallelujah.

This brief hymn of praise divides neatly into three stanzas of three verses each. Excluding the hallelujahs, within each verse are two stichs. The first third of the poem speaks of the greatness of God's name. The second portion focuses on God's transcendence. And the third part stresses God's concern for affairs on earth.

Verse 1 is a general summons to God's people to praise Him. Then verse 2 speaks of the temporal extent of that praise, and verse 3 tells the geographical extent. God's name is blessed at all times and in all places. Notice the chiastic arrangement of verses 2 and 3. The first and the fourth elements are parallel and the two interior elements are parallel.

A May the LORD's name be blessed
   B From now to eternity
   B´ From east to west
A´ May the LORD's name be praised.

The middle group of verses affirms God's position above both the earth and the heavens. Everything is clear until verse 6, which can be translated several ways but with little variation in basic meaning. It may mean that God is so high above heaven and earth that He must stoop even to see them. Or it may say that this great God is, in fact, concerned with all the details of His creation, heaven and earth included. A glance at the translations will show how these different interpretations are worded.

The last three verses portray vividly the compassionate interest God has in the unfortunate. It is He who reverses fortunes, taking a man from the dung heap to the throne room. It is He who blesses otherwise barren women with babies. Because He is so lofty and because He is so near, praise the Lord.

PSALM 114

Included in Psalm 114 are a couple of the more picturesque figures of speech in the Hebrew Bible. No one can visualize the mountains and hills skipping about like rams and lambs, but such is the figure the psalmist chose to describe either the Sinai earthquake or the conquest of Canaan. The theme of Psalm 114 is God's deliverance of Israel out of Egypt and into the Promised Land. If the translation of the opening word is "after" rather than "when," the anachronism of verse 2 is eliminated. The very mention of Judah and Israel implies knowledge of the divided kingdom which existed from the death of Solomon (922 BC) to the Assyrian conquest of Samaria (722 BC). The Exodus from Egypt occurred several hundred years before Solomon.

Only one other problem attends this psalm. The last word of verse 1 is quite uncertain. Based on postbiblical Hebrew and other cognate languages, the interpretation has been "strange language." But the word may also be read as "strong" or "cruel." Compare

Isaiah 25:3 where the same words occur. Such a rereading does not affect the overall interpretation.

The four middle verses state some facts concerning the Exodus and then ask questions about those facts. The sea which looked and fled was, of course, the Red Sea. Exodus 14:21–22 records that event. The Jordan also turned back as the Israelites began their assault on the west bank. Joshua 3:14–16 records that event.

If the quaking of the mountains refers to the phenomena surrounding the giving of the Law on Sinai, it is chronologically out of order in this psalm. Others see it as a figurative way to describe the conquest of Canaan and, in particular, the miraculous overthrow of the walls of Jericho. The answer to the questions of verses 5 and 6 is the power of God, who works on behalf of His people.

Notice in verse 7, as elsewhere in this psalm, the use of staircase parallelism. The element "at the presence of God" is shared by both lines. But the first line begins with a verb, understood only in the second line. The second line modifies God's name to include Jacob. This longer title for God can be implied in the first line. So the lines are parallel, but each has something the other does not have and they balance. Verses 1 and 4 evidence the same feature.

The last of the Exodus miracles alluded to in this psalm is the water from the rock at Meribah (Ex. 17:6–7; Num. 20:11–13). Because of the strong emphasis this psalm puts on the Exodus, it is understandable why the Hebrews use it as part of the Passover ritual.

PSALM 115

The contrast between the living, creating God of Israel and the powerless, inanimate idols of the heathen is the subject of Psalm 115. Sections of the psalm sound liturgical. The repetitious series in verses 9–11 and 12 and 13 point in that direction.

The opening verse is a general introductory praise note. Two of

God's outstanding attributes, mercy and truth, are underscored. The first of these, especially, represents a whole series of virtues that "mercy" only begins to name. The Hebrew word also means loving-kindness, covenant love, steadfastness, integrity, fidelity, and promise keeping. A question comes from the mouths of the unbelieving Gentiles: Where is their God? Perhaps it was a real question. After all, there were no statues of Yahweh, the God of the Hebrews, and to this day no archaeological excavation has produced one. Those heathen, just like the ones today, had difficulty even imagining, much less worshiping, a God of spirit and truth.

Verse 3 gives the answer. God is in heaven, not in the shape of a statue. Then begins a mockery of the whole system of idolatry. Only Isaiah (44:9–20) is more pungent in his satire on images. Whereas the God of Israel does or makes whatever He pleases, these pagan gods are manmade (v. 4).

In verses 5–7 there is a list of inadequacies. Though the images appear to have all their faculties—mouths, eyes, ears, noses, hands, feet, and throats—all are inoperative. Nothing works. All is for show alone.

The first part of the psalm ends on the caustic indictment that idolaters will be just like the idols they worship, namely, dead.

With verse 9 begins a section that may have been sung antiphonally. It is quite possible that a soloist, perhaps a senior priest, sang the first half of each verse and that the choir sang the response: "He is their help and shield." "Shield" as a title for God goes back to Genesis 15:1 where God promised Abraham, "I am thy shield and thy exceeding great reward."

This group of three verses (9–11) is very similar to Psalm 135:19–20. Some think there were three distinct categories of worshipers corresponding to the three courtyards in the later temple of Herod: the priests (house of Aaron), the Jews at large (house of Israel), and the converts (you that fear the LORD). Note how the three categories of worshipers appear again in the three-fold benediction of verses 12 and 13.

From the central part of the psalm the focus turns once more to the character and attributes of God. He alone gives increase (v. 14). He made heaven and earth (v. 15). He receives no praise from dead men (v. 17).

Some sciolistic Bible students have singled out verse 16 as a condemnation of modern space travel. The verse speaks to God's sovereign, creative power, not to who belongs where. If they are correct and man has no right to the sky then, conversely, God has no right on earth, which is simply not true. Verse 17 reflects some of the pre-New Testament thinking regarding the afterlife. From the psalmist's limited perspective, death ends all participation at the sanctuary. Likewise, the ineffective service of idolaters to lifeless gods produces no praise from the true and living God.

Only the people who can sing this psalm are able to bless the Lord. And to that end they pledged themselves by averring their intentions in the closing verse of Psalm 115.

PSALM 116

In the Greek and Latin Bibles, Psalm 116 is counted as two psalms with the break after verse 9. Both halves are a testimony to God's faithfulness through a time of sickness. Note the similarity of verses 1–4 to verses 10–11. Then verses 5–9 and 12–19 are roughly parallel in their words of praise and promise.

Although the opening words may sound somewhat commercial, it is true that we cannot outdo God in love. We only love Him because He loved us first. His love to us is not prompted by our affection or obedience but by His own divine character. In particular, the author of this psalm is grateful to be alive. Over and over, this theme appears throughout the psalm. If verse 3 were in our idiom, it would be, "I was at death's door" rather than "the cords of death encompassed me."

The dire circumstances prompted a personal prayer for deliverance and health. Some Bible students see similarities between this prayer, and the one of King Hezekiah when he too was near death (Isa. 38:10–20).

Notice the figures of speech in the testimony of salvation (vv. 5–9). God delivered the psalmist's soul, perhaps saved his breath, spared his eyes from tears, and kept his feet from slipping. Then he picks up the idea of the feet to state in verse 9 that he will walk before the Lord in the land of the living.

As Hebrew poetry this psalm has some unusual forms, so the sense of the first line of verse 10 may be, "I believe and certainly will speak." By revocalizing the second verb, the Anchor Bible offers, "I remained faithful though I was pursued."

Verse 11 has the rather nasty remark that "all men are liars." Since this is the only time in the Bible the word in question occurs in this form, perhaps a milder sense is correct. The Revised Standard Version has "Men are all a vain hope," while Moffatt suggests, "All men are a failure."

The balance of the psalm is filled with promises of service and devotion. Only verse 15, a familiar one, interrupts the series. Here are some of the psalmist's "renderings" (v. 12) to the Lord for His benefits. He says in verse 13 that he will take the cup of salvation, a very beautiful picture in itself (cf. Ps. 23:5b). He will call on God's name (vv. 13, 17b). He will pay his vows (vv. 14, 18). He confesses his servant role (v. 16), and he will offer sacrifices of thanksgiving in the public courts of God's house in Jerusalem (vv. 14, 18, 19).

Now what does verse 15 mean? Often it is cited in connection with martyrs who die for their faith. Sometimes we hear it quoted at the funerals of faithful Christians, especially if they are elderly. The meaning of all the Hebrew words is clear, but the meaning of the entire verse is difficult. Can it mean that God is anxious to see His followers die? Or does He hate to see them die? How can death be described as precious? Most likely the real meaning lies close to all the suggestions in this paragraph. It is no small concern to God. He, like the apostle Paul and us, must have mixed feelings about the death of godly people (cf. Phil. 1:23). To die and be with God in person will be sheer bliss. To live and serve is privilege and duty. The verse simply underscores, from God's perspective, the importance of this event which ushers the saint from a life of sickness, servitude, and struggle to one of relief, release, and rejoicing. Is it not comforting to know that God is more concerned with our death than we are?

PSALM 117

As is commonly known, Psalm 117 is the shortest chapter in the Bible. Coincidentally, it comes two chapters before the longest, which is Psalm 119. Furthermore, it is the middle chapter of the Bible, with 594 chapters preceding it and 594 following. Cardinal Hugo de Sancto Caro divided the Bible into chapters in the year 1250, and we do not know if he planned it this way or not. Such a phenomenon certainly should not be used as a proof for inspiration or the like.

Psalm 117 is a summons to all nations to praise the Lord. Notice the chiasmus with the opening and closing words "Praise the LORD."

Two attributes are singled out—God's mercy and truth. Psalm 115:1 mentioned the same two characteristics of the Deity. The first one, in particular, is a rich word carrying the basic meaning of faithfulness to covenant promise. Each attribute is also modified with an adjective. His loving-kindness is great and His truth is everlasting. Hallelujah!

PSALM 118

Psalm 118 is a hymn of thanksgiving to the Lord for salvation. While a particular military victory may have occasioned its composition, the terms are very general and can refer to all sorts of divine deliverance, physical and spiritual. Several verses in the psalm are familiar because they appear in the New Testament. Matthew (21:42) and Mark (12:10–11) quote both verses 22 and 23, while Luke (20:17) and Peter (1 Peter 2:7) use only verse 22. Luke, in Acts 4:11, again alludes to the figure of the rejected stone.

All four evangelists cite verses 25–26 in their passion narratives. (See Matt. 21:9; 23:39; Mark 11:9–10; Luke 13:35; 19:38; John 12:13.) In addition, verses 6–7 appears in Hebrews 13:6. Some scholars see similarities between this psalm and the song of Moses in Exodus 15. Compare verses 14 and 28 with Exodus 15:2 and verses 15 and 16 with Exodus 15:6. Because of this, some date Psalm 118 early while others, noting the allusion to the temple (e.g., v. 26), date it later. Several obvious changes in subject matter divide the poem into several parts. Verses 1–4 constitute an invitation to praise. Next follow three sections (vv. 5–9, 10–12, 13–18) which speak of God's deliverance from trouble, hostilities, and death. Verses 19–29 read like a temple liturgy with at least two speakers. One is the priest who allows only the righteous to enter the temple. The other is the psalmist who himself enters and worships.

The use of repetition is quite remarkable throughout this psalm. The opening and closing verses are identical. The same refrain as in those two appears in verses 2, 3, and 4. Verses 6 and 7 open the same way. Except for the last words (in Hebrew) of verses

8 and 9, these two are identical. The last stichs of verses 10, 11, and 12 match, as well as the verbs in the first stichs. The expression "the right hand of the LORD" is used three times in verses 15 and 16. Both "gate" and "righteous" are in verses 19 and 20.

After the theme verse (1) which begins and ends the psalm, there is a threefold invitation to reflect God's mercy. The house of Israel, the house of Aaron, and those who fear the Lord represent the Jewish laity, the clergy, and the converts, respectively. Once more the most notable attribute receives the focus. The phrase "His mercy endures forever" occurs five times in this psalm but twenty-six times in Psalm 136. The Hebrew word is *ḥeseḏ* and the fullest meaning is "faithfulness to covenant promise." Since God promised love, mercy, and kindness, various translations use one or more of these for their interpretation of this very full term.

The nature of the trouble mentioned in verse 5 is unknown. Most likely it had to do with military confrontation, and the psalmist is speaking in the first person for the entire nation. Notice the contrast between the "tight spot" ("distress") and the "open space" in verse 5, a vivid way of expressing trouble and release. The next four verses are two pairs. Because the Lord is on the side of the righteous, they need not fear human enemies. Compare the remarks on Psalm 112:8 regarding the elliptical phrase at the end of verse 7.

It is not bad or wrong to trust men; it is just better to trust the Lord. People fail. Governments wane. Weapons prove inadequate. But God never fails.

The verb "cut down" or "cut off" appears three times in verses 10–12 (see RSV). Everywhere but here and in Psalms 90:6 and 58:7 it means circumcise. However, the form of the verb is unique to these three verses.

Some Bible translators avoid the question of the addressee in verse 13 by choosing not to read the Hebrew but some other ancient version. It cannot be God who tries to trip up the believer. He is mentioned in the third person in the same verse. Perhaps it is death personified (cf. v. 18). Whoever that enemy was, God proved Himself the strong Savior.

The voice of rejoicing sings three tributes to the right hand of God (vv. 15–16). As with us, the right hand is the position and sign of favor and blessing (cf. Ps. 110:1). Rodin the sculptor did the hand of God—it is a right hand. He also carved the hand of Satan—it is a left hand. When Rembrandt painted Jeremiah bemoaning the destruction of Jerusalem, only the prophet's left hand and foot appear—a symbol of the unhappy, unfortunate, inauspicious events of the exile.

Verses 19 and 20 read like a conversation at the temple gate. First the worshiper asks entrance. Then the gatekeeper cites the qualifications for entrance (cf. Ps. 15).

The circumstances which prompted verse 22 are uncertain. It is possible there was a prominent stone rejected by the masons that eventually became the cornerstone. In any event, the New Testament writers apply this to Christ, who indeed was rejected by many only to become the cornerstone of the church (cf. Eph. 2:20).

Likewise, the occasion behind verses 25 and 26 is not known. Perhaps these verses were sung in connection with pilgrims making their way to the annual festivals in Jerusalem. The Hebrew words for "save now" are approximately *hosanna*. We know, of course, that the most significant Person to make His way to the temple was the Lord Jesus Christ, the Messiah Himself.

Many Bible students continue to have the Messiah in mind as they read verse 27. Hence they see Christ, the Lamb of God, as the sacrifice bound to the horns of the altar.

The psalm ends with notes of praise, thanksgiving, and exaltation.

PSALM 119

Psalm 119 is outstanding in several ways. It is the longest psalm and the longest chapter in the Bible. Its 176 verses are almost double the next longest chapter, Numbers 7 with its eighty-nine verses. Psalm 119 is two chapters away from the middle chapter of the Bible, Psalm 117.

The 176 verses are divided into twenty-two groups or stanzas of eight verses. Each of the eight verses within a stanza begins with the same letter of the Hebrew alphabet. In this way each of those twenty-two letters begins eight consecutive verses. The letters are in alphabetical order. Some editions of the English Bible have the Hebrew letters printed, others have the name of the letter written out at the head of each stanza. Hence verses 1–8 all begin with *aleph,* verses 9–16 with *beth,* verses 17–24 with *gimel,* and so on to the end of the psalm.

Of the 176 verses, 114 are found completely or in part in one of the Dead Sea Scrolls. This helps in those few places where there are textual problems.

The psalm is a magnificent hymn of praise about God's Word. Synonyms for the Bible appear in every verse except verse 122. (Four other verses, 84, 90, 121, and 132, are questionable.) But several verses have two epithets for Scripture, for example, 43, 48, and 160. Some of these terms are: law, testimony, way, precept, statute, command, ordinance, and word.

Although no New Testament author quotes from Psalm 119 (with the possible exception of verse 139 in John 2:17, but cf. Ps. 69:9), several of its verses are very familiar, even from childhood. Verse 9 is:

How shall a young man cleanse his way?
By taking heed . . . to thy word.

Verse 11 has:

> Thy word have I hid in mine heart,
> That I might not sin against thee.

And verse 105 (NASB) reads:

> Your word is a lamp to my feet,
> And a light to my path.

Naturally, with the main focus on the Word of God, there are many affirmations about its truthfulness, its endurance, and its benefactions. Verse 89 stresses its immutability:

> For ever, O LORD,
> Thy word is settled in heaven.

Verse 160 (ASV) underscores its veracity and eternality:

> The sum of thy word is truth;
> And every one of thy righteous ordinances endureth forever.

Verses 99 and 165 record its advantages:

> I have more understanding than all my teachers.
> Great peace have they which love thy law.

Scholars debate whether or not there is any overall outline to the psalm. Some see a more or less miscellaneous collection of ideas focused on the characteristics of the Law of the Lord and the psalmist's attitude toward it. It is wisdom literature akin to the Proverbs. Others struggle to outline the poem and fit titles to each group of eight verses. This latter approach is unconvincing.

There are ten synonyms for the Word of God. This has prompted some Bible students to match them up with the Ten Commandments. Others count only eight different terms and assume that the writer wanted to use each one but once in each stanza. This obviously was not the case, and to make it work would require severe emendation.

A number of verses hint that the author was the victim of either some disease (e.g., vv. 25, 50, 75, 83, 143) or of some persecution (e.g., vv. 53, 61, 69–71, 78, 141). The prayer "quicken me" occurs over and over (e.g., vv. 25, 40, 88, 107, 149, 154, 159). This too may show the bad health or the dangerous situation of the psalm's author. Otherwise, clues to who wrote it are unavailable. Some say he was old and near death because of the other reasons, while others say he was a young man because of such statements as: "I have more understanding than all my teachers" (v. 99), or "I understand more than the aged" (v. 100 ASV).

One thing is certain, the author loves the Word of God. In fact, one of his verses that has been put to music is 97:

O how love I thy law!
it is my meditation all the day.

Verse 11, cited above, is also a well-known gospel song.

Rather than proceed through the psalm verse by verse, this study focuses on the different titles for God's Word.

1. Law. This is the Hebrew word *torah*. Basically the meaning is "that which is given out," hence, taught. It refers not merely to the Decalogue or to the Pentateuch but to the entire corpus of information God has given. It occurs in verse 1 and in twenty-four other places in Psalm 119.

2. Testimonies. This word refers to God's statement about Himself and the world in general. The term describes the ark of the covenant in the tabernacle and later in the temple, and the tablets of the Ten Commandments kept in the ark. Overtones of the legal system are here as well as in the other synonyms. His testimonies are His record of the things He knows to be true. Variations of the root appear in verse 2 and in twenty-two other places in the psalm.

3. "Way" translates two different Hebrew words. The one used in verses 3, 14, 27, 30, 32, 33, and 37 is the usual word. It means everything from a path to a highway.

4. The second word for "way" is behind the translation in verse 15. It comes up several other times but not as a synonym of Scripture.

5. Of the twenty-four occurrences of the word "precepts" in the Bible, twenty-one are in Psalm 119. This is a suitable translation, the only other good option being "charge."

6. In verse 5, and twenty other times, we read the word "statutes." This term has the force of an inscribed royal decree. In the Pentateuch it is often coupled with one of the other words in this list, usually "commandment." As in our legal system, it is a more particularized legal requirement rather than a broad statement demanding good behavior.

7. "Command" or "commandment" occurs twenty-two times in the psalm. Even though this is the number of stanzas, its appearances are not distributed one to each stanza. This Hebrew word is widely known in English as the second element in the expression Bar Mitzvah, literally "son of a command," meaning a boy now old enough to be responsible. Interestingly, this word does not describe the Decalogue in Hebrew. They are called the "ten words" (Ex. 34:28; Deut. 4:13; 10:4).

8. "Judgments" (usually KJV), or "ordinances" (usually ASV, RSV,

and others), or "rulings" (usually JB), appears nineteen times in Psalm 119. As the various alternatives indicate, the word does not necessarily imply a judicial verdict of guilty. As well, it might mean exoneration or acquittal. A judge in ancient Israel was a leader, often charismatic and military, who, among many other things, adjudicated disputes.

9. The most common term for "word" in Hebrew is *dabar*. With its cognates (e.g., the verbal form *speak*), it is the most frequently used word in the language. In Psalm 119 it is used twenty-two times (but again, not evenly distributed). Both the singular and the plural occur. Once (v. 43) it is in the construction, "word of truth."

10. A less frequent term translated "word" or "promise" occurs nineteen times in this psalm. These represent over half the total in the Old Testament. It is related to a very common verb (*say*) and may have in it the idea of the spoken word.

Just as a reading of Psalm 119 may seem endless, so our praise for God and His Word should be endless. From a New Testament perspective the Word is also the incarnate Christ. To read this psalm with the Lord Jesus in mind, or even to use His name in place of the various names for the Bible, makes a very rich devotional experience. Verse 162 is a random example of this exercise. It also brings to mind the parable of the pearl of great price (Matt. 13:45–46).

> I rejoice in the Lord Jesus Christ
> As one that finds great spoil.

Another would be verse 173:

> Let Your hand be ready to help me
> Because I have chosen Jesus Christ.

Try it!

PSALM 120

Psalms 120 through 134 all have the title "a song of ascents" or degrees. Most Bible students connect this term with the ascent to Jerusalem for the annual festivals: Passover, Pentecost, and the Feast of Tabernacles. The pilgrims sang these psalms as they went (Ex. 23:14; Deut. 16:16; Luke 2:41–42). Jerusalem is on a hill, but by no means a high one. In fact, the adjacent Mount of Olives raises one hundred feet higher than the holy city itself. But because of its religious significance, Jerusalem is the highest mountain in the world.

Less popular suggestions concerning the "song of ascents" include one that has to do with a certain staircase in the temple. It had fifteen steps corresponding to these fifteen psalms. Yet another theory is that these psalms evidence frequent concatenation in which a word or a phrase connects or links pairs of verses so that the psalms proceed by stages or degrees. For example, in Psalm 120 the Lord's name is in verses 1 and 2. The words "deceitful tongue" link verses 2 and 3. The English word "dwell" connects verse 5 to 6 (although two Hebrew words are here). And "peace" occurs in both verses 6 and 7. Some of the psalms are completely concatenated. See the comments on Psalm 123 for a fine example of this.

Psalm 120 is not particularly joyous. Rather, it is a kind of lament. The psalmist is complaining about those who say false and destructive things about him. Verse 1, however, does record the fact of an answered prayer, but that is the only positive verse of the seven in this brief poem. It reflects the common propensity of people to pray only in time of trouble. It is not bad to do that—unless that is the only time we do it.

Verse 2 is either a record of that prayer or a new one for a similar problem. In particular, the psalmist wishes for deliverance from those who deceive and lie. Although it might be a prayer that his own lips be pure, this is unlikely in view of verse 6.

Verse 3 is a rhetorical question answered in verse 4. The cure of hot coals for an impure tongue is similar to the episode in Isaiah 6. There a seraph cauterized the prophet's lips with a coal from off the altar.

The psalmist laments the fact that he lives among barbarians and pagans exemplified by Meshech and Kedar. The former is a place of uncertain location to the north and west. Kedar is a tribe living in the deserts to the south and east. The reference to these faraway places strengthens the assumption that this psalm is a pilgrim's song. The next two verses expand the complaint that he lives with inhospitable neighbors. "Peace" is the best translation for *shalom*, especially in contrast to the word "war'" which ends the psalm. Nevertheless, we must still bear in mind the rich, comprehensive meaning of that term. In addition to cessation of hostilities it means health, wealth, happiness, and a right relationship with God.

The question to the modern believer is this: When they speak of war, do we speak of peace?

PSALM 121

Two poetical versions of Psalm 121 appear in the Scottish Metrical Psalter (1650), but I prefer the paraphrase and expansion which John, Duke of Argyll, made in 1909.

Unto the hills around do I lift up
  My longing eyes:
O whence for me shall my salvation come,
  From whence arise?

From God the Lord doth come my certain aid,
    From God the Lord, who heav'n and earth hath made.

He will not suffer that thy foot be moved:
    Safe shalt thou be.
No careless slumber shall his eyelids close,
    Who keepeth thee.
Behold our God, the Lord, he slumb'reth ne'er
    Who keepeth Israel in his holy care.

Jehovah is himself thy Keeper true,
    Thy changeless Shade;
Jehovah thy Defense on thy right hand
    Himself hath made.
And thee no sun by day shall ever smite;
    No moon shall harm thee in the silent night.

From ev'ry evil shall he keep thy soul,
    From ev'ry sin:
Jehovah shall preserve thy going out,
    Thy coming in.
Above thee watching, he whom we adore
    Shall keep thee henceforth, yea, for evermore.

Of the twenty different translations of the Old Testament in my library, only Luther's German edition and the King James Version do not interpret the second half of verse 1 as a question. They read the word "whence" as a relative pronoun (German, *von welehen*). Kenneth Taylor departs most drastically from a straightforward translation with the Living Bible paraphrase: "Shall I look to the mountain gods for help?" Basically, I agree with the interpretation. The psalmist in verses 1 and 2 is asserting his confidence in the Lord who created heaven and earth, including the mountains. Help does not come from the mountains but from their Creator. Canaanites and other pagans looked to the high places for spiritual strength. Our eyes must be lifted yet higher. While the Rockies and other mountain ranges can give inspiration, and though God's hand is more obvious in spectacular landscapes, they are still only the creation and not the Creator.

The theme of God's sustenance continues through this psalm. Note the six occurrences of the word "keep" in verses 3–8 (ASV). Ours is the ever-wakeful God (v. 4). Unlike Baal whom Elijah accused of sleeping (1 Kings 18:27), the Watcher over Israel never indulges in the rest that humans require.

To people living in an arid climate, the sun is a real enemy. It burns their skin. It parches their throats. It dries up their water holes. It makes midday work unbearable. For that reason God is called a shade (v. 5) so that the sun does not strike by day (v. 6). Compare Psalm 17:8; 91:1; Isaiah 25:4; 49:10; and Jonah 4:8 for this idea.

The moon parallels the sun. In general the moon was friendlier and some ancient people deified it. But others feared it too and connected the moon with lunacy. Again Psalm 91:5–6 complements this passage. God's care is ever with us protecting us night and day, through heat and cold, from enemies human and natural.

Verses 7 and 8 expand even further the idea of God's keeping power. "Soul" in verse 7 can be understood theologically, or physically in the sense of life, or both. God preserves, spares, keeps alive, and gives longevity to those He loves. The eternal dimension comes up in verse 8. God will keep the believer now and for eternity. The "coming in" and "going out" encompass all our actions. It is an aphoristic way of describing everything we do. Deuteronomy 28:6; 31:2; Joshua 14:11; and 2 Samuel 3:25

all contain a similar statement. It is even possible to read into these words notions of the cradle and the grave. God is with us when we are born and when we die. At the death of the believer the "evermore" begins.

PSALM 122

Better than any of the other pilgrimage songs (Pss. 120–134), Psalm 122 fits that category. The opening verses clearly state that those who sing this psalm are on their way to the Jerusalem temple.

The title contains the name of David (as do Pss. 124, 131, and 133 in this group). Coincidentally, David's name is in verse 5. These titles may indicate that David wrote it, that it was written for him, about him, or in his style.

As the psalms before and after it, Psalm 122 evidences staircase parallelism. "House of the LORD" and "thy gates, O Jerusalem" are synonyms. The name Jerusalem itself links verses 2 and 3. The same Hebrew word is behind the "whither" (or "to which," RSV) and the "there" in verses 4 and 5. "Thrones" appears twice in verse 5. The "peace" and "prosperity" of verse 6 echo in verse 7. "Peace" appears a third time in verse 8. The term "for the sake of" (ASV) connects the last two verses.

The psalm fits the pilgrim (or modern tourist!) who finds himself at the gate of the holy city about to ascend the final steps to his goal, the temple of God itself. Every Christian feels a surge of excitement and hears his heart beat a little faster as he first glimpses the city of God, Jerusalem the golden. The modern city is hardly "compacted together." It suffers from urban sprawl. But the ancient city, and to a certain extent the present walled, old city of Jerusalem, fit this description. It was not and still is not a large city in size, but in importance it is the navel of the earth, the center of the world. Here Abraham built an altar; here Solomon erected the temple; here the Son of God met and conquered death.

Most specifically verse 4 speaks of it as the focus of pilgrimages. This is the place, as Moses said many times in Deuteronomy, where God would choose to make His name dwell (see especially Deut. 12, 14, 16, 17).

Exactly what "thrones of judgment" are is uncertain. Perhaps the pilgrims would bring cases for adjudication when they came to Jerusalem.

The command to pray for the peace of Jerusalem is as pertinent today as it was then, maybe more so. The Christian knows, however, that no enduring peace will come apart from the Prince of Peace who lived, died, and rose there so many years ago. Though the common Israeli greeting is *shalom* (peace), and though the meaning of the word Islam is "submission," neither the Jews nor the Muslims enjoy the other's intentions.

Jerusalem means "city of peace," and that fact may be behind the repetition of the word "shalom" in verses 6–8. The pilgrim could be representing others at the temple, as the first half of verse 8 implies. Or it may mean that he is praying for his relatives and friends who live in Jerusalem all the time.

One of the countless benefits of Christianity is that God can be found anywhere. He is no longer localized in a building on a hill in the Middle East. Holy Land tours convey no religious merit, but prayer for Jerusalem's peace still avails.

PSALM 123

As noted previously, Psalm 123 is a fine example of concatenation. Each verse is connected with what precedes and follows it by at least one linking word. Notice the word "eyes" once in verse 1 and three times in verse 2. The prayer "have mercy" connects the end of verse 2 with verse 3, where it occurs twice. The phrase "filled with contempt" is repeated in both verses 3 and 4.

The beginning of this psalm is like Psalm 121: "I will lift up my eyes." In the latter the psalmist states, in effect, "I will not look to the hills for my strength but to the Lord." In Psalm 123 he is more straightforward.

Verse 2 has in it two illustrations: a servant looking to his master, and a maid looking to her mistress. In such a devoted and servile way the believer looks to his Lord. The idea of servitude continues into the New Testament, but the new covenant brings a new relationship between God and His child. His status is elevated, and although he is still a servant, he is also a brother of Christ and a joint heir with Him. After the confession of devotion and allegiance in the first two verses, the actual prayer of the psalm comes in verse 3, with a complaint in verse 4. The psalmist repeats his plea, "have mercy," and the area in which he needs pity is that of persecution. Apparently he is the object of scorn and is weary of the abuse that proud and lazy men have heaped upon him. The plaintiff began in verse 1 in the singular, "I," but from verse 2 on the petitioners are plural, "we." Such general terms as characterize these verses make it impossible to know with any assurance when the psalm was written. One theory is that it comes from the time of Nehemiah when the repairers of the temple were harassed by outsiders.

It is preferable not to try to pinpoint the situation which prompted the psalm, but to apply the Scriptures to the innumerable trials God knew His children would face. The more imprecise the problem is, the more widely applicable is the prayer of verse 3. So whatever form the persecution of the believer takes, this psalm can serve as a model for prayer.

PSALM 124

Psalm 124 is basically a hymn praising God for deliverance. Although the enemies are human, the circumstances are illustrated by near drowning and escape from a bird trap.

Verse 1 is the introduction. Verses 2–5 describe the first harrowing experience, while verses 6–8 spell out the second. Both stanzas include benedictions or phrases of praise.

Both Psalm 124:1 and Psalm 129:1 (ASV) include the little liturgical instruction, "Let Israel now say." This phrase may reflect the way the psalm was used. Very likely the leader, a musically inclined Levite, would deacon or line out the psalm. Only the first verse shows this, but we understand the procedure would continue to the end. Lack of copies or the illiteracy of the people necessitated this.

The entire first stanza is worded in such a way that it is dependent on the opening statement, "If it had not been. . . ." Starting as it does with a kind of negative, the situation is described as if it really did happen. Of course, it did not because, as a matter of fact, God *was* on their side. The water did *not* overwhelm them.

As in the preceding psalm, the specifics of the persecution are unknown. But the effort of evil men to "swallow" the good is similar to the water swallowing a man. The Hebrews were neither swimmers nor seafarers. Few people in ancient times knew how to swim or desired to learn. In fact, the word "swim" occurs only three times in the Old Testament, in Psalm 6:6; Isaiah 25:11; and Ezekiel 47:5. Deep water was a frightening thing to most Hebrews.

In a few places in the Bible the word "soul" carries the meaning of breath, throat, or neck. Verses 4b and 5 may be one of those places. If one goes under water much deeper than the *neck* he cannot *breathe.* That very physical meaning of the word "soul" is quite likely meant here.

289

"Neck" also may be the meaning in verse 7 where "soul" is the usual translation. Some of the several varieties of bird traps undoubtedly caught the bird by the neck. On the other hand, "soul" sometimes refers simply to the person himself. The word is, after all, parallel to "we" in verse 7.

In any event, the psalmist, speaking for all who sing this hymn, escaped both drowning and capture. There is no reason to think that the enemy actually put out nets or other gadgetry to trap the righteous. Rather, the snares illustrate the sneaky, deceptive, and usually cruel methods that wicked men use.

Because of God, the trap did not work, and the intended victims, the believers, escaped. So a benediction closes the hymn. The exalted phrase "who made heaven and earth" is contained also in Psalm 121:2. Though injustices, abuses, and narrow escapes characterize this life, God is still aware, concerned, and in complete control.

PSALM 125

Psalm 125 is a confession of trust in the Lord and a prayer for His blessing on the righteous. However, the wicked are the subject of verses 3 and 5.

Typical of the psalms of ascent, this one speaks in exalted terms of the city of Jerusalem. Zion or Mount Zion is the poetic term for the capital city. Mostly it occurs in the psalms and usually in passages which focus on its spiritual role in the nation. The original Mount Zion, or the city of David, today lies south of the temple area outside the walled city. Its rock base is overgrown with weeds or covered by ramshackle dwellings. What today is generally called Mount Zion, the western hill immediately south of the walled city between the Tyropean and Hinnom valleys, is somewhat of a misnomer. Scholars trace the error back to Josephus, the first-century historian who, like many of us, found it hard to believe that the lesser of the two shoulders extending south was indeed the original city.

The mountain or ridge has not moved, and that is what the psalm is saying. Furthermore, the verse states that those who trust God are as unmovable as that rocky slope.

The analogy in verse 2 compares God's protection to the surrounding mountains. This is geographically accurate, since Jerusalem is located in the middle of the hill country and every horizon is punctuated by peaks. Such mountains illustrate protection. In olden times when soldiers moved only on foot there was hardly a more formidable barrier than a mountain range. Psychologically, too, mountains are beneficial. People in the mountainous areas of the United States remark that the mountains remind them constantly of their smallness and of God's greatness.

Verse 3 is somewhat difficult to understand. It is not a prayer but a statement that wickedness will not rule. Of course, it is God's protection which stems the tide of wickedness and its resultant apostasy.

In its strict division of people into two groups, Psalm 125 is reminiscent of Psalm 1. The good will inherit good things, while the crooked merit condemnation. The word for "crooked ways" in verse 5 appears only one other time in the Bible, in Judges 5:6, where it seems to mean "back roads," perhaps "detours" in the sense of "devious paths." A cognate word in Isaiah 27:1 describes a snake.

The psalm ends, as does Psalm 128, with the simple benediction, "Peace [Shalom] to Israel!" (JB).

PSALM 126

The opening verse of Psalm 126 points to its postexilic origin. The captives had dreamed so long of returning that when it happened they could hardly believe it. In Hebrew there is a play on words. The sounds of "return" and "captives" are very similar. Some translations read "fortune" for "captive" in both verses 1 and 4, but this is a matter of interpretation and not of reading a different Hebrew word (cf. RSV, NEB, AMPC).

Certain words link the psalm into an ABC, ABC pattern. Verses 1 and 4 both speak of the Lord bringing back the captives. The former is in a temporal clause; the latter is imperative. Verses 2 and 5 both have the same Hebrew word for "joy" or "singing." And verses 3 and 6 also mention "joy," though it is translated from different Hebrew words. Note again the choice of the name Zion rather than Jerusalem. It denotes the spiritual capital of the world and the singular place of God's abode.

The first half of verse 2 is a nice parallel. The verb "filled" does double duty, carrying over from the first to the second stich. "Mouth" parallels "tongue," and "laughter" parallels "singing."

Just as in Deuteronomy 29:24–28 the nations remarked on God's punishment, so in Psalm 126:2b they noted the great things God had done for His people (cf. Ezek. 36:36). The psalm turns from a hymn of thanksgiving to a prayer at verse 4, with a plea for restoration. The rivers of the south (Negev) are empty most of the time. The Arabic word for this is *wadi,* the Spanish word is *arroyo,* and the American word is *dry gulch* or *wash.* Those few times a year when the rain falls, it falls abundantly, and the gulleys become rushing torrents. That is what is behind this prayer. The people beseech God for His overflowing blessing.

Verses 5 and 6 are a pair, with the latter an expansion of the former. The King James Version is the only translation with the word "precious" in connection with seed in verse 6. Most have "seed for sowing" or the like. But three modern translations have opted for "bag" or "pouch of seed" (NEB, NASB, ANCHOR). It is not too critical a question. The point still remains: investment is often painful, while rewards are always welcome. Every farmer must calculate how much he can spare to sow against how much he hopes to reap. With God's blessing, a plenteous harvest is certain. Verses 5 and 6 supply encouragement to evangelists. The weeping, the pleading, the intercessory prayer for the lost must precede the harvest of souls that every obedient Christian wishes to see. Jesus Himself compared sowing and reaping to the work of spreading the faith in His parable of the sower (Matt. 13). To the sower, there is a measure of risk, even loss, in the effort to strike that propitious combination of soil, seed, climate, and care which produce enduring and abundant fruit.

PSALM 127

Of the psalms of ascent only 127 is ascribed to Solomon. The explanation for this is not easy, although some see a connection between him and the word "beloved" in verse 2. That word fills the Song of Solomon. Others see Solomon as the father of many children *par excellence.* With 700 wives and 300 concubines, his family must have been enormous!

There seem to be two parts to this little poem. The first two verses spell out the fact that without God's aid, man's work is useless. The second half focuses on children as assets and the gifts of God.

The psalm opens with the well-known statements about God's necessary participation in any successful human endeavor. The Hebrew word for "house" could mean several things. The plain meaning of a dwelling is, of course, the first possibility. On a grander scale it might refer to the palace or to the temple. In this regard the verse applies to church-building programs. "House" is also used in the sense of dynasty or family. Perhaps this is the connection between the two halves of the psalm. In this sense the promise has to do with building a godly home filled with mutually loving, generous, respectful parents and children.

The second illustration, that of the watchman, also admits of several applications. We need safety not only from robbers or military foes but from the multitudes of ideas and forces that would destroy us spiritually, emotionally, and physically. These threats are both within us and without. So this is also a prayer for God's vigilance over our total being. The reference to "city" may tie in with the city "gate" in verse 5.

Verse 2 elaborates on the matter of staying awake and watching. It is not advocating a carefree abandon of all diligence, nor is it suggesting laziness. Rather, the words warn against the man who burns himself out with worries or kills himself with hard work just to have a few more shekels to spend. On the other hand, God gives the gift of sleep—sound, reviving, health-restoring, therapeutic sleep—to the ones He loves.

In the ancient world, large families, especially with many boys, were viewed as proof of God's love. Witness the dramatic events in the lives of the patriarchs in their concern over sons. Or consider the problems created when a man had only daughters such as Zelophehad (Num. 27). Sons meant more hands on the farm, more children to bear the patriarch's family name, and more voices to speak in defense of the father. In fact, the last line of verse 5 has that situation in view. The many children can defend the father in the community court which meets at the city gate. A real hand-to-hand fight is not the first meaning, although that is a distinct possibility. This heritage of the Lord is compared to a quiver full of arrows. Just as no ancient warrior would go out with just one or two arrows, so no man would be satisfied with a small number of children. Incidentally, questions of overcrowding and population explosion did not concern these people, who were far from fulfilling that cultural mandate. Furthermore, more than half the children born would not survive infancy and childhood. To have many children was a kind of insurance that a sufficient number would live long enough to perpetuate the family. The analogy of the arrows works in this dimension as well. The hunter or the soldier cannot be sure he will hit the target with each arrow, so to have several gives him a better chance. Even David had five stones in his pouch when only one was necessary to fell Goliath.

PSALM 128

Both Psalms 127 and 128 speak of the blessing of a family. Perhaps that is why they are together in the Psalter. However, Psalm 128 is broader than the preceding one and mentions both wife and children as by-products of God's blessing on those who fear Him.

This psalm divides into two halves which more or less echo each other. The first verse in the first half and the first verse in the second half (v. 4) both speak of the blessing on those who fear the Lord. In Hebrew, two different words are used. Verses 1 and 2 have the word for "happy" or "blessed," while verse 4 has the more common term for blessed. Verse 2 corresponds to verse 5. Both have the Hebrew word for "good" or "well." The last verse of each half (3 and 6, respectively) refers to children.

Also noteworthy are the three place names in verses 5 and 6. Zion is parallel to Jerusalem, while Israel is the general term for the people of God in the Old Testament, regardless of where they live.

"Blessed is every one who fears the LORD" (v. 1 NASB). This introduction to the psalm is typical of the entire collection. Psalm 1 begins in a similar way. Both Psalms (111:10) and Proverbs (9:10) state that "the fear of the LORD is the beginning of wisdom." Again remember that this fear does not exclusively mean fright but encompasses reverence, respect, and awe. The God-fearer is a person who walks in the ways of God—another idea reminiscent of Psalm 1 (vv. 1, 6).

To enjoy the fruit of one's own labor is taken for granted in our free and affluent society. But for a slave or a tenant farmer this would be an extraordinary blessing.

After independence (v. 2) comes the blessing of a fruitful wife and a large number of children. In this regard, the psalm corresponds to the preceding one. Because of the central role of wine and oil in the simple economy and diet of the Old Testament world, it is only natural that the poet compares the family to these two staples. Just as a man's wealth was counted in vineyards and olive orchards, so a man's community status was achieved by a productive wife and many offspring.

The parallel blessings in verses 5 and 6 are also noteworthy. The references to Zion and Jerusalem may indicate that this is a psalm of ascent. The blessed man of this psalm makes his annual treks to the religious capital of his nation. But more than that, he is able to go as long as he lives. Neither poor health nor poverty deprive him of this tri-annual spiritual experience. Verse 5b may be saying that he retires in Jerusalem.

Added to the fact that he reaches an old age is the blessing of seeing his grandchildren. For people whose life spans rarely went over fifty, this was a unique blessing.

Psalm 128 ends with the same benediction that closed Psalm 125: "Peace be upon Israel" (ASV). Remember the promise of Psalm 122:6? "Pray for the peace of Jerusalem: they shall prosper that love thee."

PSALM 129

Psalm 129 is one of the few imprecatory psalms (cf. Pss. 69–71, and 137). The first three verses are the complaint and the last four verses are the curse.

Like Psalm 124, Psalm 129 was probably antiphonal. The instruction "Let Israel now say" (v. 1b ASV) indicates that the congregation was to repeat the words of the leader. The complaints are in such general terms that it is difficult to determine to what they refer. Any date on the psalm would be a pure guess.

The persecution the psalmist and his countrymen suffered was a lifelong one. The agony they suffered felt like a plow gouging into their backs. Perhaps this refers to scourging, since a whip would leave lacerations like furrows in a field. Verse 4 does not really belong either with the complaint section or with the curses inasmuch as the verb is not a jussive or wish-type verb. If that were true the sentence would read, "Let him cut the cords of the wicked."

Notice that the curses or imprecations follow the statement that the Lord is righteous. Neither the righteous man nor the righteous God does these things because he is unkind or hateful but because he is so concerned with righteousness, equity, and justice.

The persecutors are the haters of Zion—the very thing the righteous pilgrim loves. Zion is not merely a city, a capital, a locus for the faithful, but it is the place where God abides, His singular choice of all the cities in the world. To hate it is to hate God, and to hate God is to hate everything He is and stands for, including righteousness, mercy, integrity, and steadfast love.

The wish of verse 5 is that the persecutors be shamed and thwarted. The wish of verse 6 is that they be like the short-lived grass that grows on the flat, earthen roofs of Middle Eastern houses after rain. The worthlessness of that grass is the subject of the next four remarks (vv. 6b–8). First, it withers before it grows up. Second, because it withers so readily, no reaper bothers to harvest it (v. 7a). Third, it does not amount to enough to bind into sheaves. And fourth, the farmers do not greet and bless each other as they work it (v. 8). Incidentally, we learn from Ruth 2:4 that the two salutations in verse 8 are the common, friendly exchanges of the workers in the field.

The point is this: No one blesses God for a worthless fistful of dried weeds. May the wicked be like that—withered, cursed, and destroyed.

PSALM 130

Psalm 130 is a prayer for forgiveness and an assertion of hope in the Lord. In several ways this psalm is like Psalm 86.

The psalm is tightly knit together with key words linking immediate and more remote verses. Note the occurrences of the divine name, Yahweh (LORD), in verses 1, 3, 5, and 7 (the form in v. 3 is shortened simply to Yah). In verses 2, 3b, and 6 the less common appellative *Adonai* (Lord) appears. The word "voice" ties together the two halves of verse 2. One of the Hebrew terms for "sin" is in verses 3 and 8. The preposition "with," in reference to God, occurs in verse 4 and twice in verse 7. "Wait" occurs twice in verse 5, while the term "soul" links verses 5 and 6. Also verses 5 and 7 share the word "hope." The same Hebrew word is the basis of "mark" in verse 3 and "watch" in verse 6. Two words, "Israel" and "redeem," are found in both verses 7 and 8.

The opening two verses are a plaintive address to a hopefully compassionate God. The depths from which the psalmist cries are figurative of the throes of despair and the slough of despondency. It is unlikely that he is literally drowning or in a deep pit.

The next two verses, 3 and 4, speak of God's forgiveness. If

He did not forgive, no man could stand because all have sinned. This results in the fear of God, as verse 4b indicates. If He alone can forgive, then on Him alone can the sinner cast himself for mercy. He is the one with whom we all must deal in this matter of sin. If we pray for forgiveness. He will forgive. If we persist unrepentantly He will judge.

In the third couplet, verses 5 and 6, the verb "wait" (twice in v. 5) must carry over to do triple duty in verse 6. (The KJV, ASV, and NASB all indicate this by using italics.) Other versions merely insert the word, recognizing that it is a common Hebrew literary device. If you have ever spent a sleepless night on a camping trip, you can appreciate the sentiment of verse 6. That first soft light in the eastern sky is a welcome sight indeed.

The last pair of verses is an admonition to Israel. It may be understood corporately (the entire nation) or individually (each person). The only hope is in the Lord. Two rich words describe His concern. One is mercy, loving-kindness, or steadfast love; the other is redemption. Because He *is* the former, He *does* the latter. Love prompts redemption, which in turn should move the redeemed to love Him back.

PSALM 131

Three psalms have only three verses each: Psalms 131, 133, and 134, making them second only to Psalm 117 in brevity. Psalm 131 is an assertion of personal humility (vv. 1–2) and an exhortation to hope (v. 3). Among the psalms of ascent or degrees only this one and Psalms 122, 124, and 133 are ascribed to David. Nothing within the poem excludes the possibility that Israel's most famous king wrote it. After an initial vocative, verse 1 consists of four parallels all containing ideas of height. The psalmist denies any proud thoughts or self-aggrandizing deeds. This attitude must precede any receiving of God's blessing. He resists the proud but gives grace to the humble.

Then David compares himself to a child nursing at his mother's breast. "Weaned" (v. 2) gives the idea of a child old enough to be on solid food and independent of his mother. The root means "full" or "satisfied," so the figure here is more likely an infant just finishing a meal at his mother's breast. Compare Isaiah 11:8 where the word is used in parallel to "suckling."

The point is this: He is quiet and satisfied with what God has given him. No cause for restlessness remains in his relationship to his Maker.

Verse 3 is similar to verse 7 of the preceding psalm. Israel is enjoined to hope in the Lord from now on and until eternity.

PSALM 132

Of the fifteen songs of ascent (120–134), Psalm 132 is the most unusual. It is the longest. It is the only one to mention the Messiah. Its style is different, and it contains David's name more than any other psalm.

On the other hand, this psalm does fit the general theme of the psalms of ascent. The focus is on Jerusalem, the city of David and the Zion of God. There is some concatenation, linking of verses with key words, though it is not as tight as in the preceding psalms. Basically, the tone is positive, festive, and uplifting.

The eighteen verses of Psalm 132 fall into four more or less distinct stanzas. The first five verses focus on David's resolve to build the temple. The next five verses sound like a hymn to accompany the arrival of the ark of the covenant in Jerusalem. Verses 11–13 major on God's promise to bless David's dynasty. The last five verses contain God's promise to bless Zion.

The record of David's intention to build a dwelling place for

God's holy ark appears in 2 Samuel 7 (cf. 1 Kings 8:17). The ark had been in Kiriath-jearim at Abinadab's house (1 Sam. 7:1, NASB). Verse 6 may have an alternate or abbreviated form of that name, Jaar (meaning "woods," as in some translations). From there the ark was taken first to the house of Obed-edom and then to Jerusalem.

David did not actually build the temple, but he is responsible for making Jerusalem the permanent resting place of the ark. To his son Solomon goes the honor of constructing the building.

The mention of the city of Ephratah (v. 6) is somewhat enigmatic. It is an alternate name for Bethlehem (cf. Mic. 5:2), the home of David. But the ark was never in Bethlehem. It may have been in the "fields of Jaar" (see RSV, NASB, et al.), if that is Kiriath-jearim.

The second stanza was apparently written and/or sung to commemorate the arrival of the ark of the covenant in Jerusalem. It is assumed that the tabernacle, the wilderness tent, still sheltered it. Verse 7 has "footstool," an interesting epithet for that sacred chest.

The author of the psalm is unknown, but it sounds like a descendant of David, perhaps one of the more faithful kings of Judah such as Uzziah, Hezekiah, or Josiah. He calls himself "anointed" in verse 10. The Hebrew word for that is Messiah; the Greek word is Christ. However, this is not why the psalm is Messianic. It is mainly because of verse 17, which John the Baptist's father alluded to (Luke 1:69). All the kings are anointed. The term does not necessarily have prophetic significance.

More references to David's dynasty appear in verses 11 and 12. The psalmist refers to 2 Samuel 7:12–16 and Psalm 89:3–4, 35–36. It was true that as long as the kings of Judah patterned their lives after the Law of God they prospered. Over and over the books of Kings and Chronicles remark how each king did or did not do what was right in the eyes of the Lord.

Whereas verses 10–12 speak of people through whom the covenant was kept, verses 13–16 focus on the place. Zion, the spiritual Jerusalem, was the resting place for the ark and the dwelling place of God on earth. This was so from the time David brought in the ark around 960 BC until the Babylonian captivity around 586 BC. The records are not clear as to the disposition of the ark after that, but we do know the temple was functioning during the time of Christ. In AD 70 the Romans under Titus took away the ark as a trophy of war. Whether it was the same one or a replica we do not know.

Notice the similarity between verses 9 and 16. This is just one example of how the psalm is integrally one. Note also the repetition of words such as dwell or dwelling, resting place, anointed, swore, and clothe.

It is at verse 17 that the psalm seems to look beyond the dynasty which ended with King Zedekiah. The sprouting horn, a symbol of strength, refers to Christ, the greater Son of David. The same figures appear in the prophecies of Isaiah (4:2); Jeremiah (23:5; 33:15); Ezekiel (29:21); and Zechariah (3:8; 6:12).

The imagery of a throne, mentioned in verse 11, is also used of Christ (Isa. 9:7; Luke 1:32; Acts 2:30; Rev. 4:2–5). And although this word for "lamp" in verse 17 is not used, the Messiah will be a *light*. (See Isa. 42:6; 49:6, Luke 2:32.)

Verse 18 has the only negative note in the psalm. As the priests of Zion were clothed with salvation (v. 16), so the king's enemies will be clothed with shame. But on the Messiah's head God's crown will shine. At the first advent of Christ He wore a crown of thorns, but at the second He will be wearing one of gold (Rev. 14:14).

PSALM 133

Psalm 133 is a simple and short psalm extolling the harmonious cooperation of brothers. The brothers may be only the priests, the Levites, but more likely they were the entire Israelite family, especially as they camped on the slopes surrounding Jerusalem during festivals. As more and more people poured into the holy city for each of the three annual feasts, the temporary shelters would spill down the hillsides just as the anointing oil dripped off Aaron's head onto his beard and garments.

That is a beautiful scene not unlike the thousands that Jesus addressed on the slopes near the Galilean Sea. Nor is it much different from the crowded parking lot of a gospel-preaching church.

The unifying theme which brought these ancient believers together was God's order that all men appear in Jerusalem for the feasts of Passover, Pentecost, and Tabernacles (Deut. 16:16). These pilgrimages were religious, to be sure, but they also provided a necessary change of pace. Here the men could meet their friends, share their problems, get caught up on the news, and fulfill their duty to God.

The two illustrations of fraternal concord are most interesting. The first picture is of Aaron's anointing. Exodus 30:22–25 has the recipe for the oil and the procedure for anointing both the sacerdotal participants and the furniture and utensils. To us it may seem like a messy procedure, but we should think more in terms of furniture polish or expensive perfumed lotions. They were costly; they were fragrant; they were the finest available in the land. Aaron was the first high priest, so he represents the spiritual dimension of the pilgrimage of this psalm.

The second picture is of the dew on Mount Hermon. Hermon is the mountain to the extreme north of the Promised Land. At its slopes the four tributaries of the Jordan begin. Snowcapped much of the year, it symbolized abundant moisture, the gift of God to a dry land. Some wonder how any plants can survive the long, rainless summers of Palestine. But the answer is the dew. Nightly, as the temperature drops, the humidity in the air condenses to provide the needed moisture for plants. As water is a gift, so God blesses His people with unity and continuing life.

John 17 parallels Psalm 133. There Jesus prayed for the unity of believers, "that they may be one, even as we are" (v. 11 RSV). He also mentions the blessing of eternal life: "And this is life eternal, that they should know thee the only true God, and him whom thou didst send, even Jesus Christ" (v. 3 ASV).

PSALM 134

The fifteen songs of ascent or psalms of degrees (KJV) end with Psalm 134. This short psalm is something of a benediction closing the collection of compositions on the same general theme. Notice that the word "bless" occurs in all three of its verses. Apparently it is some sort of a liturgical blessing similar to the high priest's benediction of Numbers 6:24–26. Just who speaks these lines is not certain. Perhaps it is the priests who bless one another. Or it may be that the worshipers and the temple functionaries exchange these lines.

The servants of verse 1 could be either the priests or the worshipers. But those who stand nightly in the house of the Lord are more likely the professional clergy. First Chronicles 9:33 mentions certain singers who worked day and night in the temple (cf. 1 Chron. 23:30).

In verse 2 there are no prepositions in the original manuscripts between "hands" and "sanctuary," so the various translations offer different ones. The American Standard Version margin even suggests "in holiness." However, on the basis of the parallelism between house of the Lord and Zion, the majority choice of "sanctuary" is probably correct.

One might ask: How can we bless God and He also bless us? The latter is more common and easier to understand. However, "bless" is a synonym for praise. The word is related to the Hebrew word for "knee." Apparently kneeling is the posture for both blessing and being blessed. It is a two-way street. We give God blessing, and He gives it to us. We give Him what He wants, namely, praise, and He gives us what we want, namely, temporal and eternal benefactions. The questions to ask ourselves are these: Is our blessing only one way? Do we want only to get and not to give? This psalm twice urges us to bless the Lord and only once wishes God's blessing on us.

PSALM 135

A careful search will reveal that almost every one of the twenty-one verses of Psalm 135 is duplicated elsewhere in Scripture. The man who penned this psalm knew well both the Psalms and the history of Israel. Here are some of the obvious or more exact quotations.

Verse 1 is like the opening verses of Psalms 113 and 134. Verse 5b is similar to Psalm 95:3. Compare verses 6, 15, 16, and 18 with Psalm 115:3–6 and 8. Verses 8, 10, 11, and 12 echo in Psalm 136:10, 17–22. Verse 13 is like Psalm 102:12.

Psalm 135 clearly divides into five stanzas. The first four verses constitute the introductory volley of praise to the Lord. The next three verses exalt the Lord as the supreme God, the One who controls the powers of nature. The longest section is verses 8–14 where the psalmist reviews God's deliverance of His people during the Exodus. Verses 15–18 approximately balance verses 5–7. They ridicule idols. Finally, the last three verses form a benediction and summons to praise. They do at the close of the psalm what verses 1–4 do at the beginning. Note that the first and last word of the psalm is "hallelujah," or in English, "Praise the LORD."

It might seem that the exhortation to praise (vv. 1–3) and later to bless (vv. 19–20) is for the professional clergy only. They are the ones who stand and serve in the courtyards of the house of God. They are of the house of Levi and Aaron. However, the command is for all the rest of Israel as well (v. 19). Ultimately, all of God's people are His servants. All believers are now Jacob and Israel (v. 4). We are God's "very own" people (Titus 2:14 NIV), to give a modern flavor to the old words "peculiar people." Verse 6 is a great one for averring the sovereignty of God. He has done whatever He pleased. This is true not only in the realm of nature, as that verse states, but also in the lives of His people. His is the only will we may not question. From a scientific standpoint, verse 7 is interesting. Long ago when this psalm was written the author showed some understanding of the water cycle. It is obvious how water gets from the clouds to the sea, but it is not so easily observed how it gets back up in the sky again. This verse tells us.

From the subject of winds and water (v. 7) it is an easy transition to the deliverance of the Israelites out of Egypt. The very clipped resume of the Exodus also hits the highlights of the Transjordan wars, specifically the defeat of Sihon and Og. Numbers 21:21–35 records these victories.

Three words in verses 13–14 deserve some comment. The first is "memorial" (KJV, ASV), translated "renown" (RSV, MLB, NEB); "fame" (AMP); "remembrance" (NASB); or "title" (NASB, ANCHOR). It is a synonym for "name." Note the parallel lines. Perhaps the word which is based on the basic root "to remember" is more of a commentary on the word "name" than the other way around.

We are remembered by our names. It is that which represents a person in his absence. It is a handle to use in place of a more elaborate description.

The second word is "judge" in verse 14. In this context the judgment is positive, not condemnatory. Therefore, several modern translations have "vindicate." "Requite," "compensate," and "rule" are other options. Simply, the Hebrew word here is much bigger than any of our synonyms. It refers to the whole judicial process and beyond, even to governmental leadership.

The third word is "repent." Again the Hebrew word behind this is much broader and encompasses the dimensions of pity, compassion, and mercy. "Repent" implies that God has sinned. He has not. But He does show pity and exercise compassion.

The taunt song of verses 15–18 is reminiscent of what Isaiah said about idols and idolaters in Isaiah 44. These caustic jibes are in direct contrast to the words of praise the psalmist has for the creating and sustaining powers of the true God (vv. 5–7).

The concluding benediction contains three identical commands to the Israelites, the Aaronites, and the Levites. While the latter two are officially responsible to lead in worship, all Israel was to praise God.

PSALM 136

No other psalm quite compares to 136 because of its unique format. Each of the twenty-six verses ends with the refrain, "His mercy is forever." This is the clearest example of a psalm used for liturgical purposes. Most likely the song leader, a Levite or descendant of Asaph, would recite the first half of each verse and the congregation would echo the refrain. Although it may seem boring to us, we should be grateful for it and take this repetition as a reminder that all we have, are, or do depends on the constant loving-kindness of God.

The key word in the refrain is that many-faceted Hebrew term, *ḥesed*. No one English word covers it; therefore many different translations exist. The King James Version reads "For his mercy endureth for ever." The American Standard Version has "For his lovingkindness endureth for ever." Moffatt offered "His kindness never fails." The Improved Bible of 1913 chose, "For his mercy is forever." The Revised Standard Version renders it, "For his steadfast love endures for ever." The Berkeley Bible gives "His covenant love is everlasting." The Jerusalem Bible is, "His love is everlasting." The New English Bible employs, "His love endures for ever." The New American Bible, very close to the King James Version, opts for "For his mercy endures forever." The New American Standard Bible follows the Smith-Goodspeed 1939 translation, "For his [loving]kindness is everlasting." The Anchor Bible reads, "For his kindness is eternal." In a few of the verses the Living Bible expands the phrase to, "For his lovingkindness to Israel continues forever." And the best known of the several versions in the Scottish Metrical Psalter repeats the refrain as:

> His mercies are forever sure
> And shall for age to age endure.

All these together scarcely can bring out the richness of the words which underscore, emphasize, and enunciate the fact that God never has been and never will be anything but reliable, kind, trustworthy, faithful, and loving to His people. Psalm 136 evidences a certain plan in its contents. The opening three verses and the closing two are somewhat of an invocation and a benediction. Note in particular the similarity between verses 2, 3, and 26. Three three-verse stanzas (4–6, 7–9, 10–12) follow, and then come three four-verse stanzas (13–16, 17–20, 21–24).

The first two stanzas after the introduction (4–9) focus on God the Creator. The next two stanzas (10–16) center on God's deliverance of His people from Egypt and, in particular, from the Red Sea episode. The last two stanzas within the body of the poem (17–24) continue the Exodus theme, with special attention to the defeat of the Amorite kings and the actual possession of the Promised Land. So the psalm roughly follows the progress of events from the creation in Genesis to the conquest of Canaan recorded in Joshua.

PSALM 137

This little psalm is, on the one hand, the most plaintive and, on the other hand, the most vindictive of all the psalms. It may come as a surprise to learn that the gentle sentiments of verses 1 and 2 are in the same psalm with the curses of verses 8 and 9, but they are.

The contents indicate an exilic or postexilic setting. A captive from Jerusalem is lamenting his own misfortune and the desolation of his holy city, Jerusalem.

The first four verses bemoan the cruel taunts the captured Israelites suffered from the heartless Babylonians. Verses 5–6 are something of a vow to honor and pray for Jerusalem. The enemy Edom is the focal point of verse 7, and vicious Babylon bears the brunt of verses 8 and 9.

The rivers of Babylon are the immortal Tigris and Euphrates and the many irrigation canals interlacing the southern Mesopotamian plain. Grief prompted the exiles to abandon their songs and harps (v. 2), but the unsympathetic captors demanded in a mocking way that the Jews entertain them with the songs of Zion (v. 3). Such happiness, however, cannot be artificially generated so far from Jerusalem.

If we were to sermonize for a moment we might remember that any captivity in the Bible, be it Egyptian, Philistine, Assyrian, or Babylonian, represents domination by evil. When the believer is far from God and the company of the saints, he likewise cannot sing the Lord's song. What could be more sad than a backslidden Christian reminded of his condition by a sinner?

In the center of the psalm are two famous verses of self-malediction. The psalmist vows never to forget Jerusalem or prefer any other city over it. The penalty he wishes on himself for such failure is the loss of his right hand and the use of his tongue.

The last three verses are a curse on Edom and Babylon for the roles they played in the destruction of Jerusalem and the exile of the Jewish people. From Obadiah 11 we learn that the Edomites, the half-brothers of the Israelites through Esau, stood aloof on the day of Judah's defeat. Amos 1:11 charges Edom with pursuing his brother (Israel) with a sword and never abating his anger. That Babylon, under the leadership of Nebuchadnezzar, destroyed Jerusalem needs no documentation. The divine wrath toward Babylon is a frequent theme among the prophets (Isa. 13, 47; Jer. 25, 50, 51; Rev. 18).

Many are bothered by the vengeful attitude displayed in verse 9. "How," some ask, "can any man of God make such a wish on his enemies?" Two explanations may help in understanding this. First, the "little ones" may not be the infants, as such, but all the children, that is, citizens of the wicked mother Babylon. On the other hand, none of these ancient conquerors were above such cruelty as dashing babies onto rocks (see 2 Kings 8:12). The second explanation is merely to understand that the psalmist was voicing God's holy displeasure toward this most sinful of all kingdoms. Intense love for God is coupled with intense hatred of His enemies. It is not easy to explain, as none of us loves God enough to hate that violently, but it does point out in some degree the way these ancient saints thought.

PSALM 138

Psalm 138 is basically a psalm of thanksgiving. The opening three verses are David's assertion that he will worship. Verses 4 and 5 speak of foreign kings joining in the praise. Then the last three verses are more of the psalmist's reflection on God's favor extended to him, weak and unworthy though he was. This psalm is like those very early ones in the Psalter. In fact, verse 2 is similar to Psalm 5:7 and verse 1 compares with Psalm 9:1.

A small problem arises with the meaning of "gods" in verse 1. The Jerusalem Bible and the New American Bible translate the very common Hebrew word for "god" as "angels." These "gods" are clearly not real deity. Perhaps they are pagan idols whom the psalmist wishes to chagrin. Or they may be some kind of super-human, celestial servants such as angels. A third possibility is that they are human judges. This would agree with the "kings" of verse 4.

Note the attributes or aspects of God mentioned in verse 2: love, truth, word, and name.

It sounds as if the kings of the earth are sympathetic in verse 4. At this point the psalm might even be considered Messianic, since it speaks of the obeisance of non-Israelites. Whenever in the Old Testament we read of outsiders coming to God there is a futuristic, church-age ring to the verses under consideration.

The closing three verses (6–8) give more of the reason for this praise. David is again, as often before, reflecting on the protection God gave him from his enemies. The oft-quoted promise of verse 8 is somewhat elliptical. Of the many ways to spell out its meaning with additional words, the New English Bible is commendable. It has "The LORD will accomplish his purpose for me." That translation brings to mind Philippians 1:6: "He who began a good work in you will carry it on to completion until the day of Christ Jesus" (NIV).

PSALM 139

No other passage of Scripture quite compares with Psalm 139 for teaching what the omnipresence and omniscience of God mean. In most beautiful terms these assuring doctrines permeate this ancient psalm of David. So rich and fascinating a work is it that Edward J. Young wrote an entire book on this psalm alone.[1]

The twenty-four verses are divided into four sections of six verses each. The first six speak of God's omnipresence. The next six spell out the dimensions of His all-knowing concern. Verses 13–18 focus on God's role in our lives from a time before birth. The concluding six verses are the psalmist's response of hatred toward sin and an invitation to God to examine him. Note the "search" that both opens and closes this magnificent psalm (vv. 1, 23).

God knows everything. He even knows what we think. Of course He knows what we say. These truths are repeated several times in different ways throughout the opening verses of Psalm 139. Then verse 6 is a kind of doxology.

That God knows so much can be both disconcerting and comforting. It is foolish to suppose we can think evil and He not know it. Certain sins are sins of the mind, such as lust and pride. But in God's sight they are just as sinful as those wicked acts the hands can do.

---

1. *Psalm 139, A Study in the Omniscience of God* (London: Banner of Truth Trust, 1965).

It is also reassuring to know that God reads our motives and understands our intentions even when others do not. How wonderful to know that God sees and sympathizes with our most unspeakable problems! This also means that He knows everyone else's thought life and that He will hold all men accountable, even for what they think.

Just as it is impossible to think anything without God knowing it, so it is impossible to be in any place where He is not present. The dimensions of height and depth (v. 8) and of east and west (v. 9) are all within God's omnipresent purview. The psalmist speaks from a position of fellowship and peace with God. That God is everywhere does not frighten him; rather, it is a comfort. Even the dimension of darkness does not hinder God's ability to see and hence protect His servant. Many a Christian soldier in a dark, distant, and dangerous place has claimed the enduring truth of verses 7–12.

Verses 13–16 expand on God's knowledge of our prenatal condition. Those who oppose abortion rightly quote these verses to show that God is intensely aware of, and carefully at work with, even the unborn. Notice the words that emphasize the mystery of a developing human life: fearful, wonderful, hidden, secret, and curiously.

This section too, like the first (v. 6), ends with a doxology (vv. 17–18). Certainly God thinks of us more often and with more intensity than we do of Him. The last phrase of verse 18 is one of several problem passages in this psalm. The gist may be, as the New English Bible has paraphrased it, "To finish the count, my years must equal thine."

The last six verses seem somewhat foreign to the rest of the psalm. Suddenly this beatific poet starts hurling caustic barbs at his enemies. Despite the traditional interpretation of this passage, maybe we should understand the wicked ones to be the carnal thoughts of the believing writer. Even if it does violence to interpret the verses that way, at least we can apply them so. We must come to hate the lusts and urgings, the promptings and pulses of the old nature that still thrive within us. Let us learn to hate those fleshly passions that take our minds off God and make us think, look, and act like unregenerate men.

This view of the maledictory section (vv. 19–22) finds support in the prayer which closes the psalm (vv. 23–24). The psalmist asks that God scrutinize his heart and mind for any of those wicked patterns and motives that he has just cursed. In some respects, these verses are like the final verses of Psalm 19. There David spelled out the good and pure thought life and prayed that such would mark him. Here he describes the vicious and godless thought process and prays that such will not depict him.

All in all this is a rich devotional psalm. The continual study of it, praying the concluding prayer, will help any believer walk "in the way everlasting."

PSALM 140

Psalm 140 is basically a prayer for protection from wicked men. A "selah" appears after each group of six stichs (vv. 3, 5, 8). We would expect others after verses 10, 11, and 13, but they are not there. Whatever the meaning of the term is, it does not always break the psalms according to sense.

Apart from the three words of petition ("deliver" and "preserve," v. 1, and "keep," v. 4), the first five verses of the psalm are David's complaint. Then verses 6 and 7 are a kind of statement of faith. Next come four verses constituting a prayer against the wicked (vv. 8–11). The last two verses correspond to verses 6 and 7 as a confession of trust. In simple outline the psalm develops like this:

A Complaint (vv. 1–5)
   B Confession (vv. 6–7)
A´ Curse (vv. 8–11)
   B´ Confession (vv. 12–13)

In other places the connivings of the enemy are compared to the setting of traps (cf. Pss. 9:15; 31:4; 35:7; 57:6; 64:5). One of several rare and hence uncertain words in this psalm is translated "adder" in the standard versions. Others are the words "desires" and "wicked device" (v. 8) and "overthrow" (v. 11).

After a well-worded complaint and a typical statement of trust in the first seven verses, the psalm takes a turn at verse 8. Here begins the imprecatory section where David prays down God's curses on his foes. As with other psalms (e.g., 69:22–28 and 137:7–9) which invoke God's wrath, the interpreter is hard pressed to explain and apply the Scripture. The usual answer is this: David so loved God and hated wickedness that he prayed for the demise of those who practiced it. This was, after all, more typical of the pre-Christian law of retaliation. As New Testament believers we should try in our passions to separate the act from the actor, the sin from the sinner.

If we cannot maintain composure while hating evil, or hate it apart from the one who practices it, then perhaps we had best withdraw from the fray, repeat verse 12 of this psalm, and wait for God to judge. It may seem as though we are losing the war against sin, but David reminds us that God will vindicate the righteous and exonerate the upright.

PSALM 141

For such a short psalm, number 141 has several difficulties in it. In fact, for the last seven of the ten brief verses there are variant readings in Hebrew and other language manuscripts, or suggested emendations to relieve the problems.

In general this is a prayer for deliverance from wicked men and sinful practices. Because "evening" is mentioned in verse 2, this is commonly thought of as an evening prayer. The title ascribes the psalm to David, but there are not enough internal clues to pinpoint the circumstances which prompted it.

Different editions of the English Bible and the commentaries outline the psalm in various ways. I prefer to see three parts: 1–2, 3–7, and 8–10. Note that the divine name occurs only in the first verse of each of these sections. The first part is an introduction or invocation. The second is the body of the prayer. And the third is a review of the whole.

In the introduction the psalmist reminds God of his urgency. It appears that the situation is growing desperate and need for divine intervention is becoming more pressing. Verse 2 compares prayer to smoke rising from incense and the lifted up evening offering.

The best known verse of the psalm is the third. Fortunately, there is no question about the meaning of this simple request, "Set a watch, O Lord, before my mouth." Who of us should not pray it more often? This begins the section where the psalmist asks not to fall into sin. Not only does he pray for a bridled tongue but also for pure intentions (v. 4a). He knows that temptations will arise to share the food and ultimately the way of life of wicked men.

Verse 5 is similar to Proverbs 27:6, "Faithful are the wounds of a friend." Some of the ancient versions read the second line of verse 5 as the opposite: "But let the oil of the wicked never anoint my head" (RSV).

The difficulties continue with verses 6 and 7. Among several suggestions are "their bones" rather than "our bones" (v. 7). The two verses then describe the downfall and demise of the wicked.

The concluding three verses review the main points of the psalm. First comes an affirmation of faith in verse 8a. Then verses 8b and 9 rehearse the prayer for protection from the traps of evil people. "Gins" were a type of snare (cf. Ps. 140:5). The last verse echoes the imprecation section (vv. 6–7).

The lesson for the modern Christian is this: Keep a sweet spirit and a close relationship with the Lord, especially when the enemy seeks to lure you into sin. In particular, adopt the attitude of verse 3. If we are interpreting the last stichs of verses 5 and 6 correctly, they suggest the same gentle demeanor, even in the face of most distressing circumstances.

PSALM 142

Psalms 140–144 are all of the "trouble and trust" variety. Although Psalm 142 is sometimes labeled a personal lament or a prayer, it still follows basically the same pattern as the two preceding psalms and the two following ones. First comes the address or invocation, then the complaint, and finally the statement of confidence.

The title of Psalm 142 is similar to that of Psalm 57—a *maskil* of David when he was in the cave. The record of this episode is either in 1 Samuel 22:1 or 1 Samuel 24:3. The former passage speaks of David hiding in the cave of Adullum in the Philistine foothills. To him were gathered the riffraff of the countryside. The latter Samuel passage has David in another cave in the Judean desert near En-gedi. On this occasion David cut off the edge of Saul's robe. Both episodes were occasioned by Saul's pursuit of David. Therefore, the title to this psalm fits well with the contents, which evidence a man wrongfully persecuted and innocently pursued.

Verses 1 and 2 constitute the introduction. Note the four first-person verbs: "I cry," "I make supplication," and "I declare" (NASB). In these two verses God is addressed in the third person:

him. In the rest of the psalm David uses the second person: you. Verses 3–7 are the actual prayer.

The assertions of trust are sprinkled through the body of the prayer. In verse 3 is the statement, "Thou knewest my path." In verse 5 are the words, "Thou art my refuge." And in verse 7 notice the expression of hope: "Thou shalt deal bountifully with me."

Not all David's complaints are about his personal enemy, Saul, although some certainly refer to him. The end of verse 3 records how his enemies set a trap. They are called "persecutors" in verse 6. The "prison" of verse 7 may be the cave where David could have been so easily trapped by Saul and his men.

The other "enemies" are of a different nature. The beginning of verse 3 seems to speak of discouragement, a formidable foe in itself. The thrust of verse 4 appears to be loneliness. And verse 6 may hint at more discouragement, or what in modern terminology is called an inadequate self-image or low ego-power.

Whatever or whoever the adversary was, David saw his only hope to be God. If the Lord did not help him avoid the snare, if God were not on his right hand, if God did not listen to his cry, if God were not stronger than his foes, if God would not send righteous friends to surround him, he would certainly perish at the hands of those who hated him.

Our problems may not appear as dramatic, but they are just as real, just as debilitating, just as overwhelming, just as frightening. Whether our enemy is a person or a set of circumstances, our only hope is in the Lord. He still desires to shower His children with good things.

PSALM 143

This psalm continues David's prayer for deliverance from his enemies. The first two verses are introductory. Again there follows a section of complaint (vv. 3–6). And again the psalm ends with a series of petitions for personal safety and for the enemy's demise (vv. 7–12).

Paul the apostle, in both Romans 3:20 and Galatians 2:16, echoes the truth of verse 2b that no one is righteous in God's sight. We often think of the Old Testament saints having an inadequate theology and perhaps even a trust in works. But this verse disabuses us of that erroneous idea. At least the enlightened saints of the older dispensation saw that salvation is totally of grace and without dependence on works. No man can measure himself by God's righteous standard and be judged adequate. So David prays knowing full well that he deserves condemnation. He has no claim on God except a plea for mercy.

Having opened the prayer and confessed in a measure his own unworthiness, David proceeds in verse 3 to outline his troubles. All of the terms are quite general, so it is impossible to determine the exact nature of the enemy's persecution. However, the "darkness" of verse 3 may allude to the cave experience mentioned in the previous psalm. In many instances caves served as graves.

Verses 5 and 6 are not exactly complaints but protestations of sincerity. David is reminding God of how faithfully he has honored and served Him. There is a certain tone of despair to verse 6, as if he were complaining of God's apathy and lack of response.

The verbs of petition begin again at verse 7. These are the first imperatives since verse 2. Count how many there are: *hurry, hide not, let hear, inform, deliver, teach, lead,* and *revive.* Verse 12 has two prayers against the adversary: "cut off" and "destroy."

Notice that after each imperative follows an affirmation of faith or a statement of his personal distress. So in verse 7, we read that his spirit is failing, in verse 8 that he trusts in God, in verse 9 that he flees to God for safety, and so on. This represents a nice balance in prayer. Often we hear only the thoughtless "bless us" or "bless them." Here is a more mature mixture of supplication, praise, thanksgiving, and confession.

Again the slightly embarrassing imprecations conclude the psalm. How can a godly man pray for God to punish the enemy? This seems especially incongruous in verse 12 where the text states, "In thy *lovingkindness* cut off mine enemies" (ASV, italics added). Once more it is that theologically rich term, *hesed*. One of the several facets of that Hebrew word is faithfulness to covenant promise. David is calling on God to keep His promise, perhaps with Deuteronomy 28:7 in mind:

> The LORD shall cause thine enemies that rise up against thee
> to be smitten before thy face: they shall come out against thee
> one way, and flee before thee seven ways.

The lever the psalmist is using is God's honor. If the Lord promised then, now is the time to fulfill. Several modern translations (such as the Jerusalem Bible and the New English Bible) focus on God's love. But the translation "love" is not quite on target. The emphasis here is on God's dependability. David is concerned both with his own safety and with God's reputation for keeping the terms of the covenant which He Himself drew up.

PSALM 144

The final volley of praise which concludes the Psalter begins Psalm 144. While 144–146 are more or less personal (with the use of *I*, *my*, *me*), Psalms 147–150 are community hymns. First the praise is personal, then the nation is admonished to exalt God, and finally everything with breath is urged to praise the LORD (150:6).

This psalm is difficult to outline, and agreement between commentators or editions of the Bible is hard to find. Many parts of the psalm are found elsewhere. Verse 1a is like 18:34 and 46; verse 2 compares with 18:2 and 47; verse 3 reads the same as 8:4; verse 4 comes from 39:6 and 102:11; verse 5 echoes 18:9 and 104:32; verse 6 is similar to 18:14; verse 7 harks back to 18:16; verse 9 is close to 33:2–3; verse 10 agrees with 18:50; and verse 15b is the same as 33:12a It is interesting too that Psalm 18, from which so many of the ideas in this psalm come, is also found in 2 Samuel 22.

The opening two verses have a military tone. Perhaps David is reflecting on a recent victory and is giving God the credit. God is his fortress, his Savior, his shield, and his refuge.

A somewhat disjointed meditation on the frailty of man follows (vv. 3–4). Verse 3 is quoted in Hebrews 2:6, but the Hebrews quotation continues with the verses that follow in Psalm 8:4.

In contrast to the finitude and insignificance of men, the psalmist records a series of commands to God. Most of these contrast the power of God to the weakness of man. First, even to reach man, there is the prayer: "Bow thy heavens, O LORD, and come down" (v. 5). Then follow several ideas relative to the demonstration of divine power in nature. Toward the end of that section (vv. 5–8) is a little gibe at the enemy.

At verse 9 the Psalm takes another tack. Once more there is a series of accolades. God is praised as the One who saves and rescues. Since He is the only One who can do that, verse 11 is a prayer that He will. This stanza, like the preceding one, ends with a remark about how deceitful are the ways of the foe (cf. vv. 8, 11).

The mention of David in verse 10 does not prove that he could not have written the psalm. The Pentateuch, written by Moses constantly refers to its author in the third person.

The last section of the psalm (vv. 12–15) is the most original, that is, these verses contain few allusions to other psalms. Also, the character is different because of the grammar. Technically, there are no finite verbs—just a list of ideal and blessed conditions. A relative pronoun begins verse 12. Therefore, some translations give the list in a straightforward, indicative style. Some use jussives (i.e., wish-type verbs, "may our sons"). Still others relate everything to the last verse. I prefer this last option as a way to understand the passage, although not necessarily as a translation. Here is how it would read:

> Happy are the people whose young sons are like grown plants,
> whose daughters are like pillars designed for a temple.

This certainly is a beatific picture: strong sons, beautiful daughters, full barns, productive cattle, and abundant fields. At the end of verse 14 are certain things blessed for their absence: no violence, no call to arms, no screaming in the streets.

The formula a nation must follow to achieve such bliss is simple. All it must do is make Yahweh, the God of the Bible, its God. It may seem overly simplistic, but such a little sentence implies a lot. It involves following His commands, honoring His Word, receiving His Son, listening to His voice, and waiting for His justice.

PSALM 145

Psalm 145 is among the alphabetic acrostics. Each verse begins with the successive letter of the Hebrew alphabet. However, the letter *nun* is missing between verses 13 and 14 so the psalm has only twenty-one verses while there are twenty-two letters in the alphabet. (Cf. Pss. 25; 34; 111; 112; 119; and each chapter in Lamentations.)

This psalm is the last one in the collection with a title. And that title is merely "Praise. Of David." The beginning of a subscription is found in a Dead Sea Scroll, but all is lost except the words, "This is for a memorial."

The hallelujah psalms begin with 146 and continue to the end, but this praise psalm is not included with the praise group in the synagogue liturgy.

No outline fits very neatly onto these verses. The reason may be that the writer was too concerned with his alphabetic device to think of sub-points and the like. The main theme which does pervade the work is the goodness and greatness of God. For the most part it is personal, with the pronoun *I* quite prominent, especially in the first six verses.

As is typical of Hebrew poetry, God is spoken of in both the second and third persons. Note the use of *you* in verse 1 and elsewhere but *his* in verse 12.

The psalm is so rich in words of praise it is hard to know what to underscore. The Scottish Metrical Psalter of 1650 has no less than six entries based on Psalm 145. A modern popular hymnal lists four anthems based on verses from this psalm. Here are the six short stanzas of a version written in 1824 by Richard Mant.

God, my King, thy might confessing,
    Ever will I bless thy Name;
Day by day thy throne addressing,
    Still will I thy praise proclaim

Honor great our God befitteth;
    Who his majesty can reach?
Age to age his works transmitteth,
    Age to age his pow'r shall teach.

They shall talk of all thy glory,
   On thy might and greatness dwell,
Speak of thy dread acts the story,
   And thy deeds of wonder tell.

Nor shall fail from mem'ry's treasure
   Works by love and mercy wrought;
Works of love surpassing measure,
   Works of mercy passing thought.

Full of kindness and compassion,
   Slow to anger, vast in love,
God is good to all creation;
   All his works his goodness prove.

All thy works, O Lord, shall bless thee;
   Thee shall all thy saints adore;
King supreme shall they confess thee,
   And proclaim thy sovereign pow'r.

Although the whole psalm can be a great benefit to worship, the following ideas should be emphasized: verse 2 suggests daily worship—not just weekly, or worse yet, twice a year. If you think you have said everything you can in praise or have exhausted your thoughts on God, remember verse 3: "His greatness is unsearchable."

Verse 4 speaks of the oral tradition. God's renown was passed from father to son through many generations. The proliferation of books and widespread literature about Him is a rather modern development.

Verses 8 and 9 focus on God's attributes and, in particular, on His goodness to the entire creation.

The word "saints" in verse 10 is built on the term *ḥesed* discussed elsewhere. It implies people who are faithful in covenant-keeping and steadfast in their love to God.

Verse 12 speaks to the matter of outreach. These saints declare to others what God has done. This, after all, is what evangelism is: simply telling the Good News of what God has done.

Verses 14–16 express some of the tenderness of God. Note especially verse 15, which speaks of all the world waiting for the light of day, the warmth of the sun, the freshness of spring, and the harvest of fall. All these benefits come from God's opened hand.

Verse 18 hints at a later dispensation when it would no longer be necessary to find God in Jerusalem or at any earthly sanctuary. He would be available to anyone, anywhere, anytime. He would be near to that person who would truly call on Him.

PSALM 146

Psalms 146–150 all begin and end with the Hebrew word "hallelujah" which means "praise the Lord." For that reason the Hebrews grouped these psalms together in their liturgy and called them a third Hallel. Other Hallels were Psalms 113–118 and Psalm 136.

This psalm falls easily into an outline. The first two verses form the introduction. Verses 3 and 4 focus on the basic untrustworthiness and brevity of men. The body of the poem describes God's works and wonders (vv. 5–9). The last verse is the conclusion.

Needless to say, this psalm and those following belong to the category of praise psalms. The opening words strike that note. Observe the synonymous parallelism, which is typical of the poetry of the Hebrew Bible. In verse 2 "I will praise" is parallel to "I will sing." The two divine names "Lord" (Yahweh) and "God" ('Elohim) balance each other. And the pair of temporal clauses complement each other: "while I live" and "while I have being" (RSV).

On the negative side, the psalmist urges us not to trust in men, either the noble ones or the base ones. The latter is the meaning of "son of man" in this context. The reason for such advice is that human beings simply do not last long. Soon each man's breath will be gone and his body will turn into dust. Verse 4 contains a rare word; in fact, it occurs only here in the Hebrew Old Testament. The King James Version and American Standard Version translate it "thoughts" while the Revised Standard Version, Berkeley, and the New American Bible offer "plans."

Verse 5 introduces the main part of the poem, which is a series of participles describing God's activity. Rather than trust in men, the happy or blessed hopes in the Lord, the God of Jacob.

Eleven active verbs follow to delineate God's manifold work. The list begins with God as the Creator and Sustainer and ends with Him as the Rewarder and Judge. The middle part of the list (vv. 7–9) mostly emphasizes the merciful and generous features of God's concern for His creation.

The divine doings seem to come in pairs, whereas the verse numbers put them in triplets. So verses 6b and 7a go together— He keeps truth and executes justice. Then the last two stichs of verse 7 are a couplet—He gives food and frees prisoners. The first two-thirds of verse 8 describe His concern for the blind and the lame. Verses 8c and 9a likewise are a couplet—He loves the righteous and preserves the stranger.

Some scholars think 8c should be linked to 9c so that God's benefits to strangers, orphans, and widows may be one group, while the righteous and the wicked are put into an antithetical pair. The Jerusalem Bible has so arranged the verses.

A number of these actions are the same as the ones Christ did (cf. Isa. 61:1; Luke 4:18; Matt. 11:5). Two, in particular, illustrate salvation. The gospel frees from the prison house of sin (v. 7c), and the opening of blind eyes describes an understanding of the Christian message.

Even in judgment God is worthy of praise. He will reward the wicked man for his deeds. This last line of verse 9 recalls the last verse of Psalm 1 (RSV): "The LORD knows the way of the righteous, but the way of the wicked will perish." Another similarity to Psalm 1 comes in the choice of the word "happy" or "blessed" (cf. Pss. 146:5 and 1:1).

A kind of benediction closes this psalm. Zion, the holy city of God, representing all true worshipers, is assured that her God will reign forever. He is not like transient men, but He is God for all generations. Praise the Lord!

PSALM 147

In the Greek and Latin Bibles, Psalm 147 comprises two psalms. The numbering which got off when they put Psalms 9 and 10 together is finally straightened out, so these versions also end with 150 psalms. The break in the psalm comes between verses 11 and 12.

This psalm of twenty verses does, however, show unity. It begins and ends with the word "hallelujah." It speaks of Jerusalem in both parts (vv. 2, 12). The major theme throughout is the concern of God for His entire creation animals and man, the heavens and the earth.

Verses 1, 7, 12, and 20 have the only imperatives. These break the psalm into three stanzas, before verse 7 and before verse 12. The second break corresponds to the division of the psalm into two parts in the Greek and Latin versions. It is also interesting to note that God's proper name, Yahweh (LORD), occurs in the opening and closing verses of each of these three stanzas. Notice it in verses 1, 2, and 6; 7 and 11; 12 and 20. Actually, in verses 1 and 20 the name is shortened to "Yah," the last syllable of the word "hallelujah."

The opening verse is an introduction to the entire poem. It can be understood either that "it [praise] is good" or "He [God] is good." In the second half of the verse it is better to understand the subject as praise because the adjective "comely" and "pleasant" do not fit well with God as the subject.

Because of the reference to exiles in verse 2, the psalm may have been composed after the return from Babylon. Verses 2, 3, 4, and 6 state a number of acts God does for the world as a whole and for people in particular. In contrast to the heathen deities who were assigned various ministries, the true God is concerned both with the stars of heaven and with the broken hearts of suffering humanity. Though He numbers and names the stars, He also upholds the meek of the earth. It is no wonder the psalmist interrupted his train of thought at verse 5 to interject a doxology. He stops to magnify God's power, might, and infinite understanding.

Verse 7 is another summons to praise and an introduction to a stanza. This time, rather than starting at the bottom with the outcasts and the crushed and ending with celestial bodies, he begins with the heavens (v. 8) and concludes with the humble worshipers (v. 11).

These verses provide an interesting insight into the ancient understanding of the lifecycle. First there are the clouds (v. 8a), then the rains on the earth (v. 8b), and finally the grass on the mountains (v. 8c). This, in turn, is food for the animals (v. 9).

The third stanza begins with particular focus on the city of God, Jerusalem (vv. 12–13). From there the scope of God's blessing involves the entire Promised Land (v. 14), and ultimately the whole earth (vv. 15–18). Zion is blessed with people once more after a seventy-year exile. Once more Canaan is filled with political peace and economic prosperity. All because, in His sovereignty, God has chosen to do it so. Verses 15–19 provide a mixture of ideas. First there is God's irresistible and irrevocable word (vv. 15, 18, 19). Also, there is the weather, likewise sent at His bidding: snow and frost (v. 16), ice and cold (v. 17), wind and water (v. 18). At verse 18 these two streams of thought cross. There the word melts the snow and ice.

The analogy between these two leading ideas is simple. God's word is a gift like the moisture that comes with snow, rain, and frost. Although the cold is welcome because it brings moisture, it may also bring discomfort (v. 17). Anyone who has spent a winter in Jerusalem in a building that is not centrally heated can appreciate this. But the word of God brings both refreshment and discomfort. That is why this analogy is particularly interesting and beautiful. It is uncomfortable to read about our sin in the Bible, but it is pleasant to learn of the remedy in Christ.

Ancient Israel alone was the recipient of the blessing of the word of God. No other nations knew of it. Today, it is with the church God has deposited His Word. But rather than selfishly hoard it, our duty is cheerfully to spread it. Who would deny water to a thirsty man? Who would withhold the gospel from a dying soul?

PSALM 148

All agree that Psalm 148 has three parts. Verses 1–6 enjoin the heavens and the heavenly bodies to praise the Lord. The middle section, verses 7–10, exhorts the creation on earth to praise the Lord. The concluding four verses address the people and urge them to praise the Lord.

A "hallelujah" opens and closes the psalm. The word "praise" occurs thirteen times in these fourteen brief verses. Most of these are in the first four verses, where each stich has the word "praise."

A few of the terms merit some comment. The "hosts" in verse 2 is parallel to "angels" and, in this instance, refers to the army of assistants whom God uses for the operation of the universe. Elsewhere it often seems to mean stars, and that is still a possibility here. Verse 4 has the superlative "heaven of heavens," which is sometimes translated "highest heavens" (RSV). A text for the fiat or command creation is verse 5b: "He commanded, and they were established."

From the heights above, the psalmist moves to the depths below in verse 7. First he mentions the sea and its inhabitants. Then in verse 8 he speaks of the elements that make up the weather. In verse 9 he describes the physical features of the land and what grows on it, and finally he considers the animals. The Jerusalem Bible uses a very succinct method to render these verses:

> Mountains and hills,
> orchards and forests,
> wild animals and farm animals,
> snakes and birds.

In the final part of the psalm the focus is on human beings in all categories. The first category is the leadership: kings, princes, and judges. Verse 12 includes both sexes and the extremes of age.

Verse 13 is a wrap-up. All the above creation—animate and inanimate, animal and human—is to praise the Lord. As the psalm begins with heaven, so in verse 13b we once again lift our eyes upward.

Whereas verses 5 and 6 reflect on God's concern for the heavenly hosts, verse 14 recollects the Lord's goodness to His people. The word "horn" symbolizes strength because the strongest animals wore horns. A large horn belongs to a particularly fine specimen of a bull or ox. So, figuratively speaking, God's people now share that kind of strength.

PSALM 149

Psalm 149 has a militaristic overtone to its basic theme of praise. This appears most notably from verse 6 onward. In fact, the psalm has a division at that point. Verses 1–5 are a series of oblique commands to praise. But verses 6–9 speak of God's people executing His judgment on the unbelieving. As with its neighboring psalms, this one opens and closes with a "hallelujah" or, in English, "Praise the LORD!" The command to sing a "new song" is found often throughout the Psalter. (Note Pss. 33:3; 40:3; 96:1; 98:1; 144:9).

The word "saints" in verses 1 and 5 is interesting. It is built from the term *hesed,* meaning faithful, loving, dependable, merciful, and a lot more. Usually the Bible speaks of God's *hesed* as an attribute that is communicable; it can be shared by us. We cannot be omnipresent but we can be kind. We cannot be omnipotent but we can be trustworthy. We cannot be omniscient but we can be loving.

From verse 2 on the verbs are jussives or wish forms commonly translated "let." Another way to translate the idiom is with "should"—"Israel should rejoice in his Creator," and so forth.

Among the media used to praise the Lord, according to verse 3, is the dance. Needless to say, this is not a reference to ballroom dancing or, for that matter, to any dance which involves couples only. The Amplified Bible modifies the term "dance" with the bracketed words "single or group." This is correct.

The secondary theme of the psalm, victory in battle, may be

hinted at in verse 4b. The term "salvation" in the Old Testament usually means deliverance from some temporal danger, such as a political foe, a dread disease, or the threat of death. Therefore, verse 4 may be speaking of God's gift of victory to His people.

The reference in verse 5 to singing for joy in bed may seem strange. At least two explanations are possible. Now that the victory has been won, God's people can relax and rejoice. Or it may mean that even at night songs of exaltation are in order. Praise is not just a daytime activity, certainly not a once-a-week exercise.

The presence of "sword in hand" in verse 6 interrupts the otherwise lofty tone of this psalm. The psalm may have been used as a battle cry, or it may refer to the end of the age when God's people will assist Him in the righteous rule of the earth. In a sense, the conquest of Canaan was a punishment on the Amorites (Gen. 15:16). And the Israelites were the agents of God to punish them.

Verse 9 has a little word that may confirm this interpretation. The judgment or verdict was already *written,* that is, the heathen deserve the sword of vengeance. God chose to give His people the honor of executing His wrath. It is difficult to reconcile this with the New Testament teaching on love of enemies, but this will have to be understood in the same way as the imprecatory psalms. Even in the exaction of punishment and the execution of justice the Lord is worthy of praise.

PSALM 150

Each of the five books within the Psalter ends with a doxology. (Note Pss. 41:13; 72:18–19; 89:52; 106:48). Psalm 150 in its entirety is a doxology. It concludes not only the fifth book of the Psalter, but the entire collection of psalms. No other psalm is quite like it for its repetition of the word "praise." None compares to the universality of the summons to honor God. The word "praise," in one form or another, occurs thirteen times within the brief scope of these six verses. Included in this count are the "hallelujahs" which open and close the poem.

In verse 1 the exhortation is to praise God on earth and in heaven. That is probably the meaning of the terms "sanctuary" and "firmament of his power." There should be an echo in heaven of the volley of praise sung in the temple. And the temple, in turn, should reverberate with the sound of the heavenly choir.

Verse 2 states the reasons for praise: God is great and has done great things.

Verse 3 begins the list of instruments of praise. The first is the *shofar* or ram's horn, commonly translated "trumpet." It is not like the modern comet with valves, but is capable of changes in notes only as the player adjusts his lips to the force of his breath.

At the end of verse 3 come the *nevel* and the *kinnor*, both stringed instruments. They are portable harps which vary in size and number of strings, the *nevel* being the larger and more complicated of the two.

The *tof* (timbrel) of verse 4 is somewhat similar to a tambourine. It belongs in the percussion family. The dance, or in Hebrew the *mahol*, though not an instrument, is nevertheless a way to express praise. This may have been highly organized choreography performed by the priests and Levites, or it may have been the jubilation of the people as a whole. Two instruments are mentioned in the last half of verse 4. The "stringed instruments" (Heb., *minnim*) are spoken of only here and in Psalm 45:8. The "pipe" ("organs," KJV) is probably a very simple flute or whistle not unlike those that children play.

Verse 5 refers to two kinds of cymbals. The Hebrew word *tsiltsel* sounds like the noise these devices make. The difference between the two types is uncertain. One may be soft and the other

loud, or one mellow and the other harsh. Or they may be the synonyms "clashing" and "clanging," as the Jerusalem Bible suggests.

The grand finale comes in verse 6 where every living thing is
urged to praise the Lord. The command is that every breath be
used either to blow a horn or sing an anthem to the everlasting
praise of God.

Ultimately this is the whole message of the book of Psalms:
Praise the Lord! The chief end of man, according to one of the
ancient creeds, is to glorify God and enjoy Him forever. And the
aim of this brief commentary on the hymnbook of ancient Israel
is the same. May it prompt the reader likewise to praise the Lord.

BIBLIOGRAPHY

INTRODUCTIONS

Archer, Gleason. *A Survey of Old Testament Introduction.* Chicago: Moody, 1974.

Harrison, Roland K. *Introduction to the Old Testament.* Grand Rapids: Eerdmans, 1969.

COMMENTARIES

Calvin, John. *Calvin's Old Testament Commentaries: Psalms.* 5 vols. 1845. Reprint. Grand Rapids: Eerdmans, n.d.

Henry, Matthew. *Commentary on the Whole Bible,* vol. 3, *Job to Song of Solomon.* 1712. Reprint. Old Tappan, N.J.: Revell, n.d.

Keil, Carl F., and Franz Delitzsch. *Commentaries on the Old Testament,* vols. 11–13, Psalms. 1867. Reprint. Grand Rapids: Eerdmans, n.d.

Leupold, H. C. *Exposition of the Psalms.* Grand Rapids: Baker, 1970.

Spurgeon, Charles H. *The Treasury of David.* Grand Rapids: Zondervan, 1970.

Yates, Kyle M. "Psalms." In *The Wycliffe Bible Commentary,* ed. Charles F. Pfeiffer and Everett F. Harrison. Chicago: Moody, 1962.

OTHER

Lewis, C. S. *Reflections on the Psalms.* New York: Harcourt Brace, 1964.

MORE FROM THE
EVERYDAY BIBLE COMMENTARY SERIES

978-0-8024-1898-2

978-0-8024-1904-0

978-0-8024-1896-8

978-0-8024-1824-1

978-0-8024-1823-4

978-0-8024-1822-7

978-0-8024-1826-5

978-0-8024-1899-9

978-0-8024-1897-5

978-0-8024-1825-8

also available as eBooks

MOODY
Publishers®

From the Word to Life®